Mastering Digital Product Management

Product vision, strategy, and Agile execution for digital dominance

Dr. Vasant Gondhalekar

Shalini Dinesh

I0049868

bpb

www.bpbonline.com

First Edition 2025

Copyright © BPB Publications, India

ISBN: 978-93-65899-818

To View Complete
BPB Publications Catalogue
Scan the QR Code:

www.bpbonline.com

Dedicated to

My son, Anish, and all the smart young pros like him

- Vasant Gondhalekar, Ph.D.

My parents, husband, and son
- Shalini Dinesh, M.S.

About the Authors

- **Vasant Gondhalekar**, Ph.D., has 30+ years of experience in aerospace and defense and off-road vehicles and 10+ years in digital transformation/products and technologies. Vasant has played multiple roles as the head of aerospace and defense for *North America* and vice president of strategic accounts at *Cyient* and at *Tech Mahindra* with profit and loss responsibility. He covered engineering, IT, and digital sales and strategy as part of his responsibility. He had a diverse career in *Cessna Aircraft* (a *Textron* company) as well, where he managed various areas in product engineering, aircraft certification, manufacturing, quality, technical publications, and the *India* engineering center, to name a few. He was also the head of engineering for Textron – Jacobsen, a Golf and Turf division, and was responsible for new product development and sustaining products. Vasant also teaches at the *University of Texas* at *Dallas* in the *Jindal School of Management*, offering graduate-level courses in digital product management and digital strategy. He earned his Ph.D. in mechanical engineering with a minor in robotics and controls from *Wichita State University (WSU)* and is well published in national and international journals. He has completed several executive programs from *Harvard, Duke, Ohio State University*, and *Thunderbird School of Management*. He enjoys art and literature, and his favorite sport is American Football. He is an ardent fan of the *Kansas City Chiefs*.

- **Shalini Dinesh** is a seasoned technical product leader with over a decade of experience delivering impactful technology solutions across logistics, SaaS, and enterprise platforms. Her career spans entrepreneurial ventures, mid-sized tech firms, and global Fortune 100 companies, where she has led end-to-end development of scalable digital products in complex operational environments. She currently serves as a senior technical product manager at *Amazon* and previously led key supply chain innovation initiatives at *Walmart*, where her contributions to digital sustainability earned her the prestigious *Dallas 40 Under 40* award. Shalini holds a master of science degree in engineering management from *Southern Methodist University* in *Dallas, Texas*. She is also a published author, keynote speaker, and mentor dedicated to empowering the next generation of product leaders. She has been invited to speak at leading universities and international conferences and actively contributes to the product management community through writing, technical book reviews, and thought leadership. Her work blends strategic insight, technical depth, and a passion for building meaningful, user-centered products. Outside of work, she enjoys cooking and going on road trips with her family.

About the Reviewers

- **Sivakumar Mahalingam** is a data, cloud, and AI solutions architect with over 14 years of experience building scalable systems across AI, data engineering, and cloud-native platforms. He has designed and delivered end-to-end solutions that integrate big data pipelines, machine learning models, and modern DevOps practices for enterprises across industries. Sivakumar holds certifications in TOGAF 10, AWS, and Azure architecture, and is deeply involved in shaping technology strategies that balance innovation with operational efficiency. His current interests include applying LLMs to automate data workflows, optimizing infrastructure for AI workloads, and driving architectural best practices in production environments. He actively contributes to the open-source community and enjoys reviewing technical content to help ensure clarity, precision, and real-world relevance.

- **Dinesh Dakshinamoorthy** is a senior technical product manager with a strong background in building innovative, scalable solutions across supply chain, logistics, and data-driven product domains. At *Amazon*, he has led end-to-end product development initiatives, from vision and roadmap definition to go-to-market strategy, while working closely with engineering, operations, and business stakeholders. He combines deep technical understanding with a passion for simplifying complex workflows, driving automation, and enabling data-informed decision-making. He is known for his strategic mindset, collaborative approach, and customer-obsessed problem-solving. In addition to his core role, Dinesh actively mentors aspiring product managers and enjoys contributing to thought leadership through technical writing and industry engagement.

Acknowledgements

We would like to express our deepest gratitude to all those who have supported and contributed to the development of this book on Mastering Digital Product Management. This journey has been both intellectually enriching and personally rewarding, and it would not have been possible without the encouragement and input of many individuals.

First and foremost, our heartfelt thanks go-to our families, whose unwavering support, patience, and belief in us provided the foundation we needed to complete this endeavor. Their understanding during long hours of writing and revision has meant the world to us.

We are immensely grateful to BPB Publications for their guidance and expertise in bringing this book to fruition. Their support and assistance were invaluable in navigating the complexities of the publishing process.

We would also like to acknowledge the reviewers, technical experts, and editors who provided valuable feedback and contributed to the refinement of this manuscript. Their insights and suggestions have significantly enhanced the quality of the book.

Last but not least, we want to express our gratitude to the readers who have shown interest in our book. Your support and encouragement have been deeply appreciated.

Thank you to everyone who has played a part in making this book a reality.

Preface

We wrote this book because we wished we had something like it when we were starting out. Digital product management is a dynamic and rewarding field, but it is often misunderstood. Too often, resources are either overly academic or purely tactical, without offering a clear, end-to-end perspective. We wanted to create something more complete, a book that starts with the basics, follows a structured path, and weaves in actionable frameworks along the way. Whether you are a student curious about product management, an experienced professional stepping into the role for the first time, or someone looking to sharpen your thinking, this book is designed to meet you where you are and help you grow.

This book comprises 10 chapters, each one carefully curated to reflect the real-world responsibilities and challenges of a digital product manager. Our goal was to break down the complexities of the role and structure them in a way that helps you build your product thinking step by step. Each chapter builds on the last, creating a full 360-degree view of what lies within the product management space, from laying out a clear product vision and mastering execution, to managing stakeholders, negotiating trade-offs, navigating legal and data concerns, and leading without authority.

We have included practical frameworks, real-life case studies, and personal insights to bring the material to life. These stories and examples are not just illustrations; they are there to help you connect the dots, so you will not only learn the what and how, but more importantly, the why. Whether you are prepping for a product interview, building your first MVP, or trying to influence across teams, we hope you will find something here that resonates.

Above all, this book is a reminder that great product managers are not born; they are built. Like any great product, the best ones evolve through curiosity, empathy, and continuous iteration. We hope this book gives you not just knowledge, but clarity, confidence, and a little inspiration for the journey ahead.

Chapter 1: Introduction to Digital Product Management- Lays a solid foundation for understanding the critical role of consistency in digital product delivery, emphasizing its importance in fostering trust, driving customer loyalty, and aligning team workflows with market demands. The chapter focuses on the dual pillars of product management and project management to ensure delivery dates and structural consistency. Both are essential for audience satisfaction and brand reliability.

Chapter 2: Product Vision from Insight to Strategy- This chapter focuses on product vision. It builds on the foundational concepts introduced in *Chapter 1, Introduction to Digital Product Management* and gets into how to move from understanding customer needs to crafting a clear and compelling product vision. It also introduces strategic frameworks like the Product Vision Canvas and includes real-world examples (such as *McDonald's* milkshake story) to illustrate how a strong vision aligns product development with both user expectations and business goals.

Chapter 3: Product Market Strategy from Ideation to Domination- This chapter dives into the core of product strategy, breaking down how great products are not only built but positioned for long-term success. It explores how innovation plays a critical role in staying ahead of the competition, and how frameworks like SWOT analysis and Porter's Five Forces help shape smarter, data-driven decisions. With real-world case studies like *Netflix* and *Canva*, readers will see how disruptive thinking and strategic planning come together to define market leaders. Whether you are crafting a brand-new product or scaling an existing one, this chapter gives you the mindset and tools to do it with purpose and clarity.

Chapter 4: Product Value and Stickiness- This chapter emphasizes that building a successful product is not just about innovation, it is about creating lasting value and ensuring customer stickiness. It further explores how digital products can drive long-term user engagement, loyalty, and growth by solving real problems and integrating deeply into users' lives. It introduces frameworks and real-world examples to illustrate how companies like *Apple*, *Slack*, *Zoom*, and *Airbnb* achieved high retention and competitive advantage.

Chapter 5: Product Journey from Concept to Market- This chapter transitions from strategic thinking to practical execution, guiding readers through how digital products evolve from an initial idea to a successful market launch. It emphasizes the importance of product roadmaps as both strategic tools and communication frameworks that align vision, user needs, and organizational goals. The chapter explores various types of roadmaps, timeline-based, features-based, and goal-based, tailored to different stages of development and stakeholder needs. It also highlights how investment criteria help prioritize initiatives by assessing customer impact, strategic fit, technical feasibility, and **return on investment** (**ROI**). Real-world case studies, like *Instagram's* product evolution, illustrate how successful road mapping supports phased growth and adaptation.

Chapter 6: Customer Centric Design- This chapter deep dives into the critical role of customer centric design in product management, emphasizing that truly successful products are grounded in deep empathy for users and a keen understanding of their needs, behaviors, and pain points. Through the contrasting case studies of *Amazon* and *BlackBerry*, the chapter illustrates how customer obsession can fuel innovation and growth, while neglecting evolving user expectations can lead to irrelevance. The chapter then transitions into practical frameworks for gathering user requirements, crafting meaningful user stories, prioritizing product features, and conducting usability testing. It highlights that customer needs must be continuously re-evaluated and integrated into the development process via an iterative, collaborative approach.

Chapter 7: Data-driven Decision-making - This chapter highlights how data empowers product managers to make informed, strategic decisions by turning raw information into actionable insights. The Data Value Pyramid explains how data evolves from basic metrics to strategic wisdom. The chapter stresses the importance of clean, reliable data and distinguishes between internal (e.g., sales, support) and external (e.g., market trends, sentiment analysis) sources. Real-world examples like *Meta's Oculus Quest* and *Spotify's* personalized features show how data guides product innovation, enhances user experience, and improves decision-making. Tools like PDM, PLM, and PIM help manage product data across development stages. In essence, data is not just for validation, it is key to building better, user-centered products.

Chapter 8: Product Development Methodology- This chapter introduces product development methodologies, focusing on how teams move from idea to execution. It contrasts the Waterfall model, known for its structured, linear approach, with Agile, which emphasizes flexibility, collaboration, and iterative progress. The chapter also highlights how **product requirement documents (PRDs)** ensure alignment across teams by detailing problems, solutions, and success metrics. Quarterly planning provides high-level direction, while sprint cycles break goals into manageable tasks, keeping teams responsive yet focused.

Chapter 9: Product Sales Strategy- This chapter transitions from product development to the strategic challenge of taking a product to market and generating scalable revenue. It emphasizes that a great product alone is not enough; success also depends on how that product is monetized, positioned, and scaled. The chapter introduces eight core business models, from traditional one-time purchases to subscription and usage-based pricing, showing how each aligns with different customer behaviors and market conditions. It explores the strategic role of cloud computing in enabling flexible, scalable delivery through models like SaaS, PaaS, IaaS, and FaaS, and explains how product managers can identify when a pivot in business model is needed. Financial evaluation tools such as ROI, annualized ROI, and the J-curve are introduced to assess product viability and growth over time.

Chapter 10: Wearing Multiple Hats- This final chapter emphasizes that successful product management extends well beyond building features or managing roadmaps, it requires mastering a diverse set of cross-functional skills. Product managers must frequently *wear multiple hats*, adapting to the demands of leadership, communication, strategy, and execution in fast-paced, often ambiguous environments. The chapter explores key complementary competencies such as project management, negotiation, stakeholder alignment, and navigating legal and compliance discussions, especially when dealing with contracts or privacy regulations. It highlights the importance of influence without authority, especially when leading cross-functional teams or aligning with executives and customers.

Coloured Images

Please follow the link to download the
Coloured Images of the book:

https://rebrand.ly/e7d3de

We have code bundles from our rich catalogue of books and videos available at https://github.com/bpbpublications. Check them out!

Errata

We take immense pride in our work at BPB Publications and follow best practices to ensure the accuracy of our content to provide with an indulging reading experience to our subscribers. Our readers are our mirrors, and we use their inputs to reflect and improve upon human errors, if any, that may have occurred during the publishing processes involved. To let us maintain the quality and help us reach out to any readers who might be having difficulties due to any unforeseen errors, please write to us at :

errata@bpbonline.com

Your support, suggestions and feedbacks are highly appreciated by the BPB Publications' Family.

Piracy

If you come across any illegal copies of our works in any form on the internet, we would be grateful if you would provide us with the location address or website name. Please contact us at **business@bpbonline.com** with a link to the material.

If you are interested in becoming an author

If there is a topic that you have expertise in, and you are interested in either writing or contributing to a book, please visit **www.bpbonline.com**. We have worked with thousands of developers and tech professionals, just like you, to help them share their insights with the global tech community. You can make a general application, apply for a specific hot topic that we are recruiting an author for, or submit your own idea.

Reviews

Please leave a review. Once you have read and used this book, why not leave a review on the site that you purchased it from? Potential readers can then see and use your unbiased opinion to make purchase decisions. We at BPB can understand what you think about our products, and our authors can see your feedback on their book. Thank you!

For more information about BPB, please visit **www.bpbonline.com**.

Join our Discord space

Join our Discord workspace for latest updates, offers, tech happenings around the world, new releases, and sessions with the authors:

https://discord.bpbonline.com

Table of Contents

CHAPTER 1
Introduction to Digital Product Management

Introduction

This chapter lays a solid understanding for the readers in one of the most fundamental truths of digital product management, that consistency matters. Whether it is about meeting delivery timelines or maintaining a predictable **user experience** (**UX**), consistency builds trust, loyalty, and credibility, three things every successful product needs to thrive in a competitive market.

Oftentimes, several professionals confuse project managers with product management. Hence, this chapter covers the basic differences and goes further beyond to explain the role of a **digital product manager** (**DPM**), and it is far from being just about features or release cycles; the role of a DPM is about balancing user needs, business goals, and technical realities. They are the connector between teams, the advocate for the user, and the person who helps move ideas from messy whiteboard sketches to actual value in users hands. Rather than relying on theory, this chapter takes a practical approach by providing a comparative analysis of product and project management, breaking down real responsibilities, and explaining how collaboration changes.

Structure

This chapter covers the following topics:

- Need for product management

- Defining digital product management
- Roles and responsibilities of a digital product manager
- Product manager vs. project manager
- Case study on ChatGPT digital product study

Objectives

By the chapter's end, you will walk away with a toolkit of practical strategies, enabling you to turn high-level goals into reliable execution, ensuring every product meets or exceeds expectations.

Need for product management

Whether you are an aspiring **product manager** (**PM**) or someone who is looking to leverage your skills as an existing PM, you are in the right place. Your role as a PM is pivotal in driving the growth and prosperity of your organization through its offerings. Think of product management as the bridge connecting the dots between understanding what your customers truly need and transforming those insights into profitable business solutions.

In today's saturated market, having effective product management is non-negotiable. It ensures that your company's products meet genuine market needs and deliver significant value to your customers while ensuring sustainable profitability.

Now, picture this: A company embarks on launching a new software app without a dedicated PM at the helm. Developers may create technically brilliant products, but their success is only possible if they genuinely address user problems or are intuitive. This is where you, as a PM, step in as the advocate for the customer. You bring invaluable user research and insights, guiding the development process to create a product that resonates deeply with your target audience by solving real-world problems effectively.

So, buckle up as we explore digital product management, where understanding your customers is not just a task but a mission-critical to your organization's triumph.

The key needs of customers fall into three main areas, namely, fast response time as no customer wants to wait, understanding their needs, and providing an experience that will be worthy of customer delight. These insights set the stage for why your role as a PM is indispensable, as you are the owner to ensure these needs are met and the experience for the customers is such that the product will continue to grow in the market.

It is essential to shift your attention away from just creating a product and instead focus on its continuous success and improvement. This involves collecting user feedback, studying market trends, and recognizing areas for enhancement. By consistently refining and improving the product, you can ensure it remains relevant and competitive in the constantly evolving marketplace.

Defining digital product management

As a DPM, your role encompasses strategizing, developing, launching, and continuously improving digital products. These products can range from mobile apps, software, websites, and online services. You are tasked with managing and overseeing the entire process to ensure the product aligns with both user needs and business objectives.

Digital essentially is a software-driven platform, managed by software developers and engineers who are typically part of the IT or the engineering departments. DPMs thus play a crucial role, emphasizing their importance in software and/or **software as a service** (**SaaS**) companies, engineering and/or IT organizations working mainly for businesses undergoing digital transformation.

As DPMs, your responsibilities span your entire product lifecycle. You start by pinpointing market opportunities and addressing user issues head-on. From there, you define the features and functionalities to make your product stand out. You take charge of its development and execution, ensuring that the right features are prioritized, deliverables are on schedule, and all necessary pre-launch, launch, and change control plans are in place. Monitoring performance and gathering user feedback is also crucial.

Your decision-making process heavily relies on data. You continuously analyze and iterate on your product to keep it relevant, user-friendly, and competitive in the digital landscape. Collaboration is critical; you will work closely with cross-functional teams, including designers, engineers, marketers, analysts, and others, rather than working in isolation and making assumptions.

In today's digital age, innovation and competition are fierce. Consumers have an array of options at their fingertips, so your product's success hinges on its ability to solve real-world problems, deliver exceptional value, and adapt to users' evolving needs and technological advancements. You are vital in navigating these challenges and driving your product toward success.

The success of a product hinges on navigating several critical areas of focus. From keeping pace with evolving technologies and leveraging data-driven decision-making to fostering seamless cross-functional collaboration, you, as a PM, must master these core aspects to create impactful products that resonate with users and drive business objectives. The following points will explore these essential responsibilities, providing a clear roadmap for excelling in this dynamic role:

- **Rapidly evolving technologies:** Let us face it, technology evolves faster than ever. What was groundbreaking yesterday might be obsolete tomorrow. As DPMs, you are constantly assessing how emerging technologies impact your product and industry. It is not just about keeping up; it is about staying ahead. To do that, you need a mindset of continuous learning, curiosity, and a willingness to take calculated risks on what is next.

Think about AI, for instance. It is no longer just a buzzword; it is revolutionizing industries. Chatbots, personalization engines, image recognition, and predictive algorithms are just the beginning. However, integrating AI into your product is not as simple as flipping a switch. You are faced with questions like: *Does this technology solve a real problem for my users? How does it align with my product's vision? Do we have the resources and talent to implement it successfully?*

o **Example**: Consider how *LinkedIn* uses AI to recommend connections or job postings. As the PM for such features, you would need to ensure the AI aligns with user needs, avoids biases, and continually improves through feedback. That means staying involved in every stage from defining the algorithm's goals to collaborating with engineers on implementation and marketing teams on how to present it to users.

It is not just AI. Blockchain is reshaping finance, 5G is enabling lightning-fast connectivity, and **augmented reality/virtual reality (AR/VR)** is creating immersive UXs. Each of these technologies presents both opportunities and challenges. As a PM, your role is to discern which technologies add real value to your product and then act decisively.

However, that is only part of the story. Technology often disrupts industries entirely. Similar to how cloud computing transformed SaaS, and smartphones redefined UXs. It is your responsibility to ensure your product adapts to these seismic shifts, not as a follower but as a leader in space.

- **Data-driven decision-making:** You can quantify user behavior and understand market trends in the digital landscape. You are skilled at utilizing data analytics to pinpoint customer needs, monitor your products' performance, and ultimately, make well-informed product development and strategy decisions. Here is a truth you already know in digital product management: data is your superpower. Today, you can measure nearly everything: clicks, swipes, conversions, churn rates, user behaviors, and even the time it takes for users to scroll through your app. However, here is the catch: Having data is not enough. What sets great PMs apart is the ability to interpret that data, draw actionable insights, and use them to make impactful decisions.

You are not just looking for numbers; you are looking for patterns, stories, and truths about your users. *Are customers abandoning their shopping carts?* Maybe the checkout flow is too complicated. *Are users spending less time on your platform?* That could signal disengagement or competition drawing their attention.

o **Example**: Let us say you are managing a fitness app. Data shows a significant drop in user engagement after two weeks of downloading the app. Instead of guessing why, you dig deeper: *Are users struggling with the onboarding process? Are fitness plans too generic?* By conducting A/B tests or surveys, you discover that users are overwhelmed by too many options upfront. Your decision should be to simplify onboarding by asking users to select just one fitness goal. This is not just data-driven, it is user-centered problem-solving.

As you know, it is not just about tracking metrics; it is about choosing the right metrics. Vanity metrics like downloads or page views might look good on a dashboard, but do not always reflect your product's health. As a DPM, you focus on metrics that truly matter—retention, **customer lifetime value (CLV)**, and the **net promoter score (NPS)**.

Here is another thing: Data is not just for fixing what is broken. It is also a lens into future possibilities. Predictive analytics, for instance, helps you anticipate user needs and trends. Maybe your e-commerce platform shows that customers searching for eco-friendly products have grown by 25% month over month. That insight could guide your team to prioritize a sustainability-focused product line.

Let us not forget the ethical side. As PMs, you have a responsibility to ensure user data is collected and used responsibly. Transparency, consent, and data security are not just compliance checkboxes; they are integral to building trust with your users.

- **Cross-functional collaboration:** Building and maintaining a successful digital product requires seamless collaboration between diverse teams: Design, engineering, marketing, and customer support. As a DPM, you are the central hub, fostering communication and ensuring everyone is aligned toward a common goal. If there is one thing you have likely learned, it is this: Product management is not a solo journey. You are at the center of a bustling intersection, bringing together engineers, designers, marketers, customer support teams, and more. Collaboration is your secret weapon, but let us be honest, it is also one of your biggest challenges.

Think about the sheer diversity of perspectives in your team. Engineers are laser-focused on feasibility, designers are championing UX, marketers are pushing deadlines for campaigns, and customer support teams are fielding real-world frustrations. As the PM, it is your job to unite these voices into a coherent strategy, and that is no small feat.

- **Example**: Imagine you are leading a cross-functional team to launch a new subscription feature for a music streaming app. Designers want to create an elegant, distraction-free interface; engineers are concerned about backend scalability; and marketing wants to promise users unlimited downloads. Your role is to balance these competing priorities. By facilitating open communication and ensuring every team understands the user's pain points, you guide them to a solution that is both technically feasible and user-friendly.

However, collaboration does not stop at managing competing priorities. It is also about creating a shared sense of ownership. When teams feel involved early, whether it is brainstorming during the discovery phase or offering feedback during testing, they are more invested in the product's success.

Another challenge you have probably encountered is remote or distributed teams. With workforces spread across cities, countries, and even time zones, collaboration becomes more complex. Tools like Slack, Jira, or Miro can help bridge these gaps, but it is your leadership that makes the difference. Regular check-ins, clear documentation, and fostering a culture of transparency are what keep teams aligned.

Here is the key takeaway: Successful cross-functional collaboration is not just about coordination, it is about fostering empathy. When engineers understand the user's emotional journey or when designers see the constraints developers face, the team operates more as a cohesive unit. As the PM, you are the glue that holds these perspectives together, ensuring everyone is working toward a shared vision.

The growth of digital economy is practically in all industries. Businesses across industries are thus keen to capitalize on this growth, and a good part of all technology spending is directed toward driving transformative initiatives, emphasizing the demand for innovative strategies and solutions in the digital economy.

The role of the DPM has evolved significantly over the years. Success in product management requires a shift in mindset and practices to align with modern user expectations and organizational goals. The following section illustrates three key transformations that shape the role of PMs today: The transition from feature-driven to user-centric design, the move from siloed processes to collaborative teamwork, and the evolution from intuition-based decisions to data-driven strategies.

- **From feature-driven to user-centric:** Think back to the early days of digital product management. The goal was often to add as many features as possible, to outdo the competition, or simply because stakeholders demanded it. It was all about quantity, stacking features to make a product feel complete. However, we know this approach often leaves users overwhelmed and frustrated.

Today, that mindset has shifted entirely. Your focus is no longer on *what can we add?* But on *what problem are we solving for our users?* Being user-centric means everything you do is rooted in understanding and addressing the needs, goals, and pain points of your audience. It is about creating a meaningful experience, not just building features for the sake of it.

You can achieve this by listening to your users, engaging in continuous research, and gathering feedback at every stage of development. You are not just building a product, you are solving real problems in a way that resonates with your audience.

Think about this: Imagine you are managing a health-tracking app. Instead of cramming in every feature, step counters, calorie trackers, sleep monitors, you prioritize the features that your users need most, like an easy way to track their fitness goals. You simplify the experience, making it intuitive and actionable. That is the heart of being user-centric: solving the right problem, not all the problems.

You have also had to learn to say no. As a PM, you face constant pressure from stakeholders who want to add just one more thing. By championing the user's needs, you ensure that every decision adds value and aligns with your product's vision.

- **From siloed to collaborative:** Product management was once a solo act, where long lists of requirements were handed off to engineering or UX designers with little to no collaboration. This linear process was often marked by miscommunication and misaligned priorities, leading to significant frustration.

  Now, things are different. Today, you are not just working with teams, you are leading them. You are the central hub, connecting engineering, design, marketing, sales, and customer support. Your job is to make sure everyone is aligned, working toward the same vision, and that every voice is heard.

  Collaboration is no longer optional; it is essential. Your product's success depends on it. By fostering open communication, encouraging transparency, and aligning everyone with common goals, you are creating an environment where great ideas flourish.

  Picture this: You are launching a new payment feature for your app. Engineers are concerned about backend scalability, designers are advocating for a sleek and simple UI, and marketing is eager to announce the feature yesterday. As the PM, you are the one who brings everyone together. You mediate competing priorities, create a shared understanding of the product's goals, and guide the team toward a solution that works for everyone.

  Agile and Scrum have likely become staples in your day-to-day. You have embraced sprint planning, daily stand-ups, and retrospectives not just as processes but as tools to ensure constant collaboration and adaptability. With distributed teams becoming more common, you have mastered digital tools like Slack, Jira, and Miro to keep everyone connected and on track.

  Here is the real secret: Effective collaboration is not just about coordination—it is about empathy. When you help your team understand each other's challenges, they are more willing to work together. As a PM, you are the bridge that connects these perspectives and builds a culture of trust and shared ownership.

- **From intuition-based to data-driven:** Let us talk about how you make decisions. Years ago, it was all about gut instinct or experience. While intuition is still valuable, you now have something far more powerful at your fingertips: Data. You can track every click, swipe, and conversion. Here is the thing: You have learned that simply having data is not enough. Your success depends on how well you interpret it, uncover patterns, and turn those insights into action.

You have probably had moments where data completely changed your approach. Maybe you noticed a drop in user engagement and used heatmaps to pinpoint friction in your product's design. Or maybe you ran an A/B test on two onboarding flows and discovered one drove significantly higher retention. These are not just numbers—they are stories your users are telling you about what they need.

Consider this: Let us say you manage an e-commerce platform. Your analytics show that users frequently abandon their carts. Instead of guessing why, you dig into the data and discover the issue: Hidden shipping fees during checkout. Armed with this insight, you simplify the process and make fees transparent upfront. The result is higher conversions and happier customers.

However, being data-driven is not just about solving problems, it is also about predicting them. With tools like predictive analytics, you can anticipate trends and user behaviors before they happen. This allows you to stay ahead of the curve and build products that meet future needs.

Of course, you also face the challenge of navigating the ethical side of data. Protecting user privacy, being transparent about data usage, and ensuring that your decisions do not unintentionally reinforce biases are all part of your responsibility. As a PM, you have embraced these challenges because you know that trust is the foundation of any great product.

As a PM, you will remain at the forefront of innovation, navigating the complexities of that digital world and ensuring your products deliver exceptional value to your users and contribute significantly to the success of your organization.

Roles and responsibilities of a digital product manager

Imagine yourself as the architect of the digital world, wielding the power to craft experiences that shape how people interact and navigate the online landscape. That is the essence of a DPM. A multifaceted professional who wears many hats to bring successful digital products to life.

As a DPM, you will be the scout, constantly scanning the digital horizon to unearth hidden opportunities and unmet user needs. You will analyze trends, competitor offerings, and user behavior, becoming a detective and piecing together the puzzle to identify lucrative gaps in the market. However, your role continues beyond that.

Once a potential goldmine is discovered, you will step into the shoes of a visionary, crafting a compelling roadmap that lays out the product's purpose, target audience, and the impact it aims to create. This roadmap becomes the guiding light, ensuring everyone involved stays on the same path as the product takes shape.

A successful digital product is not built in a silo. You will also be the bridgebuilder, fostering communication and collaboration between diverse teams: Designers, engineers, marketers, and customer support. Each team brings a unique piece to the puzzle, and you will ensure they all fit together seamlessly.

Speaking of puzzles, you will also be a master researcher, constantly seeking to understand the intricacies of the user's world. You will become the user's voice through interviews, surveys, and usability testing, ensuring their needs, frustrations, and aspirations are heard loud and clear. This understanding forms the foundation for crafting products that resonate with your target audience.

However, the journey does not end with the launch. As a data detective, you will leverage the power of analytics to decode user behavior and measure product performance. You will analyze data like a seasoned analyst, identifying areas for improvement and using those insights to continuously refine and iterate on the product, ensuring it remains relevant, user-friendly, and delivers exceptional value.

As a PM, you must be ready to wear multiple hats: An architect, a visionary, a bridge builder, a researcher, and a data detective, all rolled into one. If you are passionate about the digital world, driven by user needs, and possess a knack for bringing diverse perspectives together. The world of digital product management might be the perfect adventure for you.

To understand better, let us explore the critical hats a DPM wears:

- **Visionary and strategist:** As DPMs, you are tasked with spotting market opportunities by thoroughly scanning the digital landscape. It is your job to analyze market trends, study competitor offerings, and closely observe user behavior to uncover unmet needs and potential market gaps. Once you have pinpointed an opportunity, it is up to you to craft a crystal-clear product vision. Your vision should outline the product's core purpose, identify the target audience, and define the desired impact. This vision will guide every step of the development process, from shaping the product roadmap to prioritizing features and setting timelines. Your goal is to ensure steady progress toward realizing your product's vision.

  Your role extends far beyond merely overseeing development tasks. Recognizing that strategy lies at the heart of your responsibilities is crucial. Before exploring the development process, you must meticulously identify and understand the problem you are solving. This means understanding user needs, market dynamics, and competitor landscapes.

  By thoroughly grasping the problem, you are better equipped to assess its significance. Not every situation demands a solution, and not every solution is worth pursuing. You must evaluate whether solving the identified problem aligns with your organization's goals and resources. Additionally, understanding the target audience is paramount. To tailor a resonating solution, you must empathize with their pain points, desires, and behaviors.

Furthermore, comprehending where your product stands in the market is indispensable. This involves conducting thorough market research to gauge the competitive landscape, identify potential gaps, and pinpoint differentiation opportunities. Knowing your product's unique value proposition and positioning it effectively is crucial in capturing market share and sustaining long-term success.

Ultimately, the goal of the product extends beyond its mere existence. Your product should aim to create a meaningful impact, enhance efficiency, improve UXs, or address societal challenges. Your product vision is a guiding light, outlining the overarching purpose and desired outcomes. By aligning every decision and action with this vision, you pave the way for a product that meets and exceeds expectations, delivering tangible value to users and the organization.

- **User advocate and researcher:** Understanding your users need are paramount for your product success as DPMs to ensure your products genuinely resonate with them. It would help if you took the lead in conducting various user research techniques, such as interviews, surveys, and usability testing, to gain deep insights into your users need, pain points, and aspirations. This knowledge serves as the foundation for creating products that truly meet the expectations of your target audience.

As DPMs, gathering and analyzing user feedback is ongoing throughout the product lifecycle. From the early stages of concept testing to analyzing usage data post-launch, you should actively seek out and analyze user feedback. This feedback loop is crucial for you to pinpoint areas for improvement and continuously iterate your product to enhance its usability and overall user satisfaction.

Let us get into understanding user needs and common mistakes early PMs might encounter during customer interviews.

Imagine you are a new PM excitedly diving into your first customer interview. You have prepared your questions meticulously and are eager to gather insights that will shape your product. However, as the interview progresses, you ask leading questions, inadvertently guiding the conversation toward confirming your assumptions rather than truly understanding the user's perspective.

This is a common pitfall for early PMs, the temptation to seek validation for preconceived ideas rather than remaining open to discovering genuine user needs. When you fall into this trap, you risk overlooking valuable insights that could lead to a more successful product.

Let me share a story to illustrate this point.

Example study on Sarah, a freelance app product manager

Meet *Sarah*, a budding PM tasked with developing a new productivity app for freelancers. Excited to kick-off her user interviews, Sarah dives in with questions to confirm her assumptions about what freelancers need most. She asks leading questions like; *do you struggle with time management?* or *would you find a task prioritization feature helpful?*

As Sarah continued her interviews, she noticed a pattern emerging. Many freelancer's express frustration not with time management, as they initially assumed, but with managing client expectations and payments. It becomes evident that Sarah's preconceived notions were leading her astray, and she was not genuinely uncovering the core needs of her target users.

Sarah's experience demonstrates valuable lessons you can apply.

Firstly, remain open-minded during customer interviews. Avoid leading questions that steer the conversation toward confirming your assumptions. Instead, ask open-ended questions like, *can you walk me through a typical day as a freelancer?* or *what are the biggest challenges you face in your work?*

Secondly, actively listen to your users. Please pay attention to the nuances of their responses and do not be afraid to dig deeper into unexpected areas. Sometimes, the most valuable insights come from what users do not explicitly say.

Finally, iterate and refine your approach. Use the insights gathered from customer interviews to adjust your product strategy iteratively. Understanding user needs is an ongoing process, not a one-time task.

By avoiding common pitfalls like seeking validation for assumptions and actively listening to your users, you will be better equipped to develop products that truly resonate with your target audience.

Effective collaboration and data-driven decision-making are essential qualities for a successful DPM. Managing cross-functional teams, aligning stakeholders, leveraging data insights, and championing the product vision require strong leadership and strategic execution. The following sections get into the critical responsibilities of a DPM, illustrating how collaboration, analytical thinking, and ownership drive product success:

- **Cross-functional collaborator:** Your success hinges on effective collaboration among diverse teams: Designers, engineers, marketers, and customer support. You are pivotal in facilitating communication and alignment across these teams, ensuring everyone shares the same vision for the product. One valuable tip for you is to identify the person accountable for each team, outlining their roles and expectations. This fosters clarity and maintains consistency. Consider using a platform like *Confluence* to keep all meeting notes and details updated for easy team reference.

    Managing stakeholders is another critical aspect of your role. You are tasked with overseeing the expectations of executives, investors, and partners. Effective communication of product progress, addressing concerns, and securing buy-in for critical decisions are essential throughout the development process.

Keep stakeholders informed of updates and changes to maintain transparency. Neglecting to communicate risks early or failing to update stakeholders on modifications made. Keep everyone in the loop to ensure smooth progress and successful outcomes.

The story is about Sarah, a PM for a freelancing app who aims to make an impact on her role. She believes she has the authority to make all decisions related to product development and success as an individual contributor. However, she soon realizes she is facing collaboration and stakeholder management challenges.

Sarah struggles to establish clear communication channels among her diverse designers, engineers, marketers, and customer support team. Misunderstandings arise without a central hub for information sharing, and tasks fall through the cracks. Teams are unsure of the updates, and there is no clear direction. Some gaps that they discovered during the launch arose. Sarah soon realizes that not having a designated person responsible for each team leads to confusion about roles and expectations.

As Sarah navigates the complexities of managing stakeholders, she encounters another hurdle. She fails to communicate potential risks early in the development process, fearing it might earn her negative feedback, and her manager might lose trust and confidence in her. However, Sarah fails to understand that PMs, though they are individual contributors, must collaborate with multiple stakeholders and work as a team for a successful product. Also, they should communicate challenges/risks and ask for the help needed at the early stage rather than waiting for someone to ask them for an update. She fears that if she mentions the delivery risks, her stakeholders may lose trust or enthusiasm, but she fails to understand that it is a risk as a team!

Influencing and persuading your team to embrace the product vision is paramount for success as a PM. While you are responsible for the product's success, you cannot achieve it alone. Your team's collective efforts are essential for bringing the vision to fruition.

Imagine yourself in Sarah's shoes once again. She realizes that dictating tasks to her team members is not enough to inspire their best work. Instead, she finally understands the importance of passionately influencing and persuading them to align with the product vision.

Sarah could have empowered her team members to see the bigger picture by communicating the why behind the product's goals and objectives.

As a PM, you must actively seek input and feedback from your team members, valuing their perspectives and ideas. You should encourage product ownership among your team members by fostering an environment of collaboration and inclusivity. This sense of ownership will fuel their dedication and commitment to delivering a high-quality product. Remember that you may steer the ship; the collective efforts of the entire team propel it forward. Influencing and persuading your team to embrace the product vision will set the stage for success, fostering a collaborative environment where everyone feels invested in the journey.

- **Data-driven decision maker:** You will encounter a few challenges, especially regarding wrangling with data. Initially, you might find it daunting to sift through the vast amount of data available, unsure which metrics truly matter for your product's success. Integrating various data sources and ensuring their accuracy can also present hurdles, mainly if your data collection methods are disjointed or inconsistent.

To overcome these challenges, start by defining clear objectives for your product and identifying the specific **key performance indicators** (**KPIs**) that align with those objectives. This clarity will help you focus your data efforts and avoid getting lost in irrelevant metrics. Next, streamline your data collection processes by implementing standardized methods and tools. Establishing a robust data infrastructure from the outset will ensure data accuracy and facilitate more accessible analysis and decision-making down the line. Identifying KPIs at the outset of your digital product management journey is paramount for several reasons. Firstly, it provides you with a clear roadmap for measuring the success and impact of your product. By defining KPIs early on, you establish specific metrics that align with your overarching goals, ensuring that every decision and action is purpose-driven.

Moreover, knowing how and when data will be collected and monitored is essential for maintaining accountability and tracking progress effectively. Establishing a robust data collection strategy from the beginning allows you to gather the necessary insights promptly. Determine the data collection methods, whether it is through automated tools, manual forms, or a combination of both, and ensure that they are seamlessly integrated into your product development process.

Once data collection begins, it is crucial to establish a monitoring cadence that suits the nature of your product and its lifecycle stage. Regular monitoring of KPIs provides real-time visibility into your product's performance, enabling you to identify trends, spot potential issues, and make informed adjustments as needed. The frequency of monitoring may vary depending on factors such as the complexity of your product, the pace of market changes, and the availability of resources. However, as a general rule of thumb, aim to monitor KPIs at regular intervals, whether daily, weekly, monthly, or quarterly, to ensure that you stay on track towards your objectives.

If you find yourself in a situation where you do not need access to data or are having trouble measuring specific metrics, save time. Instead, take a proactive approach to address these gaps. Consider alternative data sources, implement manual data collection methods, or work with other teams or stakeholders to gather the necessary insights. Sometimes, automated processes may not be available, or it might not be feasible to collect data directly. So, it is essential to have simple manual methods, like sending out a feedback form, to gather feedback surveys from your users outside the app. We have all been in situations where we have struggled to get data, but it is crucial to identify what we need to do and when to do it. Successful DPMs are adaptable and resourceful, and embracing creative solutions to overcome data challenges will ultimately strengthen your decision-making capabilities and drive the success of your product.

- **Product owner and champion:** As DPMs, you are pivotal in safeguarding the essence of your product's vision. It is not just about owning the roadmap and backlog; it is about being the driving force behind every strategic decision that shapes the trajectory of your product's journey. Picture yourself at the helm, prioritizing features and crafting each step on the roadmap to align with overarching goals and user needs. You are not just managing a backlog; you are curating a roadmap that serves as a blueprint for success, ensuring that every task undertaken by your team contributes meaningfully to the product's evolution.

  However, your responsibilities do not end there. You are the vigilant overseer, constantly monitoring the pulse of your product's performance in the digital landscape. After launch, you understand the depths of user engagement data, deciphering patterns and insights that reveal the true heartbeat of your product. Based on the data and user feedback, you are now armed with knowledge; you can identify areas for enhancement, seizing every opportunity for growth and refinement. Your role extends beyond mere observation; you catalyze continuous improvement. Armed with a steadfast commitment to excellence, you lead the charge in championing optimization efforts that keep your product relevant and ahead of the curve. You ensure your product remains a beacon of innovation in a sea of competition through iterative analysis, experimentation, and adaptation cycles.

As a DPM, you are the guardian of your product's destiny. With your unwavering dedication and strategic foresight, you chart a course toward success, guiding your team toward realizing your shared vision and delivering unparalleled value to your users.

Product manager vs. project manager

Imagine yourself working in the fast-paced world of digital products, surrounded by cutting-edge technology and innovative ideas. However, within this exciting space, two distinct roles often need clarification: Digital products and project managers. While their titles share a digital prefix, their responsibilities and mindsets diverge significantly.

Digital product managers

Think of a PM as a digital product's lifecycle architect. Their gaze extends beyond the immediate horizon, constantly envisioning the product's long-term success. They delve into market trends, user needs, and competitor landscapes, clearly showing the product's purpose, target audience, and desired impact. This vision acts like the *North Star*, guiding every decision throughout the product's journey, from the initial spark of an idea to its eventual launch, optimization, and even potential sunsetting.

PMs are the champions of user understanding. They actively seek user feedback through various research methods, becoming the user's voice within the organization. This deep empathy ensures that the product they envision is not just technically sound, addresses real user needs, and resonates with their aspirations.

The following is an illustration of a product roadmap, which acts as a strategic document that outlines the vision, direction, milestones, and initiatives for a product over time. Building a product roadmap will help you align business objectives and market needs, prioritize tasks, allocate resources effectively, and communicate the product's trajectory to your stakeholders. The roadmap evolves continuously, reflecting changes in market conditions, user feedback, technological advancements, and business goals.

The following figure outlines a strategic roadmap at a high level for product development, segmented into quarters. It highlights the progressive rollout of features, emphasizing a structured approach to prioritizing immediate needs, upcoming enhancements, and long-term goals to align with user requirements and organizational objectives. These high-level features can then be further expanded into specific features-based on the finalized user needs.

PRODUCT ROADMAP

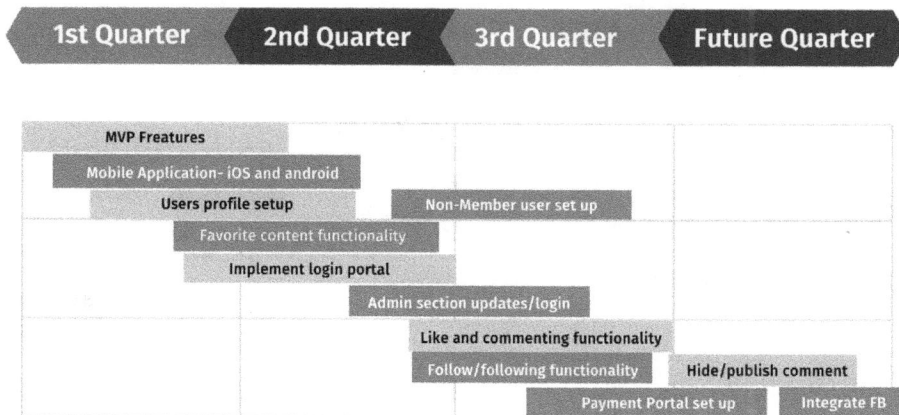

Figure 1.1: Product roadmap illustration

Digital project managers

Project managers, on the other hand, excel in the nitty-gritty of project management. They are the conductors of specific projects within the broader product roadmap. Their focus is laser-sharp, ensuring that individual features or functionalities are delivered on time, within budget, and meet the highest quality standards. They meticulously plan projects, manage resources, and navigate potential risks, ensuring smooth and successful execution.

A project roadmap is a strategic document that outlines a project's high-level plan and critical milestones, visually representing its objectives, timeline, deliverables, and dependencies. It guides the project team and stakeholders, informing everyone about the project's progress, potential risks, and resource allocation. The roadmap enables proactive decision-making to stay on track towards achieving the project's goals.

If you are wondering what makes the project and product roadmap differ, both track the deliverables. To briefly state, a project roadmap outlines tasks and deliverables for a specific project. In contrast, a product roadmap details a product's strategic direction and features over time. The project roadmap is temporary and tied to a particular project, while the product roadmap is ongoing and evolves with the product's lifecycle.

The following figure illustrates a sample project roadmap that spans multiple teams and outlines the high-level tasks. These tasks are then further expanded with specific tasks to develop the features:

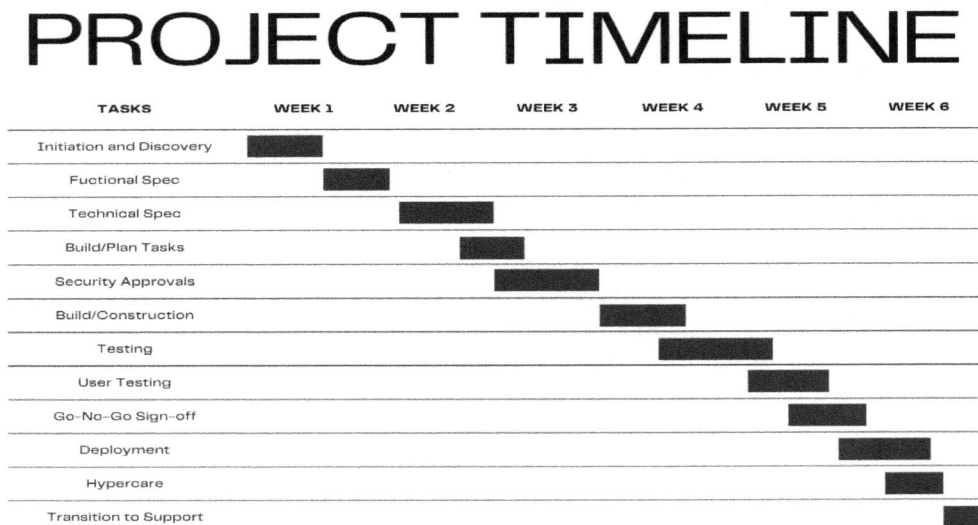

PROJECT TIMELINE

TASKS	WEEK 1	WEEK 2	WEEK 3	WEEK 4	WEEK 5	WEEK 6
Initiation and Discovery	▇					
Fuctional Spec	▇					
Technical Spec		▇				
Build/Plan Tasks		▇				
Security Approvals			▇			
Build/Construction				▇		
Testing				▇		
User Testing					▇	
Go–No–Go Sign-off					▇	
Deployment						▇
Hypercare						▇
Transition to Support						▇

Figure 1.2: *Project roadmap illustration*

Skillset spectrum: Visionaries vs. executors

The skill sets of these two roles also differ. PMs thrive on strategic thinking, constantly evaluating the long-term vision and making decisions that propel the product toward its ultimate goal. They are also masters of communication, effectively articulating the product vision to diverse stakeholders, from executives to designers. Their data analysis and interpretation skills also empower them to translate user insights and market trends into actionable product decisions.

On the other hand, project managers possess a strong foundation in project management methodologies. They excel at organization, prioritization, and meeting deadlines, ensuring the project stays on track. Their communication and interpersonal skills are crucial for building strong relationships with team members and managing stakeholder expectations effectively. Additionally, a basic understanding of technical aspects related to digital product development can be advantageous in their role.

Both product and project managers play distinct yet complementary roles in the success of digital products. You must clearly understand their unique strengths and areas of expertise to create a well-rounded team equipped to navigate the complexities and challenges of the digital landscape. Imagine a product vision meticulously crafted by a DPM, brought to life through the project execution expertise of a digital project manager. This powerful combination paves the way for innovative digital products that function flawlessly and resonate deeply with users.

Skills for a product manager

Imagine yourself as the maestro behind a groundbreaking digital product, the one calling the shots and harmonizing the efforts of talented teams. That is the essence of a PM. To honestly conduct this digital symphony, you will need a unique blend of skills–technical know-how and interpersonal finesse. We are talking about both the hard skills (like technical knowledge) and the soft skills (communication and teamwork) that make PMs thrive. So, grab your metaphorical baton because we are about to explore the essential skills that equip PMs for success, with a few extras you might not have expected thrown in for good measure!

Excelling as a PM requires a diverse and robust skill set that will enable you to navigate the complexities of product development effectively. From strategic thinking and user empathy to data-driven decision-making and technical acumen, each responsibility plays a pivotal role in delivering successful products. The following points outline the essential skills and approaches every PM must master to thrive in this position:

- **Strategic thinking and vision:** As a PM, one of your most critical responsibilities is to establish a clear strategic vision for your product. This begins in the early stages of the product lifecycle, often before the product even exists. During this stage, you will analyze the market landscape to identify gaps and opportunities. For example, imagine you are working on a SaaS platform for small businesses. You will examine competitors' offerings, study industry trends, and consider emerging technologies such as AI or automation tools. This market research enables you to define where your product can uniquely deliver value.

  Once the opportunity is clear, you will craft a product vision that aligns with business goals and resonates with the target audience. At this stage, you will work closely with executives to ensure the vision supports company objectives, such as revenue growth or market expansion. Engineers and designers will also weigh in assessing technical feasibility and initial design directions. From here, you prioritize high-level features, allocate resources, and set the product's strategic direction, which feeds directly into the product roadmap.

For example, if you are launching a new mobile banking app, your strategic vision might focus on creating a user-friendly experience that simplifies personal finance management. This vision helps guide decision-making as the team moves through development, ensuring the product remains focused on solving the correct problems for your users.

- **User empathy and research:** You must thoroughly understand your users' needs, pain points, and aspirations. You can employ various user research methods, such as surveys, interviews, and usability testing, to gather insights that will inform product decisions.

  Furthermore, do not just collect user feedback; you must also translate it into actionable insights that guide product development. You can use these to prioritize features that address user needs and ensure the product delivers a positive and intuitive UX.

  Understanding your users is not just important; it is foundational to everything you do as a PM. This process often starts during the discovery phase, where you will employ various user research methods such as surveys, interviews, and usability testing. For example, if you are working on an e-learning platform, you might interview students and educators to uncover their pain points, such as difficulty tracking progress or finding relevant courses.

  However, it does not stop there. User empathy requires you to dig deeper, listening not just to what users say but also observing their behaviors. Tools like heatmaps, user recordings, or direct usability tests can provide critical insights into how users interact with your product. In the development stage, these insights help prioritize features that address the most pressing needs. For instance, if research shows that students struggle with navigation, you might prioritize building an intuitive dashboard before adding advanced features.

  Key stakeholders involved in this process often include designers and user researchers, who help you gather and interpret insights. Engineers also play a role, as they will need to understand user pain points to design backend systems that support user-focused solutions. By championing the user's voice throughout the process, you ensure that your product delivers a positive and intuitive experience.

- **Communication and collaboration:** Effective communication is a crucial skill for PMs. You must be able to convey ideas and information clearly and concisely to diverse stakeholders, including engineers, designers, marketers, and executives. PMs must be able to articulate the product vision, explain complex concepts, and advocate for the user's voice throughout the development process.

Collaboration and relationship-building are equally important for building strong relationships, and fostering collaboration across different teams is crucial for building a successful product. PMs act as the central hub, facilitating communication and ensuring everyone is aligned towards the shared goal of product success.

You already know that clear communication is a cornerstone of your success as a PM. At every stage of the product lifecycle, you will need to articulate ideas and decisions to a diverse group of stakeholders, engineers, designers, marketers, and executives. In the ideation phase, you are communicating the product vision and ensuring everyone understands the why behind what you are building. During development, you provide clarity on priorities, specifications, and timelines. Post-launch, you are sharing results, insights, and next steps.

Imagine you are managing the development of a new collaboration tool. Early on, you will work with designers to align on the user interface and experience, with engineers to assess technical feasibility, and with marketing to establish positioning. Each team speaks a different language, and it is your role to translate between them. For example, you might explain a design decision to engineers by tying it to technical implementation or advocate for user needs to executives by connecting them to business outcomes.

Collaboration is equally important. During sprint reviews, for instance, you will work with engineers to address blockers, designers to adjust based on feedback, and marketers to ensure upcoming launches are on track. Your ability to foster a culture of alignment and teamwork is what keeps the product moving forward smoothly.

- **Analytical thinking and data-driven decision-making:** PMs use data analytics to measure the performance of their products, track user behavior, and identify areas that need improvement. They analyze data insights to make informed decisions about product features, marketing strategies, and future iterations. So, as a PM, you must often use A/B testing and other experimentation techniques to compare options and determine the most effective approach. This data-driven approach will ensure your product decisions are based on evidence rather than intuition.

Data drives decision-making throughout the product lifecycle, but its role is particularly prominent post-launch. Once your product is live, you will monitor its performance using metrics such as retention rates, conversion rates, and user engagement. For example, imagine you have launched a new feature for a food delivery app. If data shows a drop-off during the checkout process, you will dig deeper to uncover the cause; perhaps hidden fees are discouraging users. Armed with this insight, you might A/B test a more transparent pricing display to address the issue.

During development, you will also use data to inform decisions. For instance, if you are prioritizing features, data from user research or market analysis can highlight which areas will deliver the most impact. Before launching, tools like A/B testing or prototypes help you validate hypotheses and refine the product.

Key stakeholders in this process often include data analysts, who help interpret metrics, and marketing teams, who collaborate with you on growth strategies based on the insights. Engineers also play a role, especially when implementing tracking tools or integrating new analytics solutions.

- **Technical acumen:** This is beneficial for PMs as you need a fundamental understanding of technology, although you do not necessarily need to be coding experts. This will enable you to communicate effectively with engineers, have a better insight into the technical feasibility of product features, and make informed decisions about product development. As a PM, you must remain current with emerging technologies since the tech world constantly evolves and should be adaptable and willing to learn about new technologies that may impact your product or the broader market.

It never hurts to have extra skills as a PM. Developing these skills will help you stand out as a seasoned professional. You do not need to be an engineer, but having a strong grasp of technical concepts is invaluable. This knowledge enables you to communicate effectively with engineering teams and assess the feasibility of features. For instance, if your team is considering integrating machine learning into a product, you need to understand its requirements, limitations, and impact on development timelines.

Early in the product lifecycle, your technical acumen helps you set realistic goals. During sprint planning, for example, you might work with engineers to determine whether a feature can be delivered within the constraints of a sprint. Later, during **quality assurance (QA)** testing, your familiarity with technical workflows allows you to identify and resolve issues more efficiently.

Emerging technologies are another area where technical knowledge is crucial. Let us say a competitor has adopted blockchain for secure transactions. To assess whether this makes sense for your product, you will need to understand how it works and evaluate whether it aligns with your users' needs and your business strategy. This adaptability ensures your product remains competitive in a rapidly evolving landscape.

- **Negotiation:** PMs often need to negotiate with stakeholders on various aspects of the product, such as features, timelines, and budgets. Strong negotiation skills will allow you to advocate for their vision while finding acceptable solutions for everyone involved.

As a PM, you are often in the position of negotiating with stakeholders, whether it is about features, timelines, or budgets. During roadmap planning, for instance, you might need to push back on executive demands for quick delivery while advocating for a higher-quality product that requires more time. Strong negotiation skills allow you to find common ground while keeping the product's success at the forefront.

In these situations, you will work closely with executives, engineers, and marketing teams. For example, during a major product launch, marketing might request last-minute changes to better align with a campaign. Your job is to weigh the risks, negotiate priorities, and arrive at a solution that satisfies all parties without jeopardizing the timeline or product quality.

- **The ability to say no:** PMs are bombarded with requests and ideas, and it is crucial to say no strategically. This ensures you focus on the most critical tasks and avoid scope creep that could negatively impact the product.

  Saying no strategically is one of the toughest and most important skills you will develop. Requests come from every direction: Executives wanting additional features, engineers proposing technical improvements, or users requesting niche functionality. Your ability to focus on the most critical priorities ensures the product delivers maximum value without succumbing to scope creep.

  For example, if your roadmap focuses on improving user onboarding, you might decline a request to build advanced reporting features. Explaining this decision involves tying it back to user needs and business goals. By maintaining this focus, you ensure that the team's efforts deliver the greatest impact.

- **Task management:** While only sometimes a core aspect of the role, as a PMs you may need to manage tasks and timelines, especially when leading smaller teams or working on complex projects. Strong task management skills ensure projects stay on track and deliverables are met.

  While task management may not always be your primary responsibility, it often becomes essential when leading smaller teams or complex projects. Imagine managing a product update with multiple dependencies. In these cases, you will create timelines, track progress, and ensure deliverables stay on schedule.

  Working closely with project managers (if available), engineers, and designers, you will identify blockers, reassign tasks as needed, and keep the team aligned on priorities. Your organizational skills directly influence the team's ability to deliver on time and within scope.

- **Effective communication, including the ability to be persuasive:** While sweet tongue may not be the most professional term, as a PM, you will need to be a clear communicator. You can convince stakeholders of the value of your vision and ideas while maintaining a professional and respectful demeanor.

By cultivating these diverse skills, you can become an influential leader and navigator in the digital landscape. You will now be able to bridge the user's needs and business objectives, ensuring that products function flawlessly, resonate with users, and contribute to the organization's success.

Finally, your ability to communicate and persuade is central to your success. Whether you are presenting a product vision to executives, rallying a team around a challenging goal, or convincing stakeholders to invest in a new initiative, your words carry weight.

For example, when pitching a new feature to leadership, you will need to present a compelling case backed by data, user insights, and market analysis. Your ability to connect the dots between user needs, business goals, and technical feasibility ensures your ideas resonate and gain buy-in. This skill, more than any other, enables you to inspire confidence and drive your product forward.

Case study on ChatGPT digital product study

The speed at which digital products reach a million users highlights the evolving landscape of technology adoption and consumer engagement. Some innovations experience explosive growth, capturing widespread attention almost instantly, while others take years to establish their presence. The following table provides a compelling comparison of how quickly various digital products achieved this milestone, showcasing the power of innovation, market readiness, and user demand in driving rapid adoption:

Brand	Time to reach one million users
Netflix	3.5 years
Airbnb	2.5 years
Facebook	10 months
Spotify	5 months
Instagram	2.5 months
iPhone	74 days
ChatGPT	5 days

Table 1.1: *Million users*

Table 1.1 tells us a fascinating story about how quickly some digital products reached a million users. ChatGPT, the AI-powered text generator, is the undisputed champion, going a million users in a jaw-dropping 5 days! Its innovative capabilities resonated with a large audience, highlighting the ever-growing demand for such technologies.

Now, compare that to Netflix, the streaming giant. It took them a whole 3.5 years to reach the same milestone. Remember, Netflix pioneered its field, introducing a new way to watch movies and shows. It took time for users to embrace this shift and for the service to gain widespread adoption.

Airbnb, the poster child of the sharing economy, reached the million-user mark in 2.5 years. This rapid growth demonstrates the immense potential of this innovative model. Facebook, the social media powerhouse, did even better, reaching a million users in just 10 months! This explosive growth highlights the early social media boom and the undeniable appeal of online connections.

Instagram, another social media darling, took only 2.5 months to reach a million users. This remarkable feat speaks volumes about its viral potential and the increasing popularity of photo sharing. Interestingly, the iPhone, *Apple* revolutionary smartphone, achieved the same feat in just 74 days. This rapid adoption showcases the immense excitement surrounding its launch and the paradigm shift it brought to the mobile phone industry.

While data for WhatsApp is not included here, it is worth noting that it boasts massive user bases, exceeding 2 billion and 180 million, respectively. However, the time it takes for a digital product to reach such heights can vary significantly. Several factors include the product's category, who it targets, its marketing strategy, and the overall market conditions.

ChatGPT, reaching 1 million users in 5 days, suggests exceptional product positioning and targeted marketing strategies that capitalize on the existing interest in AI technology.

These impressive cases offer valuable insights for aspiring and new PMs. Key lessons include the importance of understanding user needs, crafting a clear and compelling vision, optimizing UX, and leveraging data-driven decision-making. Each of the following listed takeaways serves as a foundation for creating impactful and successful products:

- **Understanding user needs:** Putting users at the heart of the product strategy is critical. By conducting thorough research and actively listening to user feedback, you can ensure the product addresses real needs and resonates with your target audience.

- **Crafting a compelling vision:** A clear and compelling vision articulating the product's purpose, value proposition, and impact is essential. This vision should serve as your North Star, guiding decision-making throughout the product's development and marketing.

- **Optimizing UX:** A smooth, intuitive, and enjoyable UX is crucial for user adoption and retention. You need to continuously analyze user data and feedback to identify areas for improvement and iterate on the product to optimize the experience.

- **Data-driven decision-making:** Relying on user data and market research insights is crucial for making informed decisions. Only PMs who can effectively analyze and interpret data can make strategic choices that propel the product toward success.

These are just a few essential skills you, as PMs, should focus on developing. Additionally, staying up to date with the latest trends and technologies is crucial in this rapidly evolving field. Continuous learning through online courses, attending industry events, and networking with other professionals is essential to staying ahead of the curve.

Remember, the cases you witnessed are just a glimpse into the ever-evolving world of digital products. Every success story is a testament to the talented PMs behind the scenes strategic thinking, user-centric approach, and data-driven decision-making. If you are passionate about innovation, UX, and making a difference in the digital landscape, consider embarking on this exciting journey of digital product management. The future of technology rests in the hands of the next generation of product leaders.

So, the next time you encounter a new digital product, take a moment to consider its journey. It might have taken weeks, months, or even years to reach where it is today. Each story is unique, and understanding the factors behind their success can be incredibly insightful.

Conclusion

Wrapping up this chapter, it is clear that digital product management is more than just overseeing development, about making strategic decisions, understanding users, and driving meaningful impact. The role demands a mix of vision, adaptability, and collaboration, all while staying ahead in an ever-evolving digital landscape. Whether you are crafting a roadmap, working with cross-functional teams, or leveraging data to refine your product, your ability to balance these responsibilities will define your success. As you move forward, remember that great product management is not just about launching products—it is about continuously improving them to create lasting value for both users and businesses.

Looking ahead to the next chapter, we will focus on the foundation of product vision. You will learn how to move from understanding customer needs to defining a strong value proposition that differentiates your product in the market. Through strategic frameworks and the Product Vision Canvas, you will learn how to craft a compelling vision that aligns with both user expectations and business goals. With real-world examples, including *McDonald* approach to understanding customer jobs with milkshakes, the next chapter will equip you with the tools to shape a clear, impactful product direction.

Points to remember

- Digital product management bridges the gap between user needs and market demands, ensuring successful product development.
- Collaboration is paramount for PMs. They cannot work alone and require effective communication and teamwork across diverse teams to achieve product success.
- Understanding user needs and market positioning is crucial. This requires both empathetic user research and thorough market analysis.
- PMs act as user advocates. They lead research efforts to understand user needs and implement continuous feedback loops to ensure the product remains user-centric.
- Effective teamwork is fostered by cross-functional collaboration and managing stakeholder expectations. This ensures everyone is aligned and working towards the same goals.
- Data-driven decisions are essential. This involves defining clear objectives, establishing robust data collection methods, and overcoming challenges creatively to leverage data insights effectively.
- PMs take ownership of the product vision. They monitor performance, lead optimization efforts, and drive continuous improvement for the product.

Multiple choice questions

1. **What is the primary role of a DPM?**
   a. Writing code for the product
   b. Strategizing, developing, launching, and improving digital products
   c. Handling customer support for digital products
   d. Managing only the marketing aspect of a digital product

2. **Why is effective product management considered essential in today's market?**
   a. To ensure products are created quickly
   b. To prioritize company revenue over user needs
   c. To ensure products meet market needs, deliver value to customers, and maintain profitability
   d. To reduce the number of features in a product

3. **Which of the following best describes the responsibility of a DPM in addressing rapidly evolving technologies?**
   a. Ignoring new technologies to focus on existing product strategies
   b. Adopting every new technology without assessing its value
   c. Assessing how emerging technologies impact the product and deciding which add real value
   d. Delegating all technology-related decisions to engineers

4. **What is an example of data-driven decision-making mentioned in the chapter?**
   a. Building features-based solely on competitor analysis
   b. Using A/B testing to improve a fitness app's onboarding process
   c. Guessing user needs based on intuition
   d. Developing a product without considering metrics

5. **What is the main challenge of cross-functional collaboration for a DPM?**
   a. Ensuring that engineers and designers communicate effectively
   b. Managing team meetings efficiently
   c. Uniting diverse team perspectives into a coherent strategy
   d. Assigning tasks to customer support teams

6. **How does being user-centric differ from being feature-driven?**
   a. User-centric focuses on solving user problems, while feature-driven focuses on adding as many features as possible
   b. User-centric prioritizes market trends, while feature-driven ignores them
   c. User-centric avoids adding features altogether
   d. User-centric relies on intuition, while feature-driven is data-based

7. **What is one ethical responsibility of DPMs when using user data?**
   a. Selling user data to third-parties
   b. Ensuring transparency, consent, and data security
   c. Avoiding the use of user feedback in decision-making
   d. Using data solely to increase profitability

8. **What was the reason behind the failure of early product management practices?**
   a. A lack of interest in user needs
   b. Overloading products with features that often-left users frustrated
   c. A focus on user retention over acquisition
   d. Ignoring business objectives

9. **How does collaboration contribute to product success?**
   a. By allowing one team to dominate the decision-making process
   b. By ensuring that all teams work toward a shared product vision
   c. By reducing the need for user research
   d. By focusing only on marketing deliverables

10. **Why is the ability to say no strategically important for DPMs?**
    a. To avoid unnecessary meetings
    b. To ensure the team focuses on the most critical priorities and avoids scope creep
    c. To delegate tasks effectively
    d. To speed up the development process

Answers

1	b
2	c
3	c
4	b
5	c
6	a
7	b
8	b
9	b
10	b

CHAPTER 2
Product Vision from Insight to Strategy

Introduction

A good product manager knows that everything starts with understanding the customer. The first step, even before building a product or a feature, is crucial to dive deep into the target audience, learning about their real-world challenges and their frustrations, and not just focus on the functionalities they may actually need. Without this insight, even the most polished product can miss the mark. Asking the right questions as to why they are frustrated or what would make their job easier.

Product development is an art based on a simple truth: A product only succeeds if it solves the right problems. That is why customer needs should always come first, without exception. The focus is not just on adding features; it is about making the customer's life easier and helping them get their jobs done better and faster.

Of course, aligning with the business vision, or goals for launching new products, whether it is to grow their market share, reach new customer segments, boost revenue, or stay competitive, is important, but only after the underlying customer need is uncovered. Great product managers step into their users' shoes, ask the tough questions, and stay relentlessly focused on solving meaningful problems, and if possible, visit the customer at their location to observe their process, to see it firsthand and not just hear them explain. That is where real value is created.

Structure

This chapter covers the following topics:

- Understanding customer needs
- Understanding value propositions
- Value proposition
- Jobs to Be Done
- Product Vision Canvas
- Kano Model
- Product vision and analysis

Objectives

By the chapter's end, you will walk away with a practical framework for translating customer insights into a compelling product vision, ensuring your product not only meets user needs but also stands out in a competitive market. You will gain actionable strategies to engage with customers, prioritize features effectively, and craft a strong value proposition, setting the foundation for long-term product success.

Understanding customer needs

Understanding customer needs is critical for any product manager, and one of the best ways to do that is by interacting with customers regularly. Consider this: *How often do you actively engage with your customers as a product manager?* Moreover, if you are an aspiring product manager, how would it usually make sense to interact with customers? If you answered anything less than once a month, it is high time you started interacting more often with your customers.

To better understand customer needs, it is recommended that you interact with your customers regularly, at least once a week. However, if that is not feasible, then at least once a month is recommended. You can do this virtually, through email, chat, or video conferencing, to connect with your customers and gather feedback on the product.

However, to get an even better understanding of customers, it is helpful if you can visit them at their place of use and observe how they interact with the product. This allows you to see firsthand how the customer behaves, how the product works, and what issues or problems they may face. By doing this, you can better understand customer needs and tailor your product to meet those needs.

Interacting regularly with customers is crucial for understanding their needs and improving your product. Whether done virtually or in person, prioritizing customer interactions is essential for building a successful product. There are several ways to interact with customers, including conducting interviews and focus groups with a targeted few, involving your customers in testing, observing data metrics to identify patterns, and sending out feedback surveys.

Imagine yourself as a digital product manager eager to gather insights that will shape the development of your latest project. *Understanding your users is critical to success, but where do you begin?* Let us look at various methods you can use to collect customer requirements and feedback in this section.

Surveys and questionnaires

Picture yourself crafting surveys tailored to your users' needs. You ask questions that matter, aiming for clear and concise feedback. You might even consider offering incentives to boost participation, after all, *who does not love a little reward for their time?* You start by defining the objectives of your survey and what specific questions you want to answer. *What insights are you hoping to gain?*

As you begin drafting your survey questions, remember the importance of clarity and simplicity. It would help to avoid jargon or complex language confusing your respondents. Instead, opt for clear, straightforward, easy-to-understand, and short questions so that the customer reads the questions and is willing to respond, rather than sending out lengthy surveys.

However, you also know that crafting the perfect survey requires more than just writing questions; it is about designing an experience that engages and motivates respondents to participate. So, you consider the length of your survey, keeping it concise enough to capture valuable insights without overwhelming your users.

Now, it is time to choose the right platform for distributing your survey. You explore various options, from dedicated survey tools to built-in survey features on social media platforms. You weigh the pros and cons of each platform, considering factors like accessibility, customization options, and analytics capabilities.

As you launch your survey, you are mindful of the importance of incentivizing participation. You consider offering rewards or incentives to encourage users to provide feedback. Whether it is a discount code, a chance to win a prize, or simply a heartfelt thank you, you recognize the value of showing appreciation for your respondents' time and effort.

However, your work continues once the survey is live; now, it is time to promote it. You leverage your communication channels, email newsletters, social media platforms, and even your product to spread the word about your survey. You are strategic in your messaging, highlighting the benefits of participating and emphasizing the impact their feedback will have on shaping the future of your product.

As responses start pouring in, you are vigilant in monitoring the data. You analyze response rates, demographic breakdowns, and open-ended feedback to uncover meaningful insights. You are also prepared to follow-up with respondents who may have provided incomplete or unclear responses, ensuring you capture the most comprehensive data possible.

Throughout the process, you must remain mindful of potential pitfalls and biases that could skew your results. You are cautious not to ask leading questions or inadvertently influence respondents' answers. Instead, you strive for neutrality and objectivity, seeking to uncover genuine insights that will inform your product decisions.

In the end, conducting a survey is not just about collecting data; it is about connecting with your users, undterstanding their needs and preferences, and using that knowledge to create a resonant product. By following these best practices and staying true to your objectives, you are well-equipped to harness the power of surveys to drive meaningful change in your digital product management journey.

User interviews

Before conducting interviews, meticulously prepare for each session. Define your objectives, outline your interview guide, and select participants representing your target audience. Setting clear goals and criteria ensures that your interviews are focused and productive.

Creating a comfortable and friendly environment is essential to building trust and establishing a positive rapport with the participants when starting an interview. To encourage open and honest communication, you should ask open-ended questions that allow your participants to share their experiences and insights freely. Avoid asking leading questions that may bias responses and instead use neutral prompts that spark meaningful conversations. By allowing participants to express themselves in their own words, you can uncover valuable insights that may have been missed.

Active listening is crucial during user interviews. Tune into participants' words, tone, and body language. Nod along, maintain eye contact, and probe deeper into areas of interest. Demonstrating genuine interest and empathy fosters a collaborative atmosphere where participants feel heard and valued.

When conversing with someone, probing for details to uncover nuances and underlying motivations is essential. Asking follow-up questions can help clarify responses, and seeking examples can help illustrate critical points. Ask them if it is possible to show what they are currently doing. Usually, people might forget all the details or realize they have not mentioned something until they see it and think about it. Also, record the responses or take pictures, as it will help you later when you record your discovery details and discuss the analysis with your team.

Exploring unexpected avenues during the conversation and delving deeper into participants' perspectives is essential to comprehensively understand their needs and preferences. Above all, show interest in what the other person is saying and try to understand what they would do differently or what makes it challenging to perform their job.

Remain neutral throughout the interview, refraining from expressing your opinions or assumptions. Adopt a curious mindset, approaching each response with an open mind and a willingness to learn. Staying neutral ensures that participants feel comfortable sharing honest feedback without fear of judgment or bias.

Wrap up each interview positively, expressing gratitude for participants' time and insights. Offer opportunities for additional feedback or questions and provide clear next steps for follow-up or further engagement. Ending the interview respectfully will leave your participants feeling valued and appreciated.

As you conduct user interviews, approach each session with curiosity, empathy, and humility. By following the best practices listed below and staying attuned to participants' needs, you can gather rich insights to inform and shape your digital product's development.

Usability testing and prototyping

As a digital product manager, you must conduct usability testing and get customer feedback before developing. Consider yourself creating a prototype of your latest digital product, eager to see how users interact with it. You start by sketching your ideas or working with your UX designer to prepare the mock samples, using wireframing tools to bring your vision to life. With each click and swipe, you craft an experience reflecting your product's core functionality.

Now, it is time to test your prototype. You invite a group of users to participate in a usability testing session, guiding them through various tasks and scenarios. As they navigate through your prototype, you observe their every move, noting areas of confusion or delight.

One of the best methods for conducting user testing is the think-aloud protocol. Encourage your users to verbalize their thoughts as they interact with your prototype, providing valuable insights into their decision-making process. Request them to speak out as they navigate the designs and what they think about them. Listen attentively as they express their preferences, frustrations, and suggestions for improvement.

However, user testing is not just about watching users interact with your prototype but also about asking the right questions. Before each testing session, prepare guiding questions to uncover specific insights. Ask users about their expectations, preferences, and pain points, guiding the conversation toward areas of interest.

Being aware of potential pitfalls and challenges is essential when conducting user testing. One common mistake is to provide users with too much guidance or context, which can bias their opinions. It is usual for early product managers to get upset when their testing fails. However, it is essential to understand why users think what they think without giving too many details about why the design was created in a particular way. If you build a design that is not easy to understand, you may be able to convince users in the testing group, but it may not be feasible to explain it to every user once it is launched to a broader audience. Therefore, the aim is to maintain neutrality and allow users to explore the prototype independently. Avoid leading questions that may influence their responses and skew the results.

Another thing to remember is that while usability is essential, it is important not to focus solely on usability issues. It is also essential to consider other aspects of the user experience, such as aesthetics, engagement, and emotional response. Pay attention to users' facial expressions, body language, and verbal cues to gain deeper insights into their overall impression of your product.

As you gather feedback from user testing sessions, remember that not all feedback is equal. Some insights may be more valuable, so prioritize input that aligns with your product goals and objectives. Use the feedback to iterate and refine your prototype, making incremental improvements based on user insights.

By embracing user testing and prototyping as integral parts of your product development process, you are laying the foundation for a user-centric approach that prioritizes usability, satisfaction, and success.

Feedback channels

Embedding feedback forms, rating systems, or in-app surveys directly into your product interface. You strategically place these prompts at critical touchpoints, ensuring they are unobtrusive yet easily accessible. Whether it is a simple thumbs-up/thumbs-down button, star rating, or a more elaborate feedback form, you give users multiple avenues to express themselves.

Imagine your users interacting with your product, performing tasks, or exploring features. At key moments, you can gently prompt them for feedback. For instance, you can include a pop-up window after they complete a transaction, requesting a quick rating or a brief comment. Alternatively, you can subtly invite them to share their thoughts as they explore a new feature. By timing these prompts effectively, you can capture feedback when it is most relevant and top-of-mind for users. However, it is important to avoid requesting feedback immediately when they interact with the application the next time. Instead, time your feedback prompts with at least a month's gap in between.

As the feedback starts pouring in, filling your inbox with comments, suggestions, and ratings. It would be best if you diligently analyzed this data, categorizing feedback into actionable insights. Start looking for trends and patterns, identifying common themes or recurring issues. By synthesizing and prioritizing feedback effectively, you should be able to focus on the most impactful changes that will enhance the user experience.

Finally, the feedback loop is closed by responding to users' comments and suggestions. You are acknowledging their input, thanking them for their feedback, providing transparent updates on any changes or improvements made based on their input, or sending out release notes after every update or when a new version is launched. Demonstrating that you value their feedback and actively listen fosters a sense of trust and collaboration with your users.

Listening sessions/focus groups

If you are working on a B2B product, focus groups are an excellent way to interact with your customers in a more interactive setting. You can meticulously plan the session, from selecting participants to designing discussion topics, ensuring representation across different demographics and user segments. Crafting discussion topics that align with your product goals and key areas of interest sets the stage for an engaging and productive session.

As the facilitator, you can select a comfortable venue and arrange seating in a circle or semi-circle to encourage conversation. You can set the stage for an engaging and productive session with refreshments and a warm welcome. Start with icebreaker questions to help participants feel at ease and build rapport, encouraging active participation throughout the discussion.

In practicing active listening, you must tune in to verbal and non-verbal cues, observing body language, facial expressions, and tone of voice to gauge participant reactions. With a keen eye for detail, you should note key insights, themes, and areas of consensus or divergence. Foster an environment where participants feel comfortable sharing honest feedback, both positive and negative; you should ask probing questions to uncover underlying motivations and preferences. Remember, the focus group is for the participants to speak and not for you to keep talking most of the time.

Remaining vigilant against biases, you should ensure diverse perspectives are heard, encouraging dissenting opinions and challenging assumptions to foster critical thinking. Capturing insights in real-time through notetaking, audio or video recording, or live transcription, you can summarize key takeaways at the end of the session and clarify any points of ambiguity.

With a plan for follow-up actions, you can ensure that participant feedback informs tangible improvements to your product. Each interaction becomes an opportunity to deepen your understanding of your users and refine your product accordingly. Approaching these sessions with empathy, curiosity, and a commitment to continuous improvement will pave the way for a product that truly resonates with your users' needs and aspirations.

Understanding value propositions

Product value proposition refers to the unique combination of benefits and value that a product offers to its target customers. It succinctly communicates why a customer should choose a particular product over alternatives available in the market. Essentially, the value proposition answers the question: *What problem does this product solve, and why is it better than other solutions?* In the first chapter, we discussed the different products and the time it took to reach 1 million users. Did you consider why and how they reached 1 million users and stood out amongst their competitors? Yes, right, because of their product value proposition.

Key elements for a strong value proposition

This section outlines the considerations and key elements for the product to offer a strong value proposition, which in turn creates business value.

Customer needs

When creating a product, it is crucial to prioritize your customer. This means identifying your target audience's challenges or pain points and demonstrating how your product can effectively address those needs. It is not enough for a product to look good; it must also have an emotional design that speaks to the customer's needs and pain points. With this, the product will serve its intended purpose.

Apple and its customer centric innovation

Apple is a perfect example of a brand that prioritizes customer needs at the core of its product development. When Apple creates products like the iPhone, Apple Watch, or AirPods, it does not just focus on aesthetics or technical specs; it zeroes in on solving real customer challenges. For instance, consider the iPhone. Apple has consistently addressed user pain points by refining its operating system to be user-friendly, secure, and intuitive. Features like Face ID emerged from the understanding that remembering and typing passwords is a hassle, offering users a seamless and secure alternative.

However, Apple does not stop at functionality. It deeply understands the power of emotional design; its products are not only practical but also aspirational. The sleek design of the iPhone and the simplicity of the Apple Watch interface evoke a strong emotional connection, making users feel that the product is a reflection of their identity and lifestyle. This is where Apple excels: By merging utility with design, it creates a bond that goes beyond basic usage.

Take the AirPods as another example. Apple recognized that tangled wires and unreliable connectivity were pain points for traditional headphone users. By creating a wireless design with seamless integration into the Apple ecosystem, Apple solved these issues effortlessly. Features like noise cancellation and spatial audio further enhance the experience, making the AirPods indispensable for their intended purpose.

Apple's success is built on its ability to deeply understand customer needs, address pain points effectively, and deliver products that not only work flawlessly but also resonate emotionally. By doing this, Apple ensures its products serve their intended purpose while building lasting loyalty with its customers.

Differentiation

Your product stands out by its unique differentiation factor, setting it apart from competitors and positioning it as a market leader. Highlight your product's unique features, attributes, or advantages that set it apart from competitors and make it a compelling choice for customers.

Tesla redefining differentiation in the automotive industry

Tesla is a prime example of a company that excels at differentiation, setting itself apart in a fiercely competitive automotive market. Unlike traditional car manufacturers, Tesla does not just sell cars; it offers a comprehensive vision for the future of sustainable transportation. Its differentiation lies in its unique combination of cutting-edge technology, environmental responsibility, and a focus on customer centric innovation.

Tesla stands out with its unique innovation and market differentiation. First, its vehicles are built on state-of-the-art electric powertrains that deliver unmatched performance and efficiency. Features like Autopilot, Tesla's advanced driver-assistance system, showcase the company's forward-thinking approach to integrating AI and automation into the driving experience. While competitors may dabble in **electric vehicles (EVs)**, Tesla's early dominance in creating long-range EVs with a robust Supercharger network solidified its position as an industry leader.

Tesla's differentiation extends beyond the vehicles themselves. The company has cultivated an ecosystem that includes solar energy products and battery storage solutions, reinforcing its commitment to sustainability. This seamless integration of products sets Tesla apart as not just a car manufacturer but a pioneer in clean energy innovation. Tesla's over-the-air software updates are another defining feature, providing customers with continual improvements and new functionalities without visiting a dealership, something few competitors offer.

At the heart of Tesla's appeal is its bold branding and visionary leadership. The company has built a reputation for innovation and disruption, making its products not just cars but symbols of progress and modernity. This differentiation makes Tesla more than a choice; it becomes a compelling choice for customers who value performance, sustainability, and cutting-edge technology.

By consistently delivering on its promise of innovation, sustainability, and unique customer value, Tesla remains a standout in the automotive industry and a benchmark for differentiation.

Value proposition

It is always important to prioritize the benefits that your product or service can bring to your customers. No matter how many features your product has, your customers will only be interested if they understand how it will benefit them. Your value proposition should communicate the positive outcomes and benefits customers can expect from using the product. These benefits can range from saving time and money to improving efficiency and enhancing quality of life. Therefore, it is crucial to emphasize and highlight the benefits of your product to attract and retain customers. In upcoming chapters, we will discuss more about the art of storytelling and how you can convey the benefits and tie the whole story together that will leave an impression on customers.

A well-defined product value proposition is a guiding principle for product development, marketing, and sales efforts.

Imagine this as the compelling narrative that captures the essence of your offering. It is the elevator pitch that convinces potential customers, clearly and concisely, why your product is the answer to their problems or desires. A critical distinction to grasp is that a value proposition goes beyond simply listing a product's features. Features are the technical aspects of your product, what it does. A value proposition, however, focuses on the benefits and why it matters to the customer. It translates those features into tangible improvements in the user's life.

For instance, a fitness tracker might feature heart rate monitoring. However, the value proposition would translate that into a benefit like achieving your fitness goals faster with real-time heart rate data that helps you optimize your workout intensity and motivates you to achieve goals by providing trends and nudging you to move.

The value proposition is essentially the promise your product makes to its customers. It serves as the bedrock for all your marketing endeavors, directing your messaging and ensuring that your target audience comprehends the exceptional value your product offers compared to the competition. By explicitly stating this value proposition, you can attract customers, build trust, and boost sales and user adoption. Therefore, the next time you come across a new product, take a moment to reflect on its value proposition. *Does it resonate with you? Does it cater to a need you have?* If the answer is yes, then that product has effectively fulfilled its purpose in the crowded marketplace. The value proposition is essentially the promise your product makes to its customers. It serves as the bedrock for all your marketing endeavors, directing your messaging and ensuring that your target audience comprehends the exceptional value your product offers compared to the competition. By explicitly stating this value proposition, you can attract customers, build trust, and boost sales and user adoption. Therefore, the next time you come across a new product, take a moment to reflect on its value proposition. Ask yourself the following questions: *Does it resonate with you? Does it cater to a need you have?* If the answer is yes, then that product has effectively fulfilled its purpose in the crowded marketplace.

Zoom's clear value proposition

Zoom is a brilliant example of a company that prioritizes the benefits its product brings to customers, making its value proposition crystal clear. In a world where virtual communication is a necessity, Zoom stands out by promising seamless, reliable, and easy-to-use video conferencing solutions that save time, enhance collaboration, and connect people effortlessly.

When Zoom entered the market, competitors already offered video conferencing tools, but many were plagued with technical glitches, complexity, or poor user experience. Zoom identified this gap and built its value proposition around delivering simplicity and reliability. Instead of focusing solely on its technical features, such as HD video or screen sharing, Zoom highlighted how these features translated into tangible benefits for users. It promised to make virtual meetings easy, accessible, and productive for everyone, a promise that resonated across industries and demographics.

Zoom's value proposition emphasizes benefits such as saving time with one-click meetings, enhancing collaboration with intuitive tools like breakout rooms, and bridging distances by connecting teams, friends, and families worldwide. During the pandemic, this value became even more relevant, as remote work and virtual gatherings became the norm. The company's ability to communicate the real-life impact of its product, helping teams stay connected, teachers reach students, and families celebrate milestones, turned it into a household name.

For example, a teacher using Zoom does not just see it as a tool with features like *virtual whiteboarding* or *screen sharing*. They see it as a way to ensure their students stay engaged and learn effectively, even from a distance. Similarly, a business team values Zoom for how it enables them to conduct productive meetings without the frustration of technical barriers or poor quality.

By focusing on the benefits its product brings, rather than just its features, Zoom has effectively established trust, built a loyal customer base, and stood out in a crowded market. It is a testament to the power of a well-articulated value proposition: One that speaks directly to the needs and desires of its customers.

You can identify the value proposition differently, but the most popular methods are using **Jobs to Be Done (JBTD)**, the value proposition canvas, and the Kano Model.

Jobs to Be Done

The JTBD framework is not credited to a single inventor. There is a shared origin story involving two key figures, *Theodore Levitt* and *Peter Drucker*, who laid the groundwork for JTBD with their writings in the years leading up to the 1990s. Their focus on understanding customer needs and the underlying processes behind purchasing decisions helped pave the way for the JTBD concept. Later, in the 1990s, *Tony Ulwick* was considered the father of JTBD in its modern form, and founded the innovation consulting firm strategy. He developed a process called **Outcome-Driven Innovation (ODI)**, which focused on understanding the desired outcomes customers seek from products and services. This concept laid the foundation for the JTBD framework. While *Ulwick* had been successfully applying JTBD within Strategy for over a decade, *Clayton Christensen*, a *Harvard Business School* professor, brought the framework to a broader audience. In his influential book, *The Innovator's Solution* (2003), *Christensen* discussed JTBD and its role in disruptive innovation. This exposure significantly increased awareness of the framework within the business and product development communities.

The JTBD theory is a robust framework that enables businesses to understand their customers' needs and develop a winning value proposition. Instead of focusing on fancy features and technical jargon, JTBD concentrates on the essential jobs your target audience tries to accomplish daily. By recognizing these JTBDs, you can create a product that becomes the ideal employee for the job.

The following are some of the ways you can use the JTBD framework effectively and utilize it as a game-changer for your product development process:

- **Uncover hidden needs:** The main objective of using this model is to help you go beyond the surface-level wants of your customers and instead understand the underlying motivations behind their actions. By focusing on the task they are trying to accomplish, you may discover hidden needs and frustrations that conventional market research methods may miss. To achieve this, it is important to try to comprehend the job they are trying to do and inquire about the reasons behind it. Do not attempt to steer the conversation towards your objectives, but instead, let them speak and express their needs and frustrations.

- **Prioritize features:** The process of identifying the most essential features that are necessary to complete a task can be a challenging task for any product manager. However, using the JTBD framework can help you identify the core functionalities that users demand and prioritize development efforts accordingly. JTBD allows you to determine which features are necessary for completing a task effectively and which are merely bells and whistles that can be ignored.

  While listening to feedback and gathering ideas from everyone and all directions is important, as a product manager, it is your responsibility to use converging methods to filter out unnecessary features and prioritize the ones that can truly help the user achieve their goal. This requires you to identify the core functionalities that will provide the most value to the end user and prioritize them over others.

  Using JTBD and converging methods can also help you avoid feature creep, which refers to the tendency to add more features to a product than what is necessary. By focusing on the core functionalities that users demand, you can ensure that your product provides the necessary value and meets users' needs. This, in turn, can help you build a product that is more likely to succeed in the market and attract more users.

- **Innovation through JTBD:** To create truly innovative products and services, it is essential to understand JTBD theory. This involves identifying the unmet needs and unfulfilled jobs of your target audience. Doing so, you can better understand their problems and the solutions they seek. With this knowledge, you can create products and services that meet their needs and exceed their expectations.

  Also, you can identify gaps in the market that other companies may have overlooked. This can create new products and services that disrupt existing markets and capture new audiences. In other words, JTBD theory can be a powerful tool for innovation and growth. The key to success is to stay focused on your customers' needs. Understanding their JTBD allows you to create solutions tailored to their needs and preferences. This can lead to increased customer loyalty, higher sales, and a stronger brand reputation.

The following figure is a sample template of how you can evaluate the needs and use the JTBD framework:

JOBS-TO-BE-DONE (JTBD)

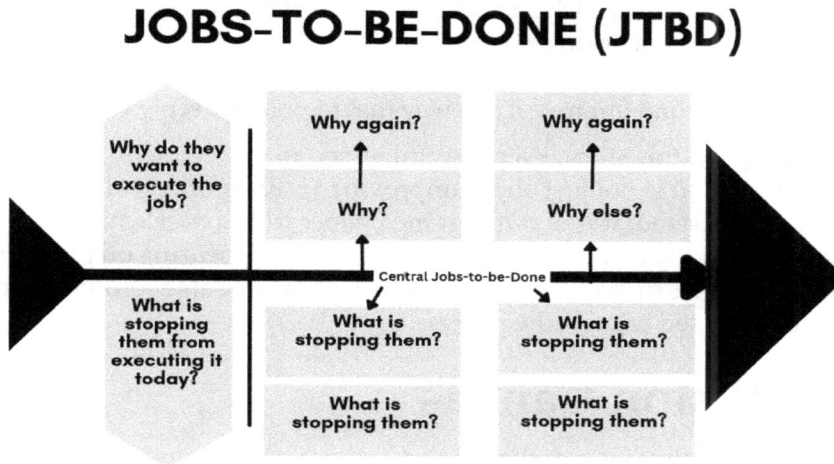

Figure 2.1: Template of JTBD framework

McDonald's case study

When it comes to understanding the JTBD framework, *McDonald* offers one of the most iconic examples, popularized by *Clayton Christensen*. The story of how McDonald's reimagined its milkshakes is not just about improving a product, it is about discovering why customers truly *hire* a product and how it solves their specific needs.

McDonald's wanted to increase milkshake sales, but first needed to understand why customers were purchasing milkshakes in the first place. Using the JTBD framework, they approached the problem from the perspective of the customer. Researchers spent hours observing and interviewing customers, asking what job the milkshake was being hired to do. The findings were both surprising and insightful.

The researchers discovered that many customers bought milkshakes early in the morning on their way to work. These customers were not seeking milkshakes for indulgence or to satisfy a sweet tooth. Instead, the milkshake was solving a very specific problem: Making their commute more enjoyable while keeping them full until lunchtime. Milkshakes were convenient to consume with one hand, lasted longer than other breakfast items like donuts, and were thick enough to occupy the customer throughout their drive.

Understanding this job allowed McDonald's to redefine its milkshake strategy. They did not just make the milkshake taste better; they focused on making it even more effective at performing its job. They experimented with making the milkshake thicker to last longer during commutes and offered additional features, like convenience-focused promotions for morning commuters.

This JTBD insight also helped McDonald's see how its milkshakes could compete, not just against other milkshakes but against entirely different products, like bagels, bananas, or even boredom during a commute. *The result?* A clearer understanding of their product's purpose, allowed them to market and improve it in a way that resonated deeply with their audience.

For product managers, this story is a powerful lesson in understanding the real job your product is hired to do. It is not just about improving features or responding to superficial customer feedback. Instead, it is about digging deeper to discover what need or problem your product solves in the context of the customer's life. By focusing on the job rather than the product, McDonald's turned a milkshake into an indispensable solution for commuters and dramatically boosted sales in the process.

Product Vision Canvas

Your Product Vision Canvas is a powerful and comprehensive strategic tool that can help you chart the course for your digital product. It is a one-page framework that allows you to define your product's purpose, target audience, and desired outcomes in a structured and organized way. Using this canvas, you can develop a compelling vision to guide your product development process towards success. It is also an efficient way to communicate your product vision and pitch to your leaders. One of the key benefits of the Product Vision Canvas is its standardized format. Unlike free-form vision boards, the canvas provides a consistent and repeatable approach to product visioning. This consistency ensures that your product initiatives are aligned with your organization's goals and values. Additionally, it ensures that your product vision is communicated effectively across teams, departments, and stakeholders. If you prefer a more collaborative approach, you can opt for a board and work with your team in person to stick ideas to the board during brainstorming and discovery sessions.

However, it is essential to remember that the Product Vision Canvas is not a rigid blueprint. It is a starting point that can be iterated and refined as you gather user feedback and market data. By adapting your canvas to reflect the latest insights, you can ensure that your product vision stays up-to-date and relevant to your target audience. By leveraging the Product Vision Canvas, you can develop a clear and shared understanding of your target audience and your product's value. This understanding not only helps you navigate the digital world but also enables you to anticipate market trends. This strategic foresight is key to steering your product toward a successful future, making the Product Vision Canvas an essential tool for product managers, designers, and developers.

Roman Pichler's product vision board is a popular and powerful strategic tool created to help product teams align on what they are building and why. It is particularly useful in the early stages of product development, when clarity and shared understanding can make the difference between building the right product and wasting time and resources. This canvas serves as a guide for defining and communicating the key components of a product strategy, combining customer insights, product definition, and business value in a single, easy-to-grasp format, especially for early product managers who have not built one before.

At the heart of the vision board is the product vision, which articulates the long-term purpose or goal of the product. It sets the tone and direction, describing the positive change the product aims to bring to users or the market. This vision serves as a North Star, ensuring everyone on the team is working toward a shared objective that goes beyond just shipping features.

Next, comes the target group, which defines who the product is being built for. This includes identifying key user segments, customer personas, or markets that will benefit from the product. Understanding the people you are designing for, what motivates them, and what challenges they face is critical to making meaningful product decisions.

Following that, the canvas focuses on user needs, the specific problems or pain points the target group experiences. Rather than guessing what users want, this section encourages teams to articulate the real-world challenges that the product should solve. It is where empathy and product thinking intersect, pushing teams to focus on outcomes over outputs. This section is particularly important to identify the key challenges faced by the user group so the solutions can be built to address a real problem that exists and not what the product manager thinks may be a problem.

Once those needs are identified, the product section outlines what the actual product is and how it will meet those needs. This includes high-level features or capabilities that are core to solving the user's problems. It is not about detailed requirements but about painting a clear picture of what makes the product valuable and different. Along with the product details, it is also important to define what success means to this product feature/ functionality, and then list out all the core metrics along with the baseline so that the success can be measured post-launch.

Finally, the vision board connects the dots back to the business through the business goals. This section outlines what the company expects to achieve by building this product, whether it is increased revenue, user growth, market expansion, or brand positioning. It is a reminder that while customer needs are central, the product also has to deliver measurable value to the business.

Altogether, Roman Pichler's vision board offers a structured way to align customer insights, product definition, and business strategy. It is most powerful when used collaboratively, revisited, and refined as the team learns more about their users and the product evolves. For anyone looking to bridge the gap between vision and execution, this canvas is an excellent starting point.

Kano Model

The Kano Model is a well-known and valuable tool in product management that will help you prioritize product features to ensure that a product delivers the most desired value to your target audience. Using this Kano Model, you can categorize the product features-based on how your customers perceive their impact on satisfaction. This model can classify product features into three categories: must have, performance, and delighters.

The must have features are those your customers expect as a bare minimum from a product. Failing to include must have features will lead to extreme dissatisfaction among customers. On the other hand, performance features are those that your customers use to evaluate the quality of a product. These features are directly proportional to customer satisfaction, meaning that the better the performance feature, the higher the customer satisfaction. Delighters are features that customers do not expect but are thrilled to have when they are included in a product. Delighters create a wow factor and will increase your customer loyalty.

Let us examine a case study that uses the Kano Model to explore customer preferences for *Star Games*. This educational video game company develops games for children to prepare them for the **State of Texas Assessments of Academic Readiness (STAAR)** exam.

Customer needs and Kano Model

Star Games conducted a Kano Model survey using paired questions to gauge customer satisfaction with various features of their educational video games to understand which features resonate the most with parents.

Here is an example of a Kano Model survey question for Star Games:

- **Functional question:** *How satisfied would you be if the game adapted its learning difficulty to your child's pace?*

- **Dysfunctional question:** *How dissatisfied would you be if the game did not offer adaptive learning difficulty?* (This assesses the same feature)

- **Results and analysis:** By analyzing responses from a large group of parents, Star Games can categorize the features into the following Kano Model classifications:

    o **Basic needs (must-be):** Some features are considered standard by customers and are crucial for their satisfaction. If any of these features are included, it can result in significant satisfaction. In the case of Star Games, some examples of such features are a safe and secure gaming environment, age-appropriate content, visually appealing graphics, and engaging gameplay that can motivate kids to prepare for their STAAR tests while making studying fun.

    o **Performance needs (one-dimensional):** The quality of features is directly related to customer satisfaction. If a feature is good, the customer is happy. Some examples of such features include the range of educational topics covered, the effectiveness of learning mechanisms, and the level of difficulty offered. In this context, adaptive learning difficulty would be considered a good feature. This means the questions would get progressively more challenging as the children correctly answer each question.

    o **Delighter needs (attractive):** The following text discusses certain features that can delight customers without causing dissatisfaction when absent. These features can be an excellent way to distinguish a product from its competitors. For instance, Star Games could consider incorporating augmented reality integration, personalized learning recommendations, instructional videos that offer shortcuts and methods to help kids understand lessons better, or the ability for parents to track their child's learning progress in detail. This could be done through alerts based on the scores they set, which would notify them if their child's score falls below a particular threshold.

o **Actionable insights:** By understanding how different features map to the Kano Model, Star Games can prioritize their development efforts.

o **Must be/basic features:** Ensure these are present and functioning well, as they are foundational for customer satisfaction.

o **Performance needs:** Improve these features to increase customer satisfaction and stand out from competitors. Adaptive learning difficulty is a prime target for improvement based on the example.

o **Delighter needs:** Invest in developing these features to create a truly delightful user experience that sets Star Games apart.

The Kano Model is a valuable tool for Star Games to prioritize the features of their educational video games based on the needs of their customers. By focusing on the essential must-be features, improving performance needs, and implementing innovative excitement needs, Star Games can develop games that resonate with parents and offer a superior learning experience for children. This case study demonstrates the effectiveness of the Kano Model in helping companies understand what matters to their customers, optimize product development, and achieve long-term success.

Product vision and analysis

When developing a digital product, a clear product vision and thorough analysis are essential. These two elements can serve as anchors to keep your product on track and prevent it from getting lost. To explain in simpler terms, a product vision is a statement that encapsulates the long-term ambition of your product and serves as a roadmap for your team. It acts as a guiding star that helps you and your team navigate through uncharted waters. It is a powerful tool that keeps you focused on your goals and motivates your team to achieve a common objective. You must understand your target audience to create a compelling product vision. You need to know their challenges, pain points, and aspirations. You need to put yourself in their shoes and understand their needs. Your product vision should be user-centric, positioning your product as the ultimate solution to their problems. Your product vision should be ambitious but feasible and grounded in reality so that you can achieve your goals. It is essential to be ambitious, but you also need to be realistic. A well-crafted product vision should inspire your team to work towards a common goal and should be achievable within a reasonable timeframe.

The best way to start identifying the product vision is for you or your team to be able to answer the most fundamental question: *What problem are you solving, and for whom?* The answer to this question should be clear and concise. Your product vision should be easy to understand and communicate internally and externally. Product vision is crucial to help you and your team stay focused on goals and motivate you towards a common objective. The vision should be user-centric, realistic, and set achievable goals. It should also be scalable, meaning it should have a long-term focus beyond just a few years. This is important as it ensures your strategy aligns with the company goals and meets customers' core needs. A well-crafted vision will inspire your team to work towards long-term goals, and it should be easy to understand and communicate.

Once you have a clear product vision, you must perform a thorough analysis to ensure your product is built on a solid foundation. This analysis should encompass various factors, including market trends, user needs, and the competitive landscape. Market trends can give you insights into what is currently in demand and what areas are ripe for innovation. User needs are critical to understanding your target audience's challenges and how your product can solve them. The competitive landscape can help you identify potential threats and opportunities and areas where you can differentiate your product from others in the market. By performing a detailed analysis, you can ensure that your product is built on a solid foundation and has the potential to succeed in the marketplace. With a clear product vision and a thorough analysis, you can confidently navigate the ever-changing landscape of digital innovation and build a product that meets the needs of your target audience.

A strong vision anticipates upcoming trends and technological advancements. Consider how your product can evolve and adapt to stay relevant as the digital world transforms. Finally, your vision should be inspiring and motivational. It should ignite a spark within your team, a rallying cry motivating everyone to strive towards a shared goal. A well-defined product vision is not just a fancy slogan; it offers many benefits. It provides a strategic direction, ensuring all decisions throughout the development process align with the long-term goals. It fosters a sense of unity and purpose within your team, keeping everyone focused on the bigger picture.

Additionally, it facilitates communication and prioritization with stakeholders by outlining the product's purpose and value proposition. This clarity will help you prioritize features and development efforts, ensuring you are not wasting resources on irrelevant tangents. Most importantly, a strong vision keeps you user-focused. By constantly referring to the target audience's needs, you ensure your product remains relevant and valuable to the people who matter most.

Let us look at a real-world example of a company with a strong product vision: *Airbnb*. Their vision statement is simple yet powerful: *To create a world where anyone can belong anywhere.* This user-centric vision addresses the fundamental human need for connection and belonging. It is future-oriented, anticipating a world without geographical limitations when finding accommodation. Most importantly, it is inspiring. It evokes a sense of community and global connection. Airbnb did not achieve its current success overnight. They started with a clear vision and a deep understanding of their target audience, travelers seeking unique and affordable accommodation experiences. They leveraged technology to connect travelers with local hosts, creating a win-win situation for both parties. By staying true to its vision and continuously iterating on its products based on user feedback, Airbnb has transformed the hospitality industry and established itself as a global leader.

Remember, your product vision is a living document. It should evolve alongside your product and the market landscape. However, by following these steps and learning from successful companies like Airbnb, you can develop a compelling vision that guides your product toward a bright future.

Conclusion

A strong product vision is the foundation of successful digital products. It defines the why behind your product, ensuring every decision aligns with solving real customer problems. Throughout this chapter, we explored how deep customer understanding, clear value propositions, and strategic differentiation drive market success. Companies like Apple, Tesla, and Airbnb did not just build products; they built solutions that resonated deeply with their users.

In the next chapter, we will shift our focus from defining the right product to strategically positioning it in the market, leveraging innovation, competitive analysis, and frameworks to ensure long-term success.

Points to remember

- Regularly gathering customer feedback is key to developing successful products and understanding their pain points.

- Utilize various methods to understand customer needs. This includes surveys, user interviews, usability testing with prototypes, feedback channels within the product, and focus groups (for B2B).

- Actively listen to customer feedback, paying attention to both verbal and non-verbal cues. Avoid leading questions and remain objective to gather unbiased insights.

- Create a unique value proposition that distinguishes your product from competitors, highlighting its benefits and value to customers.

- Use the Kano Model to prioritize product features-based on customer satisfaction. Categorize into must have, performance, and delighters.

- Understanding customer needs is ongoing. Continuously iterate and refine your product based on user insights to ensure it stays relevant and meets evolving customer needs.

- Build trust and transparency with your customers. Respond to feedback, provide development progress updates, and address concerns to demonstrate that you value their input. This fosters a positive relationship and encourages ongoing engagement.

Multiple choice questions

1. **What is the primary goal of a product vision?**
   a. To list all the features of a product
   b. To encapsulate the long-term ambition and strategic direction of a product
   c. To determine a product's technical specifications
   d. To prioritize marketing strategies

2. **According to the chapter, how often should a product manager interact with customers to understand their needs?**
   a. Once a year
   b. Once a month, at a minimum
   c. Twice a week
   d. Only during the product launch phase

3. **What is the key difference between a feature and a value proposition?**
   a. A feature is a technical aspect, while a value proposition focuses on benefits to the customer
   b. A value proposition lists features, while a feature explains the benefits
   c. Features include pricing, while a value proposition does not
   d. Value propositions focus on competitors, while features focus on customers

4. **What benefit does the JTBD framework provide to product managers?**
   a. It helps prioritize technical specifications
   b. It identifies the underlying needs and motivations of customers
   c. It tracks sales performance
   d. It develops marketing campaigns

5. **In the McDonald's milkshake example, what specific job was the milkshake hired to do?**
   a. Provide a sugary treat for dessert
   b. Replace traditional breakfast items like bagels
   c. Make a morning commute more enjoyable while keeping customers full
   d. Act as a marketing strategy to attract younger audiences

6. **What are the three categories of features in the Kano Model?**
   a. Functional, non-functional, emotional
   b. must have, performance, delighters
   c. Core, secondary, bonus
   d. Necessary, optional, luxurious

7. **Why is conducting usability testing important in product development?**
    a. To finalize the marketing message
    b. To evaluate how users interact with a prototype and identify areas for improvement
    c. To test the product against competitors
    d. To determine the exact pricing for the product

8. **Which real-world example demonstrates a clear and inspiring product vision?**
    a. Tesla's focus on product differentiation
    b. Airbnb's vision to create a world where anyone can belong anywhere
    c. McDonald's focus on milkshake improvements
    d. Zoom's emphasis on virtual connectivity

9. **How does the Kano Model help prioritize product features?**
    a. By focusing only on delighters
    b. By categorizing features-based on their impact on customer satisfaction
    c. By assigning a monetary value to each feature
    d. By comparing features against competitors

10. **What is a Product Vision Canvas used for?**
    a. To track the technical specifications of a product
    b. To define the product's purpose, target audience, and desired outcomes in a structured way
    c. To identify marketing channels for a product
    d. To map out competitor strategies

Answers

1	b
2	b
3	a
4	b
5	c
6	b
7	b
8	b
9	b
10	b

Join our Discord space

Join our Discord workspace for latest updates, offers, tech happenings around the world, new releases, and sessions with the authors:

https://discord.bpbonline.com

CHAPTER 3

Product Market Strategy from Ideation to Domination

Introduction

Product strategy is the foundation of long-term success, guiding a product's growth, differentiation, and market positioning. As a product manager, understanding how to craft and execute a strong strategy is essential in ensuring your product not only survives but thrives in a competitive landscape. This chapter explores the core principles of product strategy, emphasizing the role of innovation, competitive analysis, and strategic decision-making. Through real-world examples like *Netflix* and *Canva*, you will learn how companies leverage innovation to gain a competitive edge and redefine industries. Equipped with frameworks such as **Strength, Weakness, Opportunity, Threat (SWOT)** analysis, Porter's Five Forces, and the Improvement Kata model, you will gain practical tools to assess competition, identify opportunities, and build a resilient, forward-thinking strategy.

Structure

This chapter covers the following topics:

- Product strategy and innovation
- Product innovation
- Importance of innovation

- Disruptive innovation
- Competitive analysis
- Different types of competitive analysis
- Porter's Five Forces analysis

Objectives

By the chapter's end, you will walk away with a practical framework for developing and executing product strategy, allowing you to identify market opportunities, drive innovation, and build competitive differentiation. You will gain actionable insights into how to analyze competition, leverage disruptive innovation, and make data-driven decisions to position your product for long-term success.

Product strategy and innovation

As a product manager, you often come across the term strategy and vision. Still, you may be unable to actively participate in strategy discussions or decision-making meetings, especially in the early stages of your product career. Product strategy is a long-term growth focus that involves a detailed plan guiding the development, positioning, and growth of a single product or a portfolio of products within your company. It comprises a set of decisions and actions aimed at achieving specific business objectives and maximizing the value delivered to your customers while also ensuring that your product aligns with your company's overall vision and goals. Typically, in large companies, multiple strategic goals may be grouped into categories/pillars, and each category has a set of products or initiatives that align with the category's master goal.

At its core, if we have to lay this out, state that product strategy defines how your product will evolve, considering the competitive landscape, market trends, and customer needs and preferences. This involves thoroughly analyzing the target market, including demographics, psychographics, and behavior patterns, and understanding the product's unique value proposition, features, and functionalities.

A well-defined product strategy is essential for driving sustainable growth and competitive advantage in today's dynamic marketplace. It provides a clear roadmap for product development teams, ensuring that your efforts are focused on delivering value where it matters most. This includes prioritizing features and functionalities that align with your customer needs and preferences while considering your company's resource constraints and investment priorities.

Moreover, product strategy serves as a framework for decision-making, guiding choices related to resource allocation, investment priorities, and market opportunities. This involves continuously monitoring and evaluating the product's performance and adjusting as needed to keep it aligned with the company's overall goals and objectives. One of the most significant lessons one can learn in product management career is recognizing that a product will not always remain a top priority. The roadmap can change per business priorities at any time during the year. Imagine your product or feature was on top of the list to be developed and delivered during the next few quarters. Suddenly, the business decided that due to market situations and business challenges, the product would get moved to the backlog and would not be funded. Yes, this can happen. Therefore, always be Agile and ready to make necessary changes.

Product innovation

Let us talk about product innovation. Simply put, it is all about dreaming up and refining digital products, services, or processes to bring something fresh. Whether cooking up entirely new concepts or giving your old products a facelift with exciting new features, the end goal is to deliver solutions that your customers will love and stand out in the market among competitors. But here is the kicker: To nail product innovation, you have got to get inside your customers' heads and have a knack for spotting what is next in tech and trends. It is a rollercoaster ride from research and development to testing and finally hitting the market. Knocking product innovation out of the park can set your business apart, reel in new customers, and fuel that all-important growth.

One possible way to bring innovation is by launching an entirely new range of products to an existing business line. This could involve creating a novel idea that addresses an unmet user need or launching groundbreaking services that disrupt an existing industry.

Usually, when companies make significant improvements to an existing product, they innovate by enhancing the product's features, functionalities, or **user experience** (**UX**). This type of innovation is typically focused on improving an existing product rather than creating a new one from scratch.

Consider an outdated e-commerce platform—one clear innovation is implementing a personalized product recommendation engine. This enhancement transforms the shopping experience by tailoring suggestions for individual user preferences, driving engagement and increasing sales. This recommendation engine would analyze customer data and preferences to suggest products customers are likely interested in. The reason for the personalized approach is that it improves customer satisfaction by making it easier for customers to find the products they want, which can lead to increased sales for the e-commerce platform. To stay ahead, you must push the boundaries—leverage emerging trends, integrate cutting-edge technology, and redefine the shopping experience to set your platform apart.

Other examples of significant improvements to existing products might include adding new features to a software app, improving the user interface of a mobile app, or enhancing the performance of a piece of hardware. In each case, the goal is to make the existing product more appealing to customers and more competitive.

Again, do not think innovation is limited to user-facing aspects and what your customers can use directly. Still, on the other hand, it can also enhance the business process to improve agility by streamlining internal processes, such as developing automated workflows or implementing data-driven decision-making tools.

Importance of innovation

Innovation is the driving force behind long-term business success, allowing companies to differentiate themselves, meet evolving customer needs, and stay ahead in an increasingly competitive landscape. Businesses that fail to innovate risk becoming obsolete, while those that embrace change gain a strategic advantage. Whether through groundbreaking product development, enhanced customer experiences, or refined marketing strategies, innovation fuels growth and sustainability.

The following section explores how digital innovation creates a competitive edge, emphasizing the importance of differentiation, adaptability, and barriers to entry. It also highlights real-world examples, such as Canva, to demonstrate how innovation can revolutionize industries and establish market dominance.

It is essential to have a unique selling proposition that sets you apart from the competition, and this is where digital innovation comes into play. By continually innovating and staying ahead of the curve, you can create a competitive advantage that ensures your business is always at the forefront of your industry. Whether developing new products, refining your marketing strategy, or improving customer experience, digital innovation can help you stay ahead of the competition and make your mark in the digital marketplace.

To establish a strong competitive edge, focus on differentiation, adaptability, and create barriers to entry. The following points outline key strategies to achieve this and ensure sustained market leadership:

- **Offer unique value propositions:** Develop groundbreaking products or services that address unmet customer needs. Imagine being the first to introduce a voice-activated shopping assistant, revolutionizing the e-commerce experience.

- **Stay ahead of the curve:** As technology evolves and user expectations shift, innovation allows you to adapt and stay relevant. Consider how social media platforms constantly introduce new features to keep users engaged.

- **Erect barriers to entry:** Novel solutions make it harder for competitors to copy your success. Your innovative product or service becomes a unique selling proposition, attracting and retaining customers.

Here is an example of a product innovation to illustrate a competitive edge. Let us consider Canva, a graphic design platform. Its competitive advantage was ease of use and accessibility by revolutionizing graphic design and making it accessible to everyone. Visuals and graphic designs before Canva required expensive software and professional expertise, making the process complex and inaccessible to many. They often required expensive software and design expertise. Through a user-friendly drag-and-drop interface, pre-designed templates, and a vast library of design elements, Canva empowered anyone, regardless of design experience, to create stunning graphics; even a 9-year-old kid can use Canva efficiently. This focus on UX has cemented Canva's competitive advantage, attracting a massive user base and disrupting the traditional graphic design market.

The ROI equation shows innovation pays off

Innovation is more than just generating exciting ideas; it is a strategic investment that demands careful planning and execution. Though it involves recognizing new opportunities and creating new products, services, or processes that cater to customers' changing needs, your business would not be keen on investing in ideas and development unless there is a return on investment.

Innovation is not a one-time event; you need to consider this as an ongoing process that requires a commitment to continuous improvement and learning. You and your team should take calculated risks and invest in research and development to stay ahead of the competition. To succeed, businesses must make innovation a core part of their strategy and culture. From the top down, your company leaders would/must foster a culture of creativity and experimentation, where the best practice is where failure is viewed as a learning opportunity rather than a setback. But as mentioned earlier, innovation can be either a product or a process; following are some of the key benefits:

- **Increased revenue:** By offering cutting-edge solutions that resonate with your target audience, you can attract new customers and drive sales.

- **Improved customer retention:** Engaged customers are loyal customers. Innovation fosters a sense of excitement and keeps users coming back for more. Think about how streaming services constantly add new content to keep users subscribed.

- **Enhanced efficiency:** Innovation can also focus on streamlining internal processes. Imagine automating workflows or leveraging data analytics to improve decision-making, leading to cost savings and increased productivity.

Canva redefining digital design with innovation and ROI

Canva is a compelling example of how digital innovation translates into a measurable **return on investment (ROI)**. By making professional-looking graphic design accessible to everyone, Canva opened up a vast new market. They have attracted millions of individual users who might not have otherwise paid for design services. Additionally, their freemium model with premium features entices businesses to upgrade to advanced functionalities, generating a steady revenue stream. Canva fosters customer loyalty through continuous innovation. They consistently introduce new features, design elements, and integrations with popular tools. This keeps users engaged and prevents them from seeking alternatives. Additionally, their focus on ease of use ensures a positive UX, further encouraging retention.

Canva boasts a massive user base encompassing individuals, small businesses, educational institutions, and even large corporations. The *Sacra* website states:

Sacra estimates that Canva is at $1.7B in annual recurring revenue (ARR), up 54% from $1.1B last year. In 2021, Canva was at $750M in ARR at the end of the year, up 100% from $325M in 2020. Canva is at substantially greater revenue scale than competitors like Miro (estimated at $650M ARR) and Figma (projected at $800M ARR) but still dwarfed by the major incumbents in the creative productivity suite: see Adobe at $11B, Google Workspace at $28B, and Microsoft Office at $41B.

Canva has raised $572.6M since being founded in 2013. They have been valued at $39B since their September 2021 fundraising round led by T. Rowe Price and joined by Franklin Templeton, Sequoia Capital Global Equities, and Bessemer Venture Partners. As of today's 2023, estimates, that gives Canva a 23x forward revenue multiple—compared to Adobe at $21B in ARR (up 12%) and a $257B market cap for a 12.2x forward revenue multiple, and Figma, which Adobe acquired was on track for $400M ARR (up 100%) at $20B for a 50x forward multiple.

A shield agaist digital threats

Businesses constantly face unforeseen challenges that can cause significant disruptions if not addressed appropriately. The emergence of disruptive technologies and the increasing number of nimble competitors has made it crucial for businesses to stay ahead of the curve. Companies that fail to adapt to these changes often struggle to keep up with their competitors and may lose their market share overnight.

They need to be proactive and Agile in their approach. They must constantly assess their strategies and adapt to new technologies and market trends. This requires a deep understanding of customers' needs, preferences, and behavior and a willingness to embrace change and take calculated risks.

As a product manager, you need to adopt a growth mindset to stay competitive in the long run and develop a strategy for your product's long-term scalability and growth. Here is where innovation acts as a shield:

- **Increased adaptability:** You become more Agile by fostering a culture of innovation. You can quickly adapt to changing market trends and embrace disruptive technologies before they become threats.

- **Future-proofing your business:** Innovation ensures the digital tide does not leave you behind. By constantly evolving and anticipating future needs, you create a sustainable business model for the long haul.

Consider the previous example of how Canva constantly monitors design trends and user preferences. They readily integrate popular design elements and functionalities based on user feedback and market shifts. For instance, the rise of social media stories prompted them to introduce features specifically for creating engaging story content. The world of design software is constantly evolving. Canva readily embraces new technologies to enhance its platform. They have integrated with popular photo editing tools, cloud storage services, and social media platforms, ensuring users can leverage the latest advancements in their design workflow.

Meeting the ever-evolving customer

Customers' expectations are no longer constant and unchanging. With the ever-evolving technology, customers are constantly demanding more from businesses. You should be able to understand that customers these days expect faster response times, personalized experiences, and seamless interactions across multiple channels. Moreover, with social media's rise, customers expect companies to be more transparent and socially responsible. Therefore, as a product manager, you must stay up to date with the latest technological advancements and adapt to changing customer expectations to remain competitive. Following are some of the key points you should consider to stay ahead of the curve:

- **Deliver exceptional UXs:** By constantly refining your products and services based on user feedback, you create a delightful and intuitive experience that keeps customers happy. Think about how user-friendly interfaces and seamless transactions are now the norm in e-commerce.

- **Anticipate future needs:** Innovation is not just about reacting; it is about anticipating. By staying ahead of customer trends and identifying emerging needs, you can develop solutions that resonate deeply with your target audience.

- **Build stronger customer relationships:** Innovation demonstrates your commitment to continuous improvement and customer satisfaction. This fosters trust and loyalty, creating a stronger bond with your customer base.

In our example, Canva demonstrates agility by introducing features and functionalities catering to this diverse customer base. For instance, they offer business team collaboration features and simplified design tools for non-designers. Canva does not just react to change; they anticipate it. By staying ahead of design trends and technological advancements, they ensure their platform remains relevant and valuable to users in the long-term. For example, the growing demand for video content might lead them to introduce video editing features or integrations with popular video editing tools.

Establish innovation with the Improvement Kata model

As a product manager, it is common to feel the pressure to innovate and stay ahead of the curve in today's competitive market. However, consistently generating creative solutions and bridging the gap between ideas and reality can be challenging. To ensure a smooth launch, it is crucial to have a systematic process in place. This is where the improved SV open-source model built by *Shalini Dinesh* and *Prof. Vasant Gondhalekar* comes in a model based on the *Toyota Kata model*.

The original Toyota Kata model, developed by *Mike Rother*, provides a structured approach to fostering continuous organizational improvement. It holds valuable lessons for product managers seeking to cultivate a culture of innovation. However, it is common for product managers to overlook change control and legal alignment when bridging the gap. This may seem simple, but the gap cannot be bridged successfully without proper change control, training, and communication planning.

It is essential to bring these critical changes and legal alignments into the picture early on during discovery and keep the team informed throughout the development phase. This will help identify dependent systems or processes and prevent disruptions in the cycle chain. If one part of the chain is disrupted, it can lead to chaos. Therefore, it is crucial to maintain a smooth and structured process right from the start to ensure a successful product launch.

Before implementing any improvements, it is crucial to follow a structured approach to problem-solving. The Kata model provides a systematic framework for driving continuous improvement by defining clear challenges, understanding the current situation, setting measurable goals, and experimenting with solutions. The following steps outline how to apply this model effectively in digital product management, ensuring informed decision-making and impactful innovation:

- **Get the direction or challenge:** This is the first stage in the Kata model. This stage requires you to clearly define the challenge or pain points, that will define the direction where you need to focus on your product solution. The current situation you are trying to improve. Gather data, identify pain points, and understand the baseline performance.

- **Grasp the current situation:** This is where most amateur product managers make the mistake. They blindly follow the instructions or directions that are passed on to them from their seniors or leaders without having a firm grasp of the current situation. Talk to the end users, and the systems involved in the process, identify the end-to-end process flow, so you are aware of the full picture, before you can mark a baseline for your target condition.

- **Establish your next target condition:** First step is to define the desired outcome for your digital product. Clearly articulate the ideal future state you are aiming to achieve through your improvement efforts. This target condition should be **specific, measurable, achievable, relevant, and time-bound (SMART)**.

- **Conduct experiments to get there:** This is the heart of the Improvement Kata. Devise small-scale experiments to test potential solutions that might bridge the gap. The focus is on rapid iteration and learning from both successes and failures. Now, let us improve the above Toyota model with an additional step.

Enhanced Kata model

Shalini and *Prof. Vasant* recommend enhancing the traditional Toyota Kata model by introducing a crucial fourth step: Identify change control and legal requirements. This improvement ensures that product development is not only iterative and goal-oriented but also aligned with compliance, regulatory needs, and structured change management. By integrating this additional step, the improved 5 step model provides a more holistic and practical approach for digital product managers navigating complex product lifecycles.

Implementing changes in digital products goes beyond technical execution—it requires a structured approach to regulatory compliance and risk management. Overlooking these factors can lead to security vulnerabilities, operational disruptions, or legal consequences. By proactively evaluating potential impacts, ensuring alignment with industry standards, and maintaining clear documentation, teams can drive seamless implementation, minimize risks, and uphold product integrity. Identifying change control and legal requirements is a key consideration for effectively managing change control and compliance. If a new feature impacts user data, you should update your privacy policy and get user consent. Change control is the formal process of managing system, process, or product modifications. When adding new features or functionalities, change control procedures are often necessary to ensure a controlled and documented rollout.

Here is what you need to consider when identifying change control needs:

- **Impact assessment:** Evaluate how the proposed change influences various aspects of the product. Consider user workflows and whether additional training may be necessary.

- **System impact:** Analyze interactions with other systems and determine if dependent child systems require updates or adjustments.

- **Data impact:** Assess whether the change involves user data collection, storage, or processing user data, ensuring alignment with data privacy and security standards.

- **Stakeholder involvement:** Identify all stakeholders who may be affected, including end users who might require training or support for a smooth transition.

- **Development and operations teams:** Ensure relevant teams have updated documentation or training to support the implementation effectively.

- **Management and executives:** It is crucial to keep them informed and aligned with the change control process.

- **Regulatory compliance:** Ensure your proposed change complies with relevant legal regulations or industry standards. Examples include data privacy regulations (e.g., GDPR, CCPA). If the change involves user data collection or processing, you might need to update privacy policies and obtain user consent.

- **Security standards (e.g., HIPAA, PCI DSS):** If the change relates to sensitive data, ensure it adheres to relevant security protocols.

Disruptive innovation

Now, that we have read about innovation and its importance, let us shift gears and get to speed on what disruptive innovation is. We read that innovation can be anything, such as improving existing systems or processes, automating, etc. However, defining what truly constitutes disruptive innovation is essential If you think about why companies must invest in innovation or why they should adopt innovative strategies, then the top answer would be that it is for them to stay ahead of the curve. That is where disruptive innovation comes in. It is not about improving good products; it is about introducing something entirely new that fundamentally changes how users approach a specific task. Disruptive innovations often come from unexpected places, challenging established players and creating new markets. Innovation improves good things, while disruptive innovation creates new categories and challenges the status quo.

As the PM, the questions you should ask as you are developing a new product or refreshing an existing product should not only be around innovation, but also disruptive innovation. The following questions, while not exhaustive, will help answer the disruptive part:

- *Is there an incumbent fatigue in the market? Meaning, are the customers ready for a change? Have they been using the same product for a long time, and has fatigue started to set in for the same old product(s)?*

- *Is your product going to provide any feature that does not exist in the market today?* For example, ease of use, a step change in lower pricing for the same benefits, or satisfying an unmet need would allow you to cause disruption. Uber satisfied an unmet need, where the consumer gets to know upfront what the cost of the ride will be. It was also rolled out as a product when the existing cab industry was not expecting a digital product for cab service. Uber thus caused multifold disruption.

  Disruption does not have to be only on the technology front. It could also be how you allow the customers to consume it. If your consumption model is not offered in the current market, it can create disruption. The pay-as-you-go became very attractive to the customers.

- *Is there a technology advantage that will sustain the product for a long time, while the competition has to catch up to upgrade?* Fiber-based Wi-Fi became a game changer.

It was not too long ago that we lived in a world without streaming services. Back then, renting movies required a trip to the local blockbuster, where we would browse aisles of VHS tapes. Blockbuster was the undisputed king of video rentals, seemingly unbeatable. However, Netflix emerged as a mail-order **digital versatile disc (DVD)** rental service that offered customers a more comprehensive selection and greater convenience. Unlike blockbuster, Netflix did not directly compete with their brick-and-mortar model but offered a completely different value proposition, selection, and convenience at your fingertips. This is what we call disruptive innovation. Netflix challenged the status quo and redefined how people rented movies, ultimately leading to blockbuster's downfall.

Other classic examples of disruptive innovation in action

In the following section, you will find some of the classic examples of some common products and how they went through disruptive innovation.

Cassettes vs. CDs vs. streaming

The invention of the portable cassette in the 1970s transformed how people listened to music while moving. Before this, people had to rely on bulky players and vinyl records, which were not easily portable. The cassette tape was a game-changer as it allowed people to carry their favorite music with them, making it possible to listen to music while exercising, traveling, or commuting. However, as technology advanced, the cassette format faced a formidable challenge in the form of **compact discs** (**CDs**) in the 1980s.

CDs offered better sound quality and durability than cassettes, making them an immediate hit with music lovers. They quickly became the primary format for portable music, and people started replacing their cassette players with CD players. With the advent of digital music, CDs also started losing their market share, but they remain a popular choice for music enthusiasts who value sound quality.

Similarly, the entertainment industry witnessed another revolution with streaming services like Netflix. Streaming services offered an easy and convenient option to watch movies and TV shows from home, eliminating the need for rental CDs or DVDs. The convenience of streaming services became even more apparent during the COVID-19 pandemic as people were forced to stay indoors and look for ways to entertain themselves. Streaming services filled this void by offering a wide range of content people could watch at their own pace. The evolution of music and video formats has come a long way, and it will be interesting to see what innovations the future holds.

Bookstores vs. Kindle

Brick-and-mortar bookstores have been essential to our society for centuries, providing a unique and engaging experience for book lovers. Remember the days when we used to have a library membership, rent books, and return them on time to avoid paying a fine. It was also when we received books as gifts from friends, with a message and a signature on the first page. However, *Amazon Kindle* e-reader has significantly disrupted the industry with its technology. This portable device offers a vast library of books in a convenient format, making it easier for readers to access their favorite books while on the go.

Furthermore, the Kindle's integration with Amazon's vast digital library has allowed readers to choose from millions of books, including rare and out-of-print titles that would be difficult to find in traditional bookstores. Additionally, introducing audiobooks and other digital formats has further transformed how we consume literature.

Audiobooks, in particular, have become increasingly popular, with many readers preferring to listen to their favorite books while commuting, working out, or simply relaxing. This has opened up a new world of possibilities for people who may have difficulty reading physically or who prefer a more immersive experience. The Kindle e-reader and other digital formats have revolutionized how we read books, providing more options and making reading more accessible to a broader audience.

Kodak vs. digital camera

Remember when we were children, our parents used to have Kodak cameras with film inside, and they had to make sure the film was not removed outdoors and exposed to sunlight, while special care was also taken when printing images at photo studios. In those days, Kodak was a dominant player in the photography industry for many decades. They made capturing memories accessible to the masses through their easy-to-use film cameras and iconic yellow packaging. Kodak focused on improving existing technology and offered a variety of film types, faster shutter speeds, and more user-friendly cameras, which can be considered examples of innovation. However, they were firmly rooted in the film-based market and did not pay much attention to the invention of digital cameras in the 1970s. Although Kodak had a hand in developing early digital camera technology, it initially saw it as a niche product and did not prioritize its development. This is where the concept of disruptive innovation comes into play.

The advent of digital cameras brought with it a new set of features that appealed to a fresh user base. These users preferred convenience, affordability, and instant image sharing. While digital cameras did not necessarily produce superior image quality, film cameras offered a compelling new value proposition resonating with a growing market segment.

These disruptions all share some key characteristics:

- **Focus on a new value proposition:** Disruptive innovations do not just improve on existing products; they offer a fundamentally different way of achieving a task. Think convenience, affordability, or accessibility.

- **Target underserved users:** Disruptors often target a new user base not well-served by existing solutions. Netflix, for example, initially appealed to those who disliked the hassle of late fees and limited selection at blockbuster.

- **Start simple and improve:** Disruptive innovations often begin with a more straightforward, less feature-rich product. They focus on core functionality and gain traction before adding complexity.

The following are some steps you can take to leverage disruptive innovation as a digital product manager:

- **Identify user pain points:** *What are your target audience's frustrations and unmet needs?* Look beyond existing solutions and explore alternative ways to fulfill those needs.

  Embrace simplicity, avoid feature creep, the tendency to continuously add new features beyond the product's core purpose. Instead, focus on delivering a streamlined, impactful solution that directly addresses a user problem in a unique and innovative way.

- **Be willing to experiment:** Disruption often comes from unexpected places. Do not be afraid to experiment with new ideas and test them with real users.

Remember, disruptive innovation is not about overnight success. It is about a willingness to challenge the status quo and think outside the box. By keeping your finger on the pulse of user needs and embracing a culture of experimentation, you can position yourself as the next disruptor in the digital product landscape. So, keep your eyes peeled for opportunities, and who knows, your following digital product might just be the one to revolutionize an entire industry.

Let us explore the classic example, an intriguing case of Netflix, a company that transformed how we watch movies and TV shows. Their journey is a prime example of disruptive innovation that forever changed the entertainment industry landscape.

Case study on Netflix

A masterclass in disruption, Netflix's transformation from a mail-order DVD rental service to a global streaming powerhouse is a prime example of disruptive innovation. The company identified inefficiencies in the traditional video rental model and capitalized on emerging consumer needs, redefining how people accessed and consumed entertainment. The following sections trace Netflix's journey, highlighting key milestones that showcase its ability to adapt, innovate, and ultimately dominate the industry.

Humble beginnings of the mail-order DVD revolution

In 1997, Netflix[1] was founded as a mail-order DVD rental service, quickly gaining popularity as an alternative to traditional video rental stores. Blockbuster was the reigning giant in the video rental industry at that time with its brick-and-mortar stores. However, their limited selection of movies and TV shows and the fees they imposed on late returns caused customer frustration.

---

1. https://about.netflix.com/en

Netflix recognized an opportunity to disrupt this model by offering a more comprehensive selection of movies and TV shows and focusing on convenience. They introduced a subscription-based model that allowed customers to rent unlimited DVDs for a flat monthly fee, which were then delivered straight to their doorsteps. This eliminated the hassle of late payments and trips to the store, offering a superior UX compared to traditional video rental stores.

Netflix's focus on customer experience and convenience did not stop there. They also introduced a personalized recommendation system that suggested movies and TV shows based on the customer's viewing history, making it easier for them to discover new titles they would enjoy.

The power of disruption as convenience beats brick-and-mortar from the 1990s to the 2000s. In 1998, Netflix revolutionized the DVD rental and sales industry by launching the first-ever website that catered to a new user base that prioritized convenience and affordability over the instant satisfaction of physically browsing shelves. Rather than competing with blockbuster on features, Netflix offered a fundamentally different way of renting movies, focusing on a new value proposition. They introduced a subscription model that guaranteed predictable costs and unlimited DVD rentals without due dates, late fees, or monthly rental limits.

This innovative business model fueled Netflix's disruptive growth. In 1999, they debuted their subscription service, and in 2000, they introduced a personalized movie recommendation system that used members' ratings on past titles to predict future choices accurately. In 2005, they launched the profiles feature, allowing members to create lists for different users and moods. By 2006, Netflix had amassed 5 million members.

Streaming revolution from disruptor to leader from 2007 to present

Netflix has always been at the forefront of innovation in the streaming industry. In 2007, they launched their streaming service, which allowed viewers to watch movies and TV shows online. This bold move anticipated a shift in consumer behavior towards on-demand content consumption. Netflix continued to innovate by creating original content, expanding globally, and personalizing recommendations through sophisticated algorithms. These strategic moves solidified their position as the leader in the streaming industry, leaving traditional video rental stores like blockbuster behind. By 2017, it was operating and today, close to 73.

Additionally, Netflix began streaming content in 4K Ultra HD. Recently, Netflix released its first-ever film and series diversity study in conjunction with the *USC Annenberg Inclusion Initiative*. They also announced plans to reach net-zero greenhouse gas emissions by the end of 2022 and launched mobile games.

A closer look at the Netflix business model

Here is a breakdown of the critical elements of the Netflix business model:

- **Subscription-based revenue:** Netflix primarily relies on a monthly subscription fee to access its streaming library. This model provides recurring revenue and allows for easier user acquisition and retention strategies.

- **Content acquisition and production:** Netflix invests heavily in acquiring licenses for popular movies and TV shows. They have also become a major content producer, developing award-winning original series and films to differentiate themselves from competitors.

- **Focus on UX:** Personalization, recommendation algorithms, and a user-friendly interface are all hallmarks of the Netflix experience. Their focus on user satisfaction is a key driver of their success.

- **Global expansion:** Netflix has expanded its reach to almost every country worldwide, tailoring content and marketing strategies to diverse audiences. This international presence is a significant source of growth.

Lessons learned from the Netflix disruption

The story of Netflix offers valuable lessons for aspiring digital product managers, and some of which are listed as follows for your reference:

- **Identify user pain points:** Focus on solving real user problems, not just iterating on existing solutions.

- **Embrace new technologies:** Be willing to adapt and leverage emerging technologies to stay ahead of the curve.

- **Prioritize UX:** Obsess creating a seamless and enjoyable UX to build customer loyalty.

- **Do not be afraid to disrupt:** Challenge the status quo and explore innovative ways to deliver value to your target audience.

Understanding and applying these principles to your digital products can pave the way for innovation and potentially disrupt your chosen market. Remember, the next Netflix might just be waiting to be born!

While Netflix was once the undisputed king of streaming, the digital entertainment landscape has become a battleground. Here is a breakdown of some of the major players in the industry, who are Netflix's current competitors, and how they are vying for a piece of the streaming pie.

The major players

The streaming industry has become highly competitive, with several major players vying for audience attention. While Netflix pioneered the shift to on-demand entertainment, other platforms have emerged with distinct content strategies and value propositions. Following are some of the key competitors in the streaming landscape, each bringing unique strengths to the market:

- **Disney+:** Launched in 2019, Disney+ has emerged as a significant competitor, leveraging the immense power of the Disney library and famous franchises like *Marvel, Star Wars,* and *Pixar.* Their focus on family-friendly content and nostalgia caters to a specific audience segment.

- **Amazon Prime Video:** With Amazon Prime memberships, Prime Video offers a vast content library, including award-winning originals and licensed titles. The convenience of being included in a Prime membership makes it an attractive option for many consumers.

- **Apple TV+:** While not the most significant player in terms of content library, Apple TV+ boasts high-quality, critically acclaimed original series and movies. They aim to differentiate themselves through prestige content and a focus on Apple's user-friendly interface.

- **HBO Max:** Home to iconic HBO originals like *Game of Thrones* and a vast library of *Warner Bros.* content, HBO Max caters to a more mature audience. They aim to compete by offering a deep well of established franchises alongside compelling new productions.

- **Hulu:** A veteran of the streaming wars, Hulu offers a mix of broadcast network shows, original content, and library titles. They also have a unique live TV option, appealing to cord-cutters seeking a more traditional cable-like experience.

How Netflix maintains its lead

Even with these strong competitors, Netflix holds its ground through several strategic approaches listed as follows:

- **Content strategy:** Netflix continues to invest heavily in original content creation. They leverage data and analytics to identify audience preferences and develop shows with global appeal. Hit series like *Stranger Things* and *Squid Game* have become cultural phenomena, keeping Netflix at the forefront of the conversation. While competitors like Disney+ excel in established franchises, Netflix focuses on a broader range of genres and international productions.

- **UX:** Netflix prioritizes a seamless and user-friendly experience. Their recommendation algorithms constantly evolve, suggesting content personalized to individual user preferences. This keeps users engaged and allows them to discover new content they might enjoy. Furthermore, Netflix's global presence ensures its platform is accessible on various devices, from TVs and laptops to smartphones and tablets.

- **Global expansion:** Netflix has a near-global presence, allowing it to cater to diverse audiences with localized content and marketing strategies. This vast user base provides a strong foundation for recurring revenue and content investment.

- **Innovation:** Netflix constantly innovates, exploring new technologies like interactive content and experimenting with release strategies. Their willingness to take risks and adapt to changing viewing habits keeps them ahead of the curve.

- **A continuously evolving landscape of streaming:** The streaming industry is highly competitive, with new players frequently emerging. As we move forward, you can expect an ongoing battle for the best content. Streaming services and studios will invest heavily in producing high-quality original content and obtaining licenses for popular movies and shows. We may see more streaming services tailored to specific genres or demographics, providing a curated experience for viewers with specific interests.

As competition intensifies, pricing strategies and bundled offerings may become more prevalent. Consumers may need to subscribe to multiple services to access their preferred content. Although Netflix's position as the industry leader is not guaranteed, they are well-positioned to remain at the forefront of the streaming revolution by prioritizing high-quality original content, UX, global reach, and continuous innovation.

As an aspiring digital product manager, this ongoing battle provides valuable insights into the importance of understanding your target audience, adapting to changing market dynamics, and prioritizing a user-centric approach.

Competitive analysis

Competitive analysis is a crucial strategic process that businesses use to investigate and assess their current and potential competitors. This process involves gathering detailed information about their competitors, such as their product and service offerings, sales channels, marketing strategies, pricing models, customer experience, and overall market position. As an aspiring product manager, you need to analyze this information to gain valuable insights into your product's competitors' strengths and weaknesses and identify potential opportunities and threats in the market. Competitive analysis is a crucial tool if you have a long-term strategy for your product and are looking to stay ahead of the competition and develop effective strategies to improve your products, services, and marketing efforts.

To set your product or service apart from your competitors, it is important to understand their weaknesses and the gaps in the market. This is where competitive analysis comes in. By gathering data on your competitors, you can make informed decisions about your product development, marketing, and pricing strategies. You will be able to learn from your competitors' tactics and avoid making the same mistakes. This information will help you create a solid product roadmap, allocate resources efficiently, and steer your business in the right direction.

Components of competitive analysis

The specific details will vary depending on your industry and goals, but here are some common elements:

- **Identifying your competitors:** Determine the direct and indirect competitors that are targeting your audience and influencing market dynamics.

- **Analyzing competitor products and services:** Examine the offerings of competitors, identifying their strengths and weaknesses in comparison to your own.

- **Evaluating competitor marketing strategies:** Assess how competitors engage their audience, the marketing channels they leverage, and the effectiveness of their messaging.

- **Assessing competitor pricing:** Compare competitor pricing models with your own, evaluating the value proposition they present at different price points.

- **Customer analysis:** Analyze the target audience of competitors, understanding their demographics, needs, and preferences to refine your own market positioning.

Different types of competitive analysis

There are various approaches to conducting a competitive analysis, depending on your needs. Let us understand them in the following section.

Strength, Weakness, Opportunity, Threat analysis

The SWOT framework is a helpful tool that will allow you to thoroughly evaluate your company's internal strengths and weaknesses, considering factors such as company culture, organizational structure, management practices, and employee skills. Additionally, the framework will help you analyze the external opportunities and threats your company may face due to the competitive landscape, such as market trends, consumer behavior, technological advancements, and regulatory changes. By considering internal and external factors, companies can develop a comprehensive understanding of their current state and formulate effective strategies to improve their performance and competitiveness in the market. If you work as a product manager in a large company, you will have the advantage of hiring consultancy services to work on a complete competitor analysis and provide a detailed report.

Following is a visual illustration of the SWOT analysis:

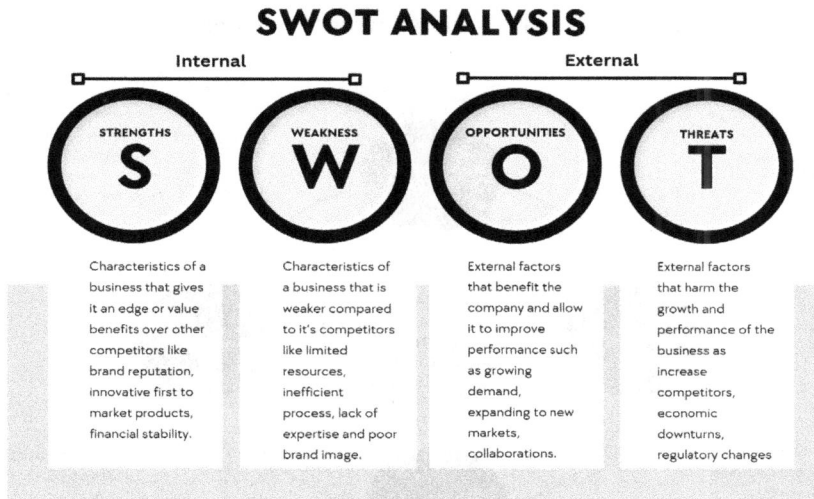

SWOT ANALYSIS

Internal		External	
STRENGTHS **S**	**WEAKNESS** **W**	**OPPORTUNITIES** **O**	**THREATS** **T**
Characteristics of a business that gives it an edge or value benefits over other competitors like brand reputation, innovative first to market products, financial stability.	Characteristics of a business that is weaker compared to it's competitors like limited resources, inefficient process, lack of expertise and poor brand image.	External factors that benefit the company and allow it to improve performance such as growing demand, expanding to new markets, collaborations.	External factors that harm the growth and performance of the business as increase competitors, economic downturns, regulatory changes

Figure 3.1: SWOT analysis framework

Porter's Five Forces analysis

Michael Porter's Five Forces model is a framework used to analyze the competitive landscape of an industry. The model examines Five Forces influencing industry profitability, including the threat of new entrants, the bargaining power of suppliers, the bargaining power of buyers, the threat of substitute products or services, and competitive rivalry.

The threat of new entrants refers to the likelihood of competitors entering and disrupting existing businesses. Factors affecting this threat include entry barriers, high capital requirements, and economies of scale.

The bargaining power of suppliers refers to the extent to which suppliers can influence pricing and other aspects of the industry. This can depend on factors such as the number of suppliers in the market and the uniqueness of their products or services.

The bargaining power of buyers refers to the extent to which buyers can influence pricing and other aspects of the industry. This can depend on the number of buyers and their willingness to switch suppliers.

The threat of substitute products or services refers to the extent to which alternative products or services can satisfy customer needs. This can depend on factors such as the availability and cost of substitutes.

Lastly, competitive rivalry refers to the intensity of competition between firms within the industry. This can depend on factors such as the number of competitors, the degree of differentiation between products or services, and the level of advertising and promotional activity.

Following figure represents the Porter's Five Forces template:

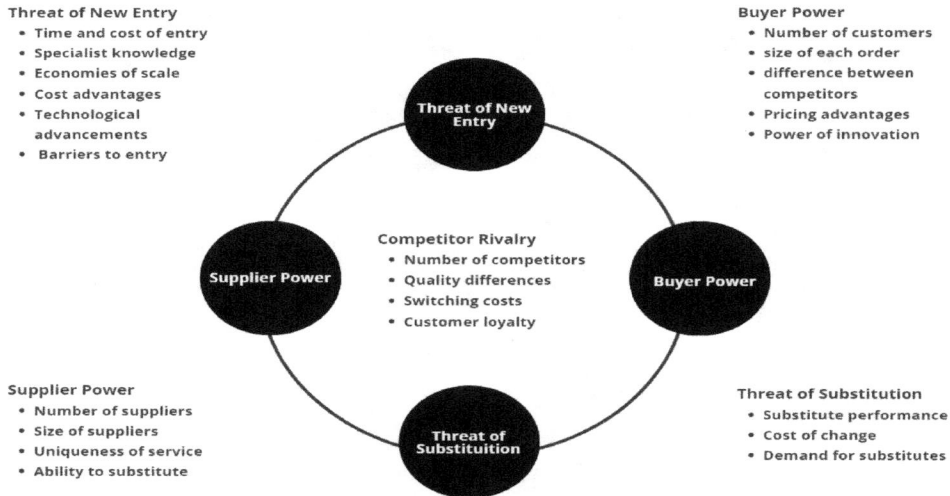

Threat of New Entry
- Time and cost of entry
- Specialist knowledge
- Economies of scale
- Cost advantages
- Technological advancements
- Barriers to entry

Buyer Power
- Number of customers
- size of each order
- difference between competitors
- Pricing advantages
- Power of innovation

Threat of New Entry

Competitor Rivalry
- Number of competitors
- Quality differences
- Switching costs
- Customer loyalty

Supplier Power

Buyer Power

Supplier Power
- Number of suppliers
- Size of suppliers
- Uniqueness of service
- Ability to substitute

Threat of Substituition

Threat of Substitution
- Substitute performance
- Cost of change
- Demand for substitutes

Figure 3.2: Porter's Five Force framework

Conclusion

In this chapter, we read the essential components of product strategy, emphasizing its role in long-term growth, differentiation, and market positioning. Innovation emerged as a key driver, with case studies like Netflix and Canva demonstrating how disruptive thinking can redefine industries. Competitive analysis frameworks such as SWOT and Porter's Five Forces provide practical tools for assessing market dynamics and positioning products effectively. Additionally, the Improvement Kata and the enhanced SV Model highlighted structured approaches to continuous product improvement, integrating change control and legal considerations. Ultimately, successful product strategy hinges on adaptability, data-driven decision-making, and an unwavering commitment to customer needs, ensuring long-term success in a competitive digital landscape.

In the next chapter, we will shift our focus from strategy to execution, exploring how to create lasting product value and user retention. You will learn how businesses ensure long-term engagement by embedding stickiness into their products, making them indispensable to customers. Through case studies like Apple, Slack, Zoom, and Airbnb, we will analyze how successful companies sustain growth by delivering unique value, fostering loyalty, and positioning themselves effectively across different market types.

Points to remember

- Product strategy defines the long-term plan for product development and market positioning, aligning with business goals.
- Innovation involves creating new products or improving existing ones to meet customer needs and gain a competitive edge.
- A strong product strategy prioritizes customer value, efficient resource allocation, and market adaptability.
- Companies like Canva and Netflix show how innovation can redefine industries and establish leadership.
- Disruptive innovation creates new markets or transforms existing ones, often challenging established players.
- Systematic approaches like the Improvement Kata model aid in executing innovative ideas while ensuring compliance and efficiency.
- Competitive analysis identifies strengths, weaknesses, and opportunities by evaluating competitors and market dynamics.
- Tools like SWOT analysis and Porter's Five Forces help structure and analyze competitive landscapes effectively.

Multiple choice questions

1. **What is the primary focus of product strategy?**
   a. Reducing development costs
   b. Creating a long-term plan for product development and market positioning
   c. Launching products as quickly as possible
   d. Avoiding competition

2. **What is an example of product innovation?**
   a. Minor bug fixes in an app
   b. Introducing a new AI-driven recommendation system in an e-commerce platform
   c. Changing a product's logo
   d. Offering a seasonal discount

3. **Which company is a classic example of disruptive innovation in the video rental industry?**
   a. Blockbuster
   b. Hulu
   c. Netflix
   d. Disney+

4. **What is the key difference between innovation and disruptive innovation?**

   a. Innovation focuses on incremental changes, while disruptive innovation creates entirely new markets.

   b. Innovation requires less investment than disruptive innovation.

   c. Disruptive innovation only applies to technology products.

   d. Innovation always targets existing markets.

5. **Which tool evaluates a company's Strengths, Weaknesses, Opportunities, and Threats?**

   a. Porter's Five Forces

   b. SWOT analysis

   c. Improvement Kata model

   d. Market segmentation

6. **How does the Improvement Kata model assist in product innovation?**

   a. By automating workflows

   b. By defining current and target conditions and breaking the gap into manageable steps

   c. By focusing solely on legal compliance

   d. By ensuring faster time-to-market

7. **What is a critical advantage of competitive analysis?**

   a. It eliminates the need for customer research.

   b. It guarantees a successful product launch.

   c. It helps identify opportunities and threats in the market.

   d. It replaces product strategy entirely.

Answers

1	b
2	b
3	c
4	a
5	b
6	b
7	c

CHAPTER 4

Product Value and Stickiness

Introduction

Building a great product is not just about launching something innovative; it is about ensuring long-term engagement and loyalty. Product value creation ensures that a product fulfills real customer needs, while product stickiness makes it indispensable in users' daily lives. A successful digital product must continuously evolve to create lasting value and keep customers coming back. This chapter explores how businesses drive customer retention by delivering unique value, crafting compelling **user experiences (UXs)**, and strategically positioning themselves in different market types. Through real-world examples like *Apple, Slack, Zoom*, and *Airbnb*, you will understand how companies sustain growth and dominate their industries by embedding value and stickiness into their products.

Structure

This chapter covers the following topics:

- Power of product value and stickiness
- Product value creation and the heart of why they use it
- The sticky formula for product success
- Market types

- New markets
- Exponential markets
- Uberization and its impact on market growth

Objectives

By the chapter's end, you will walk away with actionable insights into building products that create lasting value and foster strong customer retention. You will understand the key drivers of product stickiness, learn how to position your product in different market types, and explore strategic growth opportunities. Through case studies of industry leaders, you will gain a practical framework for maximizing product engagement and securing long-term success in an evolving market.

Power of product value and stickiness

Let us recap what we have learned so far, we have covered innovation, competitive analysis, and creating disruptive products. However, the most crucial aspect of any successful product is having customers who return time and time. This discussion will focus on two critical concepts for **digital product managers** (**DPMs**): Product value creation and product stickiness.

Product value creation refers to designing, developing, and delivering a product that meets the needs and wants of the target audience while providing them with a unique value proposition. It involves understanding your customers' pain points, preferences, and behaviors and creating a product that solves their problems, fulfills their desires, or enhances their experiences. On the other hand, product stickiness refers to the ability of a product to retain its users and encourage them to return for more. A sticky product has features or qualities that make it difficult for users to switch to an alternative product or abandon it altogether. It creates a sense of loyalty, habit, or addiction among its users.

As a DPM, having a firm grasp of these concepts is vital for creating successful products that users love and keep using. By understanding your customer's needs and preferences and designing a product that delivers value and promotes user engagement, you can ensure your product thrives in a competitive market.

Innovation is not just a buzzword; it is the lifeblood of any thriving business. It is about breathing life into fresh ideas, products, or services that resonate with the ever-evolving needs of the market. When a company pioneers innovative products, it does not just stop at meeting expectations—it raises the bar, adding layers of value that resonate with both customers and shareholders alike.

The heartbeat of any business lies in the value it delivers to its customers and shareholders. Customers become buyers and advocates when they perceive their investment brings them unparalleled value, spreading the word far and wide. For shareholders, the magic lies in financial growth; an increase in the company's stock price spells success, enriching every stakeholder involved. Creating value for your customers and shareholders is a significant aspect of your business. When your customers perceive that they are getting more value for the money they spend, they are likelier to remain loyal to your brand and recommend it to their friends and family. Shareholders, on the other hand, are interested in the company's financial performance and growth potential. When a company creates value for its shareholders, it often increases its stock price, which benefits all shareholders.

The concept of business success is deeply rooted in the ability to create and deliver value across multiple stakeholders. When the business provides value to customers, the market share goes up, which entices more people to buy the company stock, causing the shareholder value to go up. When the shareholder value goes up, the market cap for the business goes up, which in turn then benefits the employees of the company, creating better job protection and other benefits. When a company is successful, it often results in increased revenue, allowing it to invest in its employees. This can take the form of bonuses, pay raises, and other benefits that improve the quality of life for employees.

Consider the following example of a **product manager** (**PM**) working on digital document solutions within the first and middle-mile logistics space.

Shortly after launching a new product, this PM attended their first grassroots meeting with drivers. Although the majority of issues had been addressed within the first week and no critical items remained on the roadmap, a deep sense of nervous anticipation lingered. Despite conducting multiple listening sessions with office associates and driver representatives to understand user needs and propose enhancements, the uncertainty of how the product would be received remained present.

The meeting began with a simple question posed to the drivers: *Do you like the product?* followed by an introduction as the individual responsible for building it. A moment of awkward silence filled the room. To ease the tension, the PM lightheartedly joked about their confidence in the product's value. The drivers responded with laughter, and what followed was a genuine moment of connection. They confirmed their appreciation for the product and began offering thoughtful suggestions for future improvements.

This interaction revealed more than just acceptance; it demonstrated engagement, investment, and interest from the end users. The drivers were not only using the product,they were envisioning how it could evolve. In this moment, the product's stickiness was clear: It had solved real problems, built trust, and earned its place in the daily workflow of its users.

At a subsequent grassroots meeting held a few months later, the drivers enthusiastically inquired whether their feedback and comments had been reviewed. Their sentiment was clear—they felt heard. There was a strong sense of appreciation, as they acknowledged that the product team had delivered exactly what they had asked for. The enthusiasm was evident; the product was not only being used but genuinely loved.

Moments like these are often among the most meaningful in a PM's journey. Whether it is through receiving a five-star rating, a message of appreciation, or direct feedback from end users, such experiences serve as powerful indicators of product stickiness. They reflect more than satisfaction—they signal trust, engagement, and a belief that user voices are both valued and acted upon. These are the foundational elements that strengthen long-term adoption and loyalty.

Product value creation and the heart of why they use it

Think about a product you have used for years, your phone, watch, favorite jeans, sunglasses, or shoes. You stick with it for a reason. The brand's value proposition keeps you loyal, proving its worth beyond just price. This loyalty is not unique to you; countless others choose brands based on the value they consistently deliver. The same principle applies to digital products. To create lasting value, you must clearly define how your product solves real problems and fulfills essential needs, ensuring users recognize its impact and keep coming back. A digital product with a unique value proposition will attract loyal customers. Understanding the target audience's needs and pain points is crucial when designing a digital product.

Value creation does not stop at the product launch. It is an ongoing process that requires continuous improvement and innovation to keep up with the ever-changing market trends and customer demands. By staying committed to providing value to the users, a product can build a loyal customer base that will continue to support and promote the product for years to come.

Here are some key elements to consider when crafting compelling product value:

- **Identifying user needs:** It all starts with empathy. *Who are your target users? What are their pain points, frustrations, and aspirations?* Conduct user research to understand their deepest needs and how your product can address them.

- **Solving real problems:** Features should add value and overcome gaps. Focus on core functionalities that make a user's life easier, more productive, or more enjoyable.

- **Differentiation is key:** The market is crowded. *What makes your product unique?* Identify your competitive advantage and highlight the value proposition that sets you apart.

- **Make them feel valued and heard:** You must have understood why we have underlined the words valued and heard. As quoted in my above example, customers like it when their feedback comes to life, and the company is improving with each new release based on their input and opinions.

Apple iPhone 6 and 6 Plus touch disease

The iPhone 6 and iPhone 6 Plus were plagued by a hardware defect known as **touch disease**. This issue was mainly characterized by a flickering gray bar appearing at the top of the screen, eventually rendering the touchscreen unresponsive, making the affected devices nearly unusable. The impact of this defect on customers was significant, with numerous iPhone 6 and 6 Plus users reporting frustration and inconvenience due to the touchscreen issues. The issue hindered basic tasks such as typing, swiping, and accessing apps, with some users experiencing complete device failure that required repairs or replacements.

Despite these issues, many customers remained loyal to the Apple brand for several reasons, some of which are listed as follows:

- **Brand reputation:** Apple has cultivated a strong reputation for quality, innovation, and customer service. Despite the touch disease issue, many customers believed in Apple's commitment to resolving hardware issues and providing excellent support.

- **Customer service:** Apple acknowledged the touch disease problem and implemented a repair program for affected devices. Customers could bring their iPhones to Apple Stores or authorized service providers for repairs, often at no cost. The responsiveness of Apple's customer service helped alleviate some of the frustration experienced by affected users.

- **Ecosystem integration:** Many iPhone users are deeply integrated into the Apple ecosystem, which includes other Apple devices such as MacBooks, iPads, Apple Watches, and AirPods. The seamless integration between these devices, along with features like iCloud syncing and continuity, creates a sense of cohesion and convenience that encourages users to stick with Apple products despite occasional hardware issues.

- **Perceived value:** Despite the touch disease issue, customers perceived Apple products as offering superior value compared to competitors. Factors such as design, performance, software updates, and resale value contribute to this perception of value, reinforcing customers' willingness to remain loyal to the brand.

While the touch disease issue with the iPhone 6 and 6 Plus was a significant setback, many customers chose Apple products due to the combination of brand reputation, customer service, ecosystem integration, perceived value, and social influence. These factors contributed to Apple's customer base's resilience and continued loyalty to the brand.

The sticky formula for product success

Imagine a product launch. The initial buzz is exciting, but you must cultivate stickiness for long-term success. That is where the magic happens, users keep returning, engaged, and satisfied. But stickiness does not appear in a vacuum. It is the result of a carefully crafted blend of several key ingredients:

- **Innovation: The spark of something new:** Innovation is the fire starter. It is about identifying new opportunities, challenging the status quo, and developing solutions that address unmet user needs. This does not always mean inventing something entirely new. Sometimes, it is about taking an existing idea and improving upon it in a way that resonates with users. For this to happen in a smooth transition, you need to be connected with your end users by continuously monitoring their feedback and responses to know how the product is performing, gaps, and scope for growth, and addressing them promptly.

- **Value creation: Solving problems and delivering benefits:** Innovation alone is not enough. Your product needs to create genuine value for users. This means solving their problems, making their lives easier, or fulfilling a specific need. Think beyond features; focus on the benefits your product delivers.

- **Customer experience: Making it easy and enjoyable:** A smooth and enjoyable **customer experience (CX)** is crucial for stickiness. This encompasses everything from the first interaction with your product to ongoing use. An intuitive interface, straightforward navigation, and a focus on user needs are all essential elements of a positive CX.

- **Adoption: Getting users onboard:** Even the most innovative, value-driven product needs users to try it out. Developing effective marketing and user acquisition strategies is vital to driving adoption. Once users take that first step, a positive CX is crucial in keeping them engaged.

- **Stickiness: The power of retention:** This is where the magic happens. Stickiness is about keeping users engaged and coming back for more. This can be achieved through features that encourage habit formation, personalized experiences, ongoing value creation, and fostering a sense of community around your product.

- **Shareholder value: The business case for stickiness:** Sticky products are suitable for business. A loyal user base translates to recurring revenue, increased brand loyalty, and shareholder value. Investors are likelier to back companies with products that demonstrate enduring user engagement.

- **Employee value: A motivated workforce:** Working on a product that users love can incredibly motivate employees. Stickiness translates to a sense of purpose and achievement within the company. Employees feel their hard work pays off, leading to a more engaged and productive workforce.

Apple Inc. is often cited as a benchmark for brand loyalty in the consumer electronics industry. A significant portion of Apple's customer base consistently upgrades to newer models of iPhones, MacBooks, and other Apple products, despite higher price points compared to competitors. This loyalty stems from a combination of factors, including a cohesive ecosystem, an intuitive user interface, a strong emotional connection to the brand,

and exceptional customer service. The integration between devices, such as iMessage, AirDrop, iCloud, and Handoff, reinforces user commitment, making switching costs (both functional and emotional) high.

In contrast, *Samsung*, although a leading innovator in hardware and frequently ahead in adopting new technologies (e.g., foldable displays, advanced camera systems), experiences relatively lower brand loyalty. Consumers often switch between Samsung and other Android-based brands due to broader compatibility across Android devices, a competitive pricing landscape, and fewer proprietary lock-ins. While Samsung enjoys a strong market share, it does not always command the same repeat purchase behavior or emotional allegiance that Apple fosters.

This comparison illustrates how brand loyalty extends beyond product features or specifications; it is deeply influenced by CX, ecosystem cohesion, and brand perception. Companies like Apple that successfully build long-term emotional and functional value for their users often achieve stronger brand stickiness and lower customer churn.

Market types

We have explored value creation, stickiness, and other key concepts, but their impact varies across different market conditions. It is crucial to understand how strategies and implementation must adapt based on the market you are entering. Product market types define the landscape of the digital world, each presenting unique challenges and opportunities. To succeed, you must analyze these dynamics and tailor your approach accordingly.

Established markets

In existing markets, the competitive landscape is already well-established, with established competitors, well-defined customer expectations, and established market dynamics. These markets are known for their high level of competition and the availability of extensive historical data that can guide decision-making processes. As a PM operating in these markets, you must focus on product differentiation and the continuous improvement of offerings. This involves enhancing product features, improving the UX, and fine-tuning marketing strategies to remain competitive. You should aim to meet and exceed customer expectations by capitalizing on insights from market research and competitive analysis to stay ahead of the competition, sustain the market for a longer time, and gain stickiness. Established markets are characterized by well-defined boundaries and a competitive landscape where numerous players vie for market share. These markets are mature, with established customer bases, known competitors, and clearly understood needs and preferences. Entering an existing market requires a keen understanding of the current market dynamics so you can apply a strategic approach to differentiate your product from the rest of the competitors. It involves leveraging data-driven insights and deep comprehension of customer behavior to innovate and offer superior value.

The primary challenge in existing markets is differentiation. Since your customers already have options and may exhibit brand loyalty, your product must stand out through unique features, exceptional UX, or superior service. Continuous improvement is vital, involving regular updates, enhancements, and optimizations that keep the product relevant and appealing. Market research and competitive analysis become critical tools, enabling you to understand what works, identify gaps, and capitalize on opportunities others may have missed.

Strong branding and effective marketing strategies are also crucial in gaining and maintaining market share in existing markets. Building a compelling brand narrative and ensuring consistent, positive customer interactions can foster loyalty and advocacy. Focusing on customer satisfaction and leveraging customer feedback for iterative improvements can create a loyal customer base that can be instrumental in achieving long-term success.

Apple iPhone entering the smartphone market

A prime example of a product entering an existing market is the Apple iPhone. When Apple introduced the iPhone in 2007, the smartphone market was already established, with significant players like *BlackBerry*, *Nokia*, and *Motorola* dominating the scene. These companies had a firm hold on the market, with loyal customer bases and well-defined product offerings.

A clear differentiation and innovation strategy marked Apple's entry into this competitive landscape. The iPhone stood out due to its revolutionary design, combining a sleek touchscreen interface with a robust operating system supporting various applications. Unlike its competitors, which often relied on physical keyboards and less intuitive interfaces, the iPhone offered a user-friendly experience that was both visually appealing and highly functional.

One of the key differentiators for the iPhone was the introduction of the *App Store*, where the company allowed third-party developers to publish applications specifically designed for the iPhone, vastly expanding its functionality and appeal. But you must have noticed that some apps are only available in the App Store. The App Store quickly became a critical ecosystem that attracted developers and users alike, creating a vibrant community and an ever-expanding range of uses for the device.

Moreover, Apple's strong branding and marketing campaigns significantly impacted its success. The company positioned the iPhone as a smartphone and a revolutionary lifestyle device that integrated seamlessly into users' lives. Apple created immense anticipation and demand for the iPhone through compelling advertising and strategic product launches.

Despite entering an existing market with established competitors, Apple's strategic focus on innovation, UX, and ecosystem development allowed the iPhone to gain market share rapidly. It did not just participate in the market; it redefined it, setting new standards for what a smartphone could be and do. Today, the iPhone is a leading product in the global smartphone market, illustrating the potential for success when entering an existing market with a well-executed differentiation and innovation strategy.

Samsung competing with Apple in the smartphone market

Samsung's journey in the smartphone market is a testament to its ability to compete fiercely within an existing market dominated by a strong player like Apple. When Samsung entered the smartphone market, it faced significant challenges, as Apple had already established the iPhone as a benchmark for innovation and quality.

To compete effectively, Samsung adopted a multifaceted strategy focusing on innovation, diversification, and aggressive marketing. Unlike Apple, which releases a limited number of models yearly, Samsung pursued a broad product portfolio strategy. This involved releasing a wide range of smartphones catering to different market segments, from high-end flagship devices like the *Galaxy S* and *Note* series to more affordable models targeting budget-conscious consumers. This approach allowed Samsung to capture a more extensive and diverse customer base.

Samsung also focused heavily on innovation, particularly in hardware. It pioneered features such as larger screen sizes, leading to the popularization of the phablet category with its Galaxy Note series. Additionally, Samsung invested in advanced display technologies, such as **active-matrix organic light emitting diode** (**AMOLED**) screens, which offered superior color accuracy and battery efficiency compared to traditional **liquid crystal display** (**LCD**) screens. The company also pushed the envelope with features like water resistance, fast charging, and high-quality cameras, often the first to introduce these innovations.

Moreover, Samsung's global manufacturing capabilities and supply chain efficiency allowed it to scale production quickly and effectively meet the demand across different regions. Its vertical integration strategy, producing critical components like chips and displays in-house, provided a competitive edge in cost and quality control.

Marketing and branding were also critical components of Samsung's strategy. The company engaged in aggressive campaigns to market the brand. By positioning its Galaxy series as direct competitors to the iPhone, Samsung successfully created a narrative of a two-horse race in the smartphone market, compelling consumers to choose between the two leading brands.

Samsung's approach has yielded significant results. It has consistently held a substantial share of the global smartphone market, often surpassing Apple in unit sales. By focusing on a combination of innovation, product diversification, manufacturing efficiency, and strategic marketing, Samsung has managed to thrive in the highly competitive smartphone market dominated by Apple.

Together, Apple's and Samsung's examples illustrate the strategic models that helped their products succeed. Apple's approach to radical innovation and ecosystem development sets a new standard. In contrast, Samsung's strategy of broad diversification, hardware innovation, and aggressive marketing demonstrates how to compete and carve out a significant market share effectively.

New markets

When expanding into existing markets, you can benefit from your familiarity with customer needs, expectations, feedback, and the advantages and disadvantages of current products. However, breaking into new markets can be difficult due to the absence of established competition. These markets often emerge from technological developments, shifts in consumer behavior, or the discovery of previously unmet needs. Introducing a product to a new market is exciting and risky, demanding a deep understanding of the unfulfilled needs of potential customers and a commitment to innovation. To successfully launch a product in a new market, you must thoroughly understand the current processes, the future value the product will offer, shifts in user behavior, and ensure compliance with legal requirements in the specific geographic area. You could find yourself in a precarious situation without a solid understanding, dependencies, and a clear scope.

As a PM venturing into new markets, you must be a visionary, capable of seeing opportunities where others see uncertainty. This involves conducting extensive market research to identify gaps and opportunities, validating these insights with potential customers, and rapidly employing Agile development practices to iterate and refine your product offering. New markets demand high flexibility and responsiveness to feedback, as the product market fit may evolve quickly based on real-world usage and emerging trends.

One of the primary advantages of entering a new market is the opportunity to establish a strong market presence and brand loyalty from the outset. With fewer competitors, you can set the standard for quality and innovation, shaping customer expectations and capturing early adopters who can become powerful advocates for your product. However, the lack of established benchmarks also means that success is far from guaranteed. It requires a commitment to continuous learning, experimentation, and adaptation.

Marketing in new markets involves educating potential customers about the value and benefits of your product. Since these customers may be unfamiliar with the problem your product solves or how it fits into their lives, clear and compelling communication is essential. Building a community around your product, leveraging social proof, and creating memorable CXs can help drive adoption and build momentum.

Case study of Slack entering the team collaboration software market

Let us look at a prime example of a software product that entered a new market. When Slack was launched in 2013, the demand for team collaboration and communication tools was still in its infancy. While there were existing tools like Gmail, Skype, and a few enterprise solutions for team communication, none had fully addressed the growing need for a seamless, integrated, and user-friendly platform designed for the modern workplace.

Slack's founders recognized that existing tools were often cumbersome, inefficient, and poorly suited to contemporary teams' dynamic and collaborative needs. They envisioned a platform that could streamline communication, integrate with various other tools, and enhance productivity through real-time collaboration.

Slack's strategy for entering this new market involved several key elements:

- **User-centric design:** Slack focused on creating an intuitive, user-friendly interface requiring minimal training. The emphasis was on ease of use and quick adoption, ensuring that teams could use the platform immediately without significant onboarding hurdles.

- **Integration capabilities:** One of Slack's most significant innovations was its ability to integrate seamlessly with a wide range of other software tools. This meant that users could combine various aspects of their workflow, such as project management, file sharing, and notification systems, into a single platform. By acting as a hub for workplace tools, Slack provided added value that other communication tools did not.

- **Freemium model:** Slack adopted a freemium business model, offering a free tier with essential features and paid plans with additional functionality. This approach allowed teams to try Slack without financial commitment, leading to organic growth and widespread adoption.

- **Community building:** Slack invested in building a strong community around its product. This included engaging with users, incorporating their feedback into product development, and fostering a sense of belonging through user groups and forums.

- **Marketing and branding:** Slack's marketing strategy highlighted the inefficiencies of traditional communication tools and demonstrated how Slack could resolve these pain points. Through compelling storytelling and adequate social proof, Slack positioned itself as the go-to solution for team collaboration.

The combination of these strategies allowed Slack to quickly gain traction and establish a strong presence in the team collaboration market. By 2019, Slack had become ubiquitous in many organizations, revolutionizing how teams communicate and collaborate. Its success also paved the way for other innovative tools in space, further validating the new market it helped create.

Today, Slack continues to lead in the team collaboration space, competing with other major players like *Microsoft Teams*. Its journey illustrates the potential of identifying unmet needs in a nascent market, leveraging innovation and user-centric design, and building a community to achieve significant market success. Slack's entry into the team collaboration software market serves as an excellent example of how to navigate and thrive in new market territories.

Exponential markets

Now that we have discussed both the existing and new markets, there is also a market space that combines elements of both. Exponential markets are characterized by rapid growth, technological advancements, changing consumer behaviors, and emerging trends. These markets are often fueled by innovations that create entirely new categories or dramatically transform existing ones. Navigating exponential markets requires agility, foresight, and the ability to scale quickly. The potential for explosive growth in these markets is immense, but so are the challenges of staying ahead of the curve and managing the complexities of rapid expansion.

In exponential markets, the pace of change is relentless. As a PM, it is essential to recognize and respond to opportunities and threats promptly. This entails utilizing data analytics and market intelligence to spot trends and customer needs in real-time. Flexibility and adaptability are crucial, as today's effective strategies may not work tomorrow. Therefore, fostering a culture of continuous innovation and experimentation within your team is essential. Encouraging creative problem-solving and iterative development can help you stay responsive and Agile. *Can you recall products that thrived in exponential markets?* Let us pause here and name some products you think excelled in an exponential market.

Following are some examples of products that have flourished in exponential markets:

- **Airbnb:** Revolutionized the hospitality industry by offering a platform for short-term lodging, rapidly scaling to become a global leader.

- **Uber:** Transformed the transportation industry with its ride-sharing platform, quickly expanding to cities worldwide.

- **Netflix:** Disrupted traditional media by streaming digital content, scaling massively as internet speeds increased.

- **Tesla:** Pioneered the electric vehicle market with innovative technology and rapid production scale-up.

- **AWS: Amazon Web Services (AWS)** became a dominant player in cloud computing by offering scalable, on-demand cloud services.

Scalability is a crucial aspect of success in rapidly growing markets. As demand increases, it becomes essential to efficiently scale operations, infrastructure, and customer support without sacrificing quality. Investing in robust, adaptable technological solutions that can expand alongside the business is critical. This could involve utilizing cloud-based platforms, automated processes, and scalable customer service solutions. Additionally, forming strategic partnerships can offer the necessary resources and expertise to manage rapid growth effectively.

The following examples provide how various products altered existing markets and created new markets of their own:

- Products such as *Airbnb* and *Uber* created a new market in an existing industry without having to invest in any capital of their own.

- *Tesla* created a product that captured the market through its innovation and in support of a cause that many believe in, through its electric vehicles.

- *Facebook* created a market for early digital adopters in social media.

Furthermore, staying attuned to industry trends and emerging technologies is vital. Technological breakthroughs, such as **artificial intelligence (AI)**, blockchain, or the **Internet of Things (IoT)**, often shape exponential markets. Keeping up with these developments and understanding their potential impact on the market can give a competitive edge. Being proactive rather than reactive allows you to capitalize on new opportunities and pivot quickly when necessary.

Case study of Zoom in the video conferencing software market

Zoom Communications is a quintessential example of a software product thriving in an exponential market. While existent before Zoom, the video conferencing market experienced unprecedented growth due to several factors, including the global shift towards remote work and digital communication, particularly accelerated by the COVID-19 pandemic.

When Zoom launched in 2013, the market was already populated with established players like *Skype, Webex*, and *GoTo Meeting*. However, Zoom's entry was marked by its superior UX, reliability, and innovative features that addressed the pain points of existing solutions. Zoom's focus on providing high-quality video and audio, ease of use, and scalability sets it apart from competitors.

Zoom's architecture was designed for scalability from the outset. This allowed the platform to handle exponential user growth without significant performance issues. During the COVID-19 pandemic, as businesses, educational institutions, and social interactions moved online, Zoom saw a meteoric rise in adoption. The company's ability to scale its infrastructure quickly to support millions of new users was crucial to its success.

Innovation was also a key driver for Zoom. Features like virtual backgrounds, breakout rooms, and seamless screen sharing cater to diverse user needs, from corporate meetings and educational lectures to social gatherings and telehealth consultations. Zoom's intuitive interface and ability to integrate with other enterprise software make it a versatile tool for various use cases.

Zoom's freemium business model played a significant role in its rapid growth. By offering a free tier with essential features, Zoom attracted many users who could be converted to paid plans as their needs expanded. This strategy boosted user acquisition and increased brand visibility and market penetration.

The company's proactive approach to security and privacy, especially during its period of hyper-growth, was essential in maintaining user trust. Addressing security vulnerabilities quickly and transparently helped mitigate potential backlash and ensured continued user confidence.

Zoom's success in the exponential market of video conferencing software highlights several critical factors: A user-centric approach to product development, scalable infrastructure, innovative features, strategic business models, and proactive management of security and privacy.

The Zoom example illustrates how software products can thrive in exponential markets by focusing on scalability, innovation, UX, and strategic market positioning. As a PM, embracing these principles can help you navigate the rapid changes and vast opportunities inherent in exponential markets, positioning your product for sustained success and growth.

Uberization and its impact on market growth

The term uberization describes the shift of conventional service industries towards business models similar to that of *Uber*. This involves using digital platforms such as mobile apps or websites to connect customers with service providers, bypassing traditional intermediaries directly. The emphasis is on convenience, efficiency, on-demand access, and a more personalized CX. By embracing these principles, businesses can disrupt established markets and create new ones, driving significant growth and innovation.

You are partially correct if you are confused and wondering whether exponential and uberization are similar. While they relate to business innovation and growth, they represent distinct phenomena in economics and industry evolution. Uberization involves a transformation of traditional service industries through digital platforms, while exponential markets are characterized by rapid growth driven by technological advancements, changing consumer behaviors, and emerging trends. These markets often experience exponential growth, creating significant opportunities for businesses.

Key differences are as follows:

- **Focus:**
  - Uberization focuses on transforming existing service industries through digital platforms and direct connections between providers and consumers.
  - Exponential markets focus on industries experiencing rapid growth due to technological innovation and emerging trends.
- **Drivers of growth:**
  - Uberization is driven by adopting business models emphasizing convenience, efficiency, and personalized experiences.

- o   Exponential markets are driven by technological advancements, changing consumer behaviors, and the emergence of new trends.
- **Nature of innovation:**
  - o   Uberization involves innovation in service delivery and business models within existing industries.
  - o   Exponential markets involve breakthrough innovations that create or transform new industries.
- **Market dynamics:**
  - o   Uberization disrupts traditional business models and market dynamics within specific industries.
  - o   Exponential markets reshape entire industries and global economic landscapes.

Key aspects of uberization

First, let us look into the core aspects of uberization. It is about creating on-demand services that users can access quickly and easily through digital platforms. Think of how Uber allows you to request a ride with just a few taps on your smartphone. This model removes the friction of traditional processes and offers a seamless, user-friendly experience. It directly connects customers with service providers, eliminating the need for intermediaries, streamlining the service, and often reducing costs.

Expanding industries and markets

Uberization has the potential to expand industries and markets for significant growth. There are several key ways in which this can happen.

The main idea is to make services more accessible to customers by reducing barriers to entry. By adopting the uberization concept, more people can participate because it is easier for service providers to join. For example, anyone with a car can become an Uber driver, and anyone with a spare room can become an Airbnb host. This inclusivity expands the market and offers a broader range of services. Additionally, platforms that embrace this model prioritize UX, which attracts a more extensive customer base. The convenience and reliability of these services can turn occasional users into regular customers. For instance, the ease of booking an Uber ride has led many people to choose ride-sharing over owning a car in urban areas, thus expanding the market for personal transportation.

Uberization has led to new service offerings that were previously impractical. For instance, consider the rise of food delivery services like *Uber Eats* and *DoorDash*, which have adopted the Uber model to provide on-demand food delivery from various restaurants. This kind of innovation creates new markets and breathes new life into existing ones by introducing fresh dynamics and choices. Ordering food has become much easier, as anyone with access to technology can now place an order. Additionally, they can also participate as a food delivery provider. Digital platforms can expand rapidly, reaching a global audience with minimal additional costs. This scalability allows for quick market expansion and the ability to penetrate previously underserved regions. Uber's global presence indicates how an uberized model can grow rapidly and extensively, transcending geographical boundaries.

Airbnb created a market of its own and has now reached a market cap of $84 B+ surpassing some of the other well-known hotel brands, showcasing the power of digital product innovation.

Case study of Airbnb's transformation of the lodging and hotel industry

We have already looked deeply into the Airbnb example in the previous chapter. Now, let us consider how this has dramatically transformed the concept of lodging and the hotel industry since its inception in 2008 and caused a threat to other companies in the hotel industry. By leveraging a peer-to-peer business model, Airbnb allows property owners to rent their homes or spare rooms to travelers, creating a decentralized, flexible, and diverse marketplace for accommodations. This model contrasts sharply with the traditional hotel industry's centralized approach, where large chains own or manage most properties.

Keyways Airbnb changed the lodging concept

Airbnb has transformed the lodging industry by redefining how people find and experience accommodations. Its innovative approach offers numerous advantages that set it apart from traditional hotels, providing travelers with greater flexibility, unique experiences, and enhanced convenience. The following key factors highlight Airbnb's impact on the travel and hospitality landscape:

- **Diverse accommodation options:** Unlike traditional hotels, which typically offer standardized rooms, Airbnb provides various lodging options, from single rooms in apartments to entire homes and even unique properties like treehouses and yurts. This diversity appeals to travelers looking for unique and personalized experiences.

- **Local and authentic experiences:** Airbnb promotes staying in residential neighborhoods, allowing travelers to experience destinations like locals rather than tourists. This shift has expanded the appeal of travel, encouraging the exploration of less touristy areas and more authentic cultural interactions.

- **Affordability and flexibility:** Airbnb often provides more affordable options than traditional hotels, especially for more extended stays. The flexibility in pricing and variety of accommodations cater to different budgets and needs, making travel more accessible.

- **Technological convenience:** Airbnb's user-friendly platform simplifies the booking process. Features like user reviews, detailed property descriptions, and 24/7 customer support enhance hosts' and guests' trust and convenience.

- **Economic opportunities for individuals:** Airbnb has created new income opportunities for property owners, who can rent out their spaces with minimal overhead. This democratization of lodging supply has increased market competition and innovation.

Airbnb quickly grew into a global hospitality powerhouse by reshaping how people travel. Unlike traditional hotel chains, Airbnb capitalized on the sharing economy and digital platforms to connect travelers with unique accommodations. Its innovative technology, user-friendly interface, and focus on local experiences propelled it to become a household name, challenging established hotel brands in the global travel industry as discussed in the following sections.

Impact on major hotel brands

The rapid success of Airbnb has forced major hotel brands to rethink their business strategies to stay competitive in the evolving lodging industry. Companies like *Marriott, Hilton,* and *InterContinental Hotels Group (IHG)* have had to adapt by introducing new rental platforms, enhancing customer loyalty programs, and leveraging digital innovations to meet changing traveler expectations. The following section explores the specific impacts of Airbnb's rise on these hotel giants and the strategic responses they have implemented to maintain their market position.

Marriott International

Impact: Marriott, one of the world's largest hotel chains, has had to adapt to the competitive pressures introduced by Airbnb. The rise of home-sharing has forced Marriott to rethink its business model and innovate to maintain its market position.

Response:

Homes & Villas by Marriott: In response to Airbnb, Marriott launched its home-rental platform, Homes & Villas, offering luxury rental properties that combine the appeal of unique accommodations with the reliability of Marriott's standards.

Loyalty programs: Marriott has enhanced its Bonvoy loyalty program to include more flexible rewards and partnerships, aiming to retain customers by offering broader travel-related benefits.

Hilton Worldwide

Impact: Hilton, another global hotel giant, has seen a shift in consumer preferences towards more diverse and authentic lodging experiences, which has affected occupancy rates and revenue growth in some markets.

Response:

Focus on experiences: Hilton has increased its focus on providing unique guest experiences within its hotels, such as localized services and cultural events, to compete with the personalized touch offered by Airbnb.

Digital innovation: Hilton has invested in digital technologies, such as its Digital Key feature, which allows guests to use their smartphones to check in and access their rooms, enhancing convenience and the overall guest experience.

InterContinental Hotels Group

Impact: IHG, which operates brands like *Holiday Inn* and *InterContinental*, has faced similar challenges due to the growing popularity of Airbnb. The increased competition has pressured IHG to differentiate its offerings and appeal to a broader range of travelers.

Response:

Expansion of luxury and boutique brands: IHG has expanded its portfolio to include more luxury and boutique hotel brands, such as *Kimpton Hotels* and *Six Senses*, aiming to attract travelers seeking unique and upscale experiences.

Enhanced loyalty program: IHG has revamped its *IHG Rewards Club* to offer more personalized and flexible rewards, aiming to build stronger customer loyalty amidst the competitive landscape.

Conclusion

Airbnb's disruptive model has significantly impacted the lodging and hotel industry by introducing a diverse, flexible, and often more affordable alternative to traditional hotels. Major hotel brands like Marriott, Hilton, and IHG have had to innovate and adapt to this new reality, focusing on enhancing CXs, leveraging technology, and expanding their service offerings to remain competitive.

The advent of Airbnb has underscored the importance of flexibility, authenticity, and personalization in the travel industry. As a result, traditional hotel chains are increasingly incorporating these elements into their operations, seeking to balance the reliability and standardization of hotel stays with the unique and localized experiences that modern travelers crave. This ongoing evolution signifies a broader trend toward a more dynamic and diversified lodging market shaped by the changing preferences and expectations of global travelers.

The next chapter transitions from theory to execution, focusing on the product journey from concept to market. It outlines the essential steps in roadmap development, stakeholder alignment, investment prioritization, and pre-launch planning. Readers will gain a structured approach to turning product ideas into market-ready solutions while ensuring strategic alignment, customer relevance, and organizational readiness.

Points to remember

- Product value creation focuses on solving customer problems and delivering a unique value proposition that enhances user satisfaction and loyalty.
- Product stickiness refers to the ability of a product to retain users by fostering loyalty, habitual use, or creating a strong emotional connection.
- Value creation is an ongoing process requiring continuous improvements and adapting to customer needs and market trends.
- Creating value benefits customers, shareholders, and employees, forming a cycle of success that drives business growth and satisfaction.
- Apple's iPhone demonstrated successful value creation through innovation, brand loyalty, and integration within its ecosystem, even during product issues like touch disease.
- Product stickiness is achieved through elements such as innovation, value delivery, CX, and ongoing engagement with users.
- Established markets require differentiation through innovation, strong branding, and customer centric features to compete with incumbents.
- Entering new markets demands a clear understanding of customer needs, validation through research, and creating awareness about the product's unique value.
- Exponential markets are characterized by rapid growth and demand Agile strategies, scalability, and continuous innovation to thrive.
- Companies like Zoom thrived in exponential markets by offering scalable, user-centric solutions during unprecedented growth phases.
- Uberization transforms industries by leveraging digital platforms for efficiency, on-demand services, and bypassing traditional intermediaries.

Multiple choice questions

1. **What is product stickiness?**
   a. A product's ability to solve unique problems
   b. A product's ability to retain users and encourage habitual use
   c. A product's focus on features over user needs
   d. A product's reliance on innovation for market entry

2. **Why is value creation crucial in product management?**
   a. It ensures rapid product launches.
   b. It focuses on meeting shareholder expectations exclusively.
   c. It delivers solutions that enhance user satisfaction and drive loyalty.
   d. It prioritizes competitor analysis over user needs.

3. **Which company is an example of disruptive innovation in the lodging industry?**
   a. Marriott International
   b. Hilton Worldwide
   c. Airbnb
   d. InterContinental Hotels Group

4. **What characterizes exponential markets?**
   a. Stability and established customer expectations
   b. Rapid growth driven by technological and consumer behavior shifts
   c. Minimal competition and slow adoption rates
   d. A focus on incremental product improvements

5. **How did Slack create a foothold in a new market?**
   a. By focusing on physical collaboration tools
   b. By prioritizing unique features over UX
   c. By creating a user-centric design and seamless integration capabilities
   d. By reducing the scope of its offerings

6. **What is uberization?**
   a. The focus on internal process improvement through automation
   b. The transformation of traditional industries using digital platforms for on-demand services
   c. The disruption of emerging markets through new technologies
   d. The creation of high-cost premium services

7. **What is a core benefit of entering a new market?**
   a. Gaining an established user base
   b. Minimal risk and reduced investment needs
   c. The opportunity to establish a strong market presence early
   d. Reliance on existing competitors to validate the market

Answers

1	b
2	c
3	c
4	b
5	c
6	b
7	c

CHAPTER 5

Product Journey from Concept to Market

Introduction

After laying the foundation of **digital product management** (**DPM**), such as identifying customer needs and building effective market strategies, this chapter shifts focus to practical execution. It explores critical stages in the product lifecycle, beginning with one of the most essential tools in a **product manager's** (**PM**) toolkit, the product roadmap.

A roadmap is more than a planning document; it connects vision, strategy, and execution. Building an effective roadmap begins with the customer. Understanding who the product serves enables product teams to identify, analyze, and prioritize user needs, which in turn drives development decisions. A customer-first approach ensures that each feature aligns with business goals and creates meaningful value.

Tip: **When asked how to prioritize a feature, begin by emphasizing that the process starts with the customer. From there, explain how priorities are determined based on user needs, business value, technical feasibility, and other relevant factors.**

Roadmap development plays a pivotal role in effective product management. This chapter explores key methodologies and frameworks for crafting resilient and strategic roadmaps that clearly define the product vision, set tangible goals, and outline critical milestones. A well-constructed roadmap ensures alignment with both the broader organizational strategy and evolving market opportunities.

Investment criteria act as a strategic compass throughout the product lifecycle. Product initiatives are prioritized and funded based on carefully evaluated metrics and strategic relevance. These criteria help ensure that every investment decision supports overarching business objectives and responds to dynamic market demands.

Laying a strong foundation before launching a product is essential. This includes conducting thorough market research, performing in-depth competitive analysis, and establishing clear strategic positioning and messaging. These preparatory activities are critical to ensuring a smooth market entry, fostering early adoption, and building stakeholder confidence in the product's potential for success.

Structure

This chapter contains the following topics:

- Product roadmap introduction
- Investment criteria

Objectives

The objective of this chapter is to guide aspiring and current PMs through the critical transition from strategy to execution by introducing the practical tools and frameworks that bring a product to life. This chapter aims to deepen understanding of how a product journey evolves from an initial concept into a tangible market offering. It emphasizes the strategic value of a well-constructed roadmap, illustrating how it aligns product vision with business objectives, user needs, and cross-functional collaboration. Through exploration of various roadmap types, stakeholder engagement strategies, and real-world case studies, readers will learn how to define and prioritize features, manage interdependencies, and plan effective release timelines. Additionally, the chapter introduces investment criteria as a structured lens for evaluating and prioritizing product initiatives based on impact, feasibility, and business alignment. By concluding with pre-launch activities, the chapter equips PMs with the knowledge to ensure organizational readiness and a successful go-to-market execution. Ultimately, this chapter serves as a bridge between high-level strategy and day-to-day implementation, laying the groundwork for building impactful, customer-driven products.

Product roadmap introduction

A product roadmap is a vital strategic tool in product management. It outlines the plan for developing a product over time, providing a dynamic framework that defines the product's strategic direction and vision within a specific timeframe. The roadmap aligns business objectives with customer needs and technological capabilities. More than just a timeline, a well-crafted roadmap highlights key milestones, prioritized features, and strategic initiatives, offering a comprehensive view of how the product will evolve in response to ever-changing market demands.

One of the roadmap's core functions is to serve as a powerful communication tool. It facilitates alignment across cross-functional teams, stakeholders, and investors. Common tools for building roadmaps include Asana, Jira, Trello, Productboard, or internally developed platforms. Even in the absence of these, a roadmap can be created using Excel or Word. It visually communicates priorities, sequencing, and deliverables, ensuring that all stakeholders share a clear understanding of direction and progress.

When used effectively, a product roadmap supports strategic planning, prioritization, and responsiveness to market shifts. It also fosters transparency and accountability, guiding decision-making from early ideation through development, launch, and beyond. As a living document, the roadmap allows teams to monitor progress and share updates with stakeholders during business reviews, approval sessions, or routine status meetings.

Types of roadmaps

There are three primary types of product roadmaps: timeline-based, Features-based, and goal-based, each serving a distinct purpose in product management.

A timeline-based roadmap emphasizes the scheduling and sequencing of product releases and milestones over a defined time period. It is particularly useful for visually outlining tasks and deadlines, functioning similarly to project management tools. This roadmap helps communicate the development timeline to stakeholders such as dependent PMs and development teams. It is especially valuable when building digital products that rely on **application programming interface (API)** integrations with upstream or downstream systems, where cross-team coordination is essential.

A Features-based roadmap focuses on prioritizing and scheduling product features-based on criteria such as customer needs, business priorities, and market trends. This roadmap type is commonly used within product and engineering teams to ensure development efforts are strategically aligned. It plays a critical role in optimizing resource allocation, sequencing releases, and delivering user value over time. Features-based roadmaps are typically used during collaborative planning discussions with engineering partners to align on feature development and execution timelines.

A goal-based roadmap connects product development initiatives directly to broader organizational objectives and strategic goals. It links specific initiatives to desired business outcomes, such as revenue growth, customer acquisition, or market expansion, and incorporates **key performance indicators (KPIs)** to track progress. This type of roadmap is particularly effective for communicating high-level strategy to executive stakeholders and strategic planning teams, ensuring that each product initiative supports long-term business success.

Selecting the appropriate roadmap type depends on the product's development stage, the organization's strategic needs, and team priorities. Each type offers unique advantages in clarity, stakeholder alignment, and strategic direction, empowering product teams to effectively plan, execute, and deliver impactful solutions that align with user needs and business objectives.

Product roadmap audience/users

Product roadmap's effectiveness will rely heavily on internal and external stakeholders who will depend on the roadmap for strategic direction and alignment.

Internal stakeholders

The product development process is driven by internal stakeholders who rely on the product roadmap to guide their contributions and ensure alignment. At the center of this framework is the product management team, responsible for creating the roadmap, defining the product vision, setting strategic goals, and prioritizing features.

The development team, including engineers, developers, and technical leads, uses the roadmap to understand the sequencing of features, manage interdependencies, and allocate resources effectively. UX and UI designers leverage the roadmap to align their design solutions with user needs and product priorities, while marketing teams use it to plan campaigns in sync with product releases. Together, these internal stakeholders ensure that each phase of product development is cohesive, coordinated, and strategically aligned.

External stakeholders

External stakeholders also play a critical role in the success of your product and depend on the roadmap for strategic insights and alignment. Customers refer to the roadmap to understand upcoming features that may enhance their experience and address key pain points. Product partners and integrators rely on roadmap transparency to coordinate development efforts and ensure compatibility with planned updates. Investors and shareholders use the roadmap to assess the product's strategic direction, growth potential, and expected return on investment. Additionally, regulatory bodies may review the roadmap to verify that product development aligns with industry standards and compliance requirements, particularly in highly regulated environments.

Engaging stakeholders effectively

To engage diverse stakeholders effectively, PMs must establish clear communication channels, promote transparency, and encourage collaboration throughout the roadmap planning and execution process. Providing regular updates on progress, changes, and adjustments helps ensure that all stakeholders remain informed and aligned with strategic goals. Additionally, implementing feedback mechanisms allows for the collection of valuable insights, which can be integrated into the roadmap to ensure it remains relevant and responsive to evolving needs.

By understanding and prioritizing the expectations of both internal and external stakeholders, PMs can shape a roadmap that drives innovation, supports market success, fosters trust and collaboration, and ultimately delivers meaningful value to users and the business.

Roadmap development

Building a product roadmap can be daunting, especially for new or aspiring PMs. However, visualizing the roadmap as analogous to constructing a house can simplify the process. Just as building a home begins with a solid foundation and essential structures like the basement and walls, product development starts by identifying the **minimum viable product** (**MVP**) or **minimum lovable product** (**MLP**) features essential for the product to function effectively. These foundational features represent the core capabilities and are critical to long-term success.

Developing a software product follows a similarly structured approach. The initial phase centers on defining core functionalities, much like laying the groundwork for a house. These features fulfill the product's primary purpose and deliver immediate value to users. Once the foundation is set, the next step is to plan subsequent development phases.

This planning includes mapping dependencies between features and tasks. Just as plumbing or electrical systems in a house depend on the structural framework, software development requires careful sequencing to ensure that features integrate smoothly and dependencies are addressed early.

A product roadmap is essential to this process. It acts as a strategic blueprint that outlines the product's vision, development goals, and key timelines. Typically spanning months or quarters, the roadmap is divided into phases or iterations. Each phase focuses on delivering a targeted set of features or improvements, prioritized based on customer needs, business objectives, and market opportunities.

Key considerations in developing a software product roadmap

To develop a successful and actionable product roadmap, PMs must consider several critical components that go beyond listing features and assigning dates. The roadmap should be grounded in research, aligned with strategic goals, and flexible enough to accommodate change. The following elements are essential to building a roadmap that drives clarity, execution, and measurable success throughout the product lifecycle:

- **Identifying and prioritizing features:** Based on market research, user feedback, and business objectives, prioritize the product features that will deliver the most value to your users and align with the broader strategic goals.

- **Mapping dependencies:** This is where most beginners make mistakes, fail to identify dependencies between features and tasks, or forget to consider the dependency teams and their alignments or commitments before planning your roadmap, which leads to missed deliverables. So, take care when determining the sequence in which they must be developed and released.

- **Setting timelines and milestones:** Define timelines and milestones for each development phase, ensuring realistic expectations and accountability. Not only should you consider the product development time, but you should also consider changing control, deployment, and launch activities, so you know how the product has reached, the success, and gathering the feedback before rolling out the next set of features or enhancements.

- **Define key metrics for success:** You may wonder why you must identify metrics while prepping the roadmap. Being an efficient PM, you must envision what the success of your product or feature will look like and how you will measure it while you form a plan. Metrics such as customer conversion rate, retention rate, **net promoter score (NPS)**, **customer satisfaction (CSAT)**, **customer lifetime value (CLV)**, dwell time reduction, crash reduction, improving efficiency, increased productivity, etc. are critical for measuring success, but these are just samples; your metrics will be related to the type of product you are working on, the industry and various other factors. These metrics should be selected based on specific business objectives and customer needs, guiding ongoing evaluation and adjustment of the roadmap.

- **Communication and alignment:** Ensure stakeholders across the organization, including PMs, developers, designers, and executives, are aligned on the roadmap's objectives and timelines. Regular updates and communication help maintain transparency and manage expectations.

Instagram product roadmap evolution case study

In its evolutionary journey from a simple photo-sharing app to a multifaceted social media platform, *Instagram's* product roadmap has navigated through strategic phases to enhance user engagement, monetize the platform, and foster continuous innovation.

Phase one foundation and MVP launch

During the initial year of its inception, Instagram focused on establishing a robust foundation with essential features to attract early adopters. The MVP included user profiles with basic bio information, photo uploads, and a news feed displaying photos from followed users. This phase required meticulous backend development to ensure seamless user authentication and photo storage capabilities.

Phase two enhancing user engagement

In the next couple of years, building upon its success, Instagram aimed to deepen user engagement through innovative features. The introduction of *Instagram Stories* revolutionized content consumption by offering ephemeral posts, complemented by the Explore tab for discovering new content and users. The addition of direct messages provided a private communication channel, further enhancing user interaction and retention.

Phase three monetization and business growth

During the fourth and fifth years, with a solid user base in place, Instagram shifted its focus towards monetization while safeguarding user experience. This phase introduced sponsored posts and advertising options, empowering businesses to reach their target audiences effectively. Insights and analytics tools were integrated to support business profiles, offering valuable metrics for optimizing marketing strategies. Additionally, shopping features were introduced to facilitate e-commerce within the app, enhancing its utility as a sales platform.

Phase four continuous innovation and expansion

To stay competitive in the rapidly evolving social media landscape, during the years that followed, Instagram prioritized continuous innovation and expansion. The launch of *IGTV* catered to users' increasing demand for long-form video content, while enhanced security and privacy features safeguarded user data. Integration with parent company *Facebook* and other platforms facilitated cross-platform sharing, broadening Instagram's reach and functionality. This phase is characterized by ongoing iterative updates and feature enhancements based on user feedback, technological advancements, and emerging market trends.

Throughout its evolution, Instagram's product roadmap has exemplified a strategic approach to DPM, balancing innovation with user-centricity, scalability with monetization, and responsiveness to market dynamics. By adapting and iterating upon its roadmap, Instagram continues to shape the future of social media and digital communication worldwide.

Investment criteria

In product roadmap development, investment criteria are the specific guidelines used to evaluate and prioritize which product features, enhancements, or initiatives should be pursued. These criteria will help you, as a PM and stakeholders, determine how to allocate limited resources, such as time, budget, and talent, across various competing projects and ideas.

For instance, investment criteria might include factors such as customer value (how a feature solves a significant problem or meets a need), market potential (the size and growth prospects of the target market), strategic alignment (how closely a feature aligns with the company's long-term goals), and revenue potential (whether the feature or product will generate significant revenue or open new revenue streams). Technical feasibility, cost, risk, and scalability are also often considered.

By using these criteria, you can ensure that resources are directed toward initiatives most likely to drive meaningful business outcomes, customer satisfaction, and competitive advantage. Essentially, investment criteria act as a filter, ensuring that each step of the product development process remains aligned with strategic objectives and maximizes return on investment.

Maybe you might not be involved in these conversations and decision-making while you are still in your early product career stage, but it is beneficial to know this work.

Investment criteria template for product development

When evaluating new product initiatives, it is essential to apply a structured decision-making framework. The following figure is a simple investment criteria template for product development, and outlines five key pillars: strategic alignment, customer impact, market opportunity, technical feasibility, and **return on investment (ROI)** and success metrics, to help PMs and stakeholders assess potential investments with clarity and confidence.

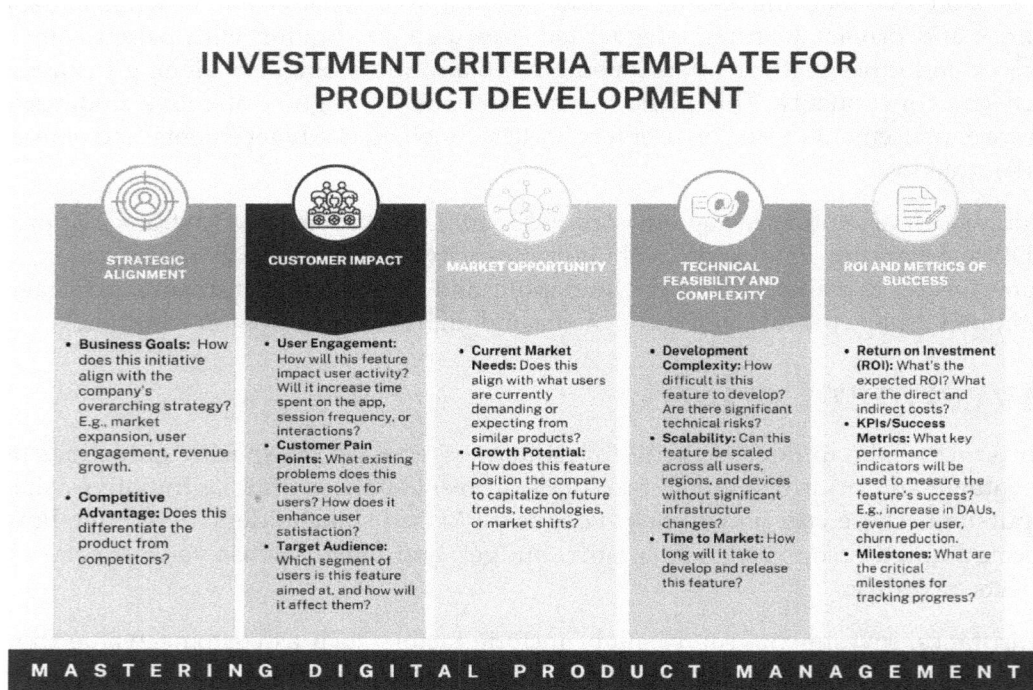

Figure 5.1: Investment criteria template

The template above can be applied to the earlier Instagram example to explore the different criteria that would be considered during the product development decision-making process.

Instagram investment criteria case study

To understand how theoretical investment principles translate into practical decision-making, it helps to examine a real-world example. The following section illustrates how Instagram, one of the most influential digital platforms, might assess new product features using a variety of investment criteria. From strategic alignment and customer impact to technical feasibility, monetization, and competitive differentiation, this example demonstrates how a comprehensive evaluation guides the prioritization of product initiatives.

- **Strategic alignment:** Features closely aligned with Instagram's overall business goals and its parent company, *Meta's* long-term strategy, are considered high priority. Strategic alignment ensures product initiatives support broader corporate objectives, such as ecosystem integration or market expansion.

  o **Example**: Cross-platform messaging between *Instagram, Facebook Messenger*, and *WhatsApp* is a prime example of strategic alignment with Meta's vision of creating a unified messaging ecosystem. By allowing users from these different platforms to communicate seamlessly, Meta is working toward increasing user engagement across its network while fostering data integration and advertising opportunities.

  o **Expansion**: Instagram might prioritize developing features that facilitate easier integration with *Meta's Horizon Workrooms* or **virtual reality (VR)** initiatives, which could eventually blend social networking with VR. An example could be allowing users to create and share 3D or VR content directly within the Instagram app. Another strategic feature might involve more in-depth integration of Instagram and Facebook Ads, allowing advertisers to manage campaigns across both platforms from a single dashboard.

- **Customer impact:** This criterion assesses how much a new feature or product enhancement will increase user interactions, time spent on the app, or daily active users. High engagement ensures users return to the platform frequently, creating a sticky ecosystem.

  o **Example**: Instagram Stories, introduced in 2016, significantly boosted user engagement by allowing users to post temporary photos and videos that disappear after 24 hours. This feature encouraged frequent interactions, especially among younger users who enjoy casual, low-pressure sharing. Introducing interactive elements like polls, question boxes, and music stickers amplified engagement, making the feature more dynamic and participatory.

  o **Expansion:** Instagram would prioritize features that foster regular content creation, commenting, liking, sharing, or messaging between users. For instance, the decision to add *Instagram Reels* aimed to capture the growing trend of short-form videos and boost daily user engagement by encouraging creators to post more content. A feature such as personalized recommendations in the Explore tab, based on users' past interactions, would also score high, as it keeps users exploring new content, extending their time on the app.

- **Market opportunity:** This criterion measures how well a feature fits current trends in the social media landscape. Features that capture or anticipate user behavior trends or capitalize on emerging technologies allow Instagram to stay competitive.

- o **Example**: The introduction of Instagram Reels directly responded to the rising popularity of *TikTok* and short-form video content. As more users gravitated toward creating and consuming quick, entertaining videos, Instagram aligned its roadmap to incorporate this trend, ensuring it remained relevant in the social media market.

- o **Expansion**: Instagram might prioritize features like integrating **non-fungible tokens** (**NFTs**) into the platform, enabling users to buy, sell, and showcase digital art directly on their profiles. This would capitalize on the growing interest in digital assets. Additionally, Instagram could develop voice and audio-based features, following trends like those seen with the rise of *Clubhouse* and *Twitter Spaces*, by allowing users to create live audio chats or podcasts within the app.

- **Technical feasibility and scalability:** This criterion assesses whether the feature can be quickly developed and scaled to Instagram's massive global user base. Technical challenges, development time, and infrastructure costs are vital factors. Features that can be scaled across millions of users with minimal technical risk are highly valued.

  - o **Example**: The introduction of Instagram Stories was technically feasible due to its similarity to *Snapchat's* ephemeral content model. It scaled quickly across Instagram's existing infrastructure. It leveraged Instagram's existing photo and video-sharing capabilities without requiring a complete system overhaul, making it both a feasible and scalable product decision.

  - o **Expansion**: Instagram might prioritize features like advanced AI-driven filters and **augmented reality** (**AR**) effects. While these features require development work, they can be implemented without fundamental changes to the platform's core architecture. On the other hand, building features like blockchain integration for decentralized identity verification or privacy control might be deprioritized if they introduce significant technical complexity without clear, scalable benefits.

- **ROI and metrics of success:** This criterion evaluates the potential ROI and how success will be measured. It involves setting clear KPIs and benchmarks to track the effectiveness of a product or feature. PMs must define these metrics early to understand the value a feature will bring to both the users and the business. ROI can be measured in various ways, such as increased user engagement, growth in active users, operational efficiency, or customer retention, depending on the product goals.

  - o **Example**: Instagram Reels not only aimed to increase daily user engagement but also sought to capture a portion of the short-form video content market. Metrics of success for this feature could include user adoption rates, time spent on Reels, increased ad revenue from Reels, and new user sign-ups driven by the feature's popularity.

- o **Expansion**: For a new feature like NFT integration, Instagram could measure success through metrics like the number of NFT transactions, user engagement with digital art, and the growth of NFT creators using the platform. Additionally, if Instagram introduced voice-based features, success could be gauged by tracking user engagement in audio rooms, listener retention, and potential partnerships with creators for exclusive audio content. Establishing these KPIs would allow the product team to assess whether the feature meets its objectives and delivers a positive ROI.

- o **Bonus item**: Not all products are the same, and based on their business model, niche, and position in the market, the investment criteria would differ. For instance, since Instagram is in a mature stage with monetization potential, let us add a couple of bonus criteria that could be considered as follows.

- **Monetization potential:** This evaluates how a feature will contribute to Instagram's revenue, mainly through advertising, e-commerce, and paid partnerships. Revenue-generating features significantly impact Instagram's ability to sustain and grow its platform.

  - o **Example**: Instagram's shopping feature lets users buy products directly from the app. Brands can tag products in posts, stories, and reels, enabling a seamless shopping experience for users. This has opened up a new revenue stream by blending social interaction with e-commerce, allowing businesses to advertise and sell directly through Instagram, taking advantage of user browsing habits.

  - o **Expansion**: Instagram might invest in features integrating social commerce, such as virtual try-on features using AR, where users could try-on products like clothing or accessories before purchasing. Another example would be expanding advertising tools for small businesses by introducing analytics dashboards that give detailed insights into how their ads and posts perform, making Instagram a more valuable platform for paid advertising.

- **Competitive differentiation:** This criterion measures how much a feature sets Instagram apart from competitors. Features that are innovative or exclusive to Instagram will help the platform maintain a competitive edge and attract more users.

  - o **Example**: Instagram filters and AR effects were key differentiators that set the platform apart from other social media apps. Users could apply artistic filters to their photos and videos or use playful AR effects, making the content creation experience more engaging and unique compared to other platforms like Twitter or Snapchat at the time.

   o   **Expansion**: Instagram could focus on differentiating itself by enhancing its in-app video editing capabilities, offering a more robust set of editing tools (similar to standalone apps like *Adobe Premiere* or *Final Cut Pro*) within the app itself. Another potential feature could be integrating AI-driven tools that help users automatically edit and enhance their photos and videos based on trending aesthetics, offering a competitive edge over apps that require manual editing.

Setting stage for a launch success

PMs often concentrate on the development phase, but it is equally important to prioritize the critical pre-launch activities that set the stage for a successful release. These activities encompass a wide range of tasks, including conducting market research, finalizing marketing strategies, coordinating with sales teams, validating product quality through testing and feedback, preparing customer support to handle inquiries, and building anticipation around the upcoming launch. Whether launching a new product or a major feature update, a well-executed pre-launch strategy plays a pivotal role in determining how the product is received in the market and ultimately contributes to its overall success. By giving careful attention to these preparations, PMs can help ensure a smooth, efficient, and impactful launch that resonates with the target audience. It is also essential to remember that pre-launch planning should not be left until after development concludes; stakeholders must be engaged from the earliest planning stages to ensure alignment and readiness. The following sections explore these activities in greater depth.

Understanding pre-launch activities

Pre-launch activities are tasks, strategies, and processes you carry out before a product goes live. Think of this as the final stretch, where every detail needs to be ironed out, from aligning with your change control (if it is an internal B2B product), deployment team, and marketing team to double-checking technical deployments. It is the moment when you are preparing for the big debut, ensuring the product is ready for the real-world, your internal teams are aligned, and your go-to-market strategy is solid.

These activities generally include finalizing the product, testing bugs or usability issues, planning the marketing and communications strategy, training internal teams, preparing customer support, and ensuring you have all the data and metrics to track the launch's success. Essentially, pre-launch ensures that every stakeholder is informed, every process is straightforward, and the market is primed for what is to come. At this point, one might wonder when planning should begin and when stakeholders should be involved. The answer is early, right from the start. They should be engaged during the product's initial kick-off and invited to weekly status updates, even if they have no active role during the initial stages. This will keep your stakeholders informed and help them plan for the correct timing.

When should product managers start planning for pre-launch

It would help to consider pre-launch activities before the product is fully built. Ideally, planning begins as early as when your product development has not even started, or in some instances, during early development stages, typically around 2-3 months before the anticipated launch. By this point, you will have a solid understanding of what the final product will look like, and you can begin by laying the groundwork for launch preparation.

Waiting until the last-minute to plan your pre-launch activities is risky. A well-coordinated pre-launch phase helps reduce the risk of last-minute surprises, ensures the team is aligned, and keeps things running smoothly. The earlier you start, the more time you will have to account for unexpected challenges, a technical issue, a miscommunication with marketing, or a delay from third-party partners.

Key stakeholders involved in pre-launch activities

Pre-launch is a cross-functional effort. As the PM, you must coordinate with several teams to ensure everyone is aligned and ready. Here is a breakdown of the key stakeholders you should involve:

- **Product team:** You will work closely with your engineers and designers to ensure the final product or feature is polished, tested, and ready for deployment.
- **Marketing and communications:** These teams will handle the go-to-market strategy, including email campaigns, press releases, social media, and customer messaging.
- **Sales and customer support:** These teams must be trained on the product's new features, use cases, and potential customer questions. Sales can help promote the product, and support will address any initial user concerns.
- **Legal and compliance:** In some cases, especially for regulated industries, you must ensure that your product complies with legal and regulatory requirements.
- **Data analytics:** Have your analytics team setup metrics and tracking so you can monitor how the product performs post-launch, including user engagement, retention, or other KPIs you have defined.

Change management is very important if you are making changes to the process in a B2B or internal product involving business customers. It is crucial to understand the current process clearly and be prepared with change control and training to help them prepare for the new launch.

The better your coordination across these teams, the smoother your launch will be. Pre-launch activities are as much about ensuring the product is ready as they are about ensuring your entire organization is prepared for it to hit the market.

Pre-launch activities checklist

Following is a template checklist to help you organize your pre-launch activities. This list is not exhaustive, but it covers the key areas that will set you up for success:

Category	Task	Owner	Status	Notes
Product readiness	Final product testing and bug fixes	Product/ engineering	Not started/in progress/complete	Finalize by date and other notes
	Usability testing—final	Product/ **quality assurance (QA)**	Not started/in progress/complete	Address feedback
	Confirm deployment plan	Engineering	Not started/in progress/complete	Deployment scheduled date
	Dependency readiness	Product	Not started/in progress/complete	List dependency owners and other notes
Marketing and communication	Develop a go-to-market plan	Marketing	Not started/in progress/complete	Include key messaging, press, and social media
	Launch marketing like ads, email campaigns etc.	Marketing	Not started/in progress/complete	Creative or ads team approval date
	Announcement to internal teams	Internal comms/ marketing	Not started/in progress/complete	Internal announcement date
Customer support	Train sales team on new features	Product/ sales	Not started/in progress/complete	Schedule training date
	Support materials like training docs and self-help videos	Customer support/ deployment team	Not started/in progress/complete	Support material readiness date

Category	Task	Owner	Status	Notes
Legal/ compliance	Final sign off on communication draft, and validate compliance updates	Legal/ compliance	Not started/in progress/complete	Ensure all regulations in place.
Data and analytics	Is the metrics dashboard ready to track key metrics	Product/ data team	Not started/in progress/complete	List key metrics and dashboard link to track
Go live confirmation	Final confirmation on deployment readiness	Product/ engineering	Not started/in progress/complete	Final check before launch

Table 5.1: Pre-launch checklist

Pre-launch activities are the final and essential step before your product goes live. It is the bridge between development and market introduction, making sure everything is in place for a smooth and successful release. Start planning early, involve the right teams, and use a detailed checklist to stay on track. One of the best ways to track this is to conduct a weekly status update call with the team present the same tracker checklist every week, and update them accordingly. The above template is a rough draft version, and it should be modified as per your team's needs. With a structured approach, you can setup your product for success from day one, and every stakeholder will stay informed and will know the status of the product development. Remember: A well-executed pre-launch plan can make all the difference in whether your product succeeds or struggles out of the gate.

Conclusion

Chapter 5, Product Journey from Concept to Market laid the groundwork for transforming product vision into reality, emphasizing the importance of strategic roadmap development, stakeholder alignment, investment criteria, and pre-launch readiness. Through real-world examples and frameworks, it illustrated how prioritization, planning, and coordination are central to bringing a product from concept to market. Whether identifying critical features, aligning roadmaps with business goals, or managing cross-functional teams, every step of the journey requires thoughtful execution. A well-crafted roadmap is not just a development tool—it is a strategic asset that unites teams, ensures alignment, and delivers meaningful value to users.

As we move forward, the focus shifts from execution to experience. In *Chapter 6, Customer Centric Design* readers will explore the essential principles of customer centric design. This next chapter gets into how product teams can craft solutions that not only function but also delight—balancing empathy, usability, and business objectives. From gathering user requirements and writing effective user stories to prioritizing features and conducting usability testing, it also offers actionable insights for building products that resonate deeply with users and stand out in competitive markets.

Points to remember

- A well-defined product roadmap is essential for guiding development, prioritizing features, and ensuring alignment with strategic goals, customer needs, and market opportunities.

- Identifying feature dependencies and carefully sequencing development tasks is crucial to avoiding delays and ensuring smooth integration.

- A product roadmap is more effective when it is flexible enough to accommodate changing business priorities, market shifts, or evolving customer needs.

- Investment criteria such as strategic alignment, customer impact, market opportunity, technical feasibility, and ROI help prioritize product features for maximum business and user value.

- Continuous innovation, whether through new products or enhancements to existing ones, drives growth, boosts customer engagement, and keeps your business competitive.

- Pre-launch activities, including market preparation, stakeholder alignment, and rigorous testing, are key to ensuring a successful product release. Early involvement of cross-functional teams is vital for smooth coordination.

- Clear communication and alignment across all stakeholders, from developers to executives, helps maintain transparency and manage expectations throughout the product lifecycle.

- Pre-launch readiness includes setting up success metrics, tracking dashboards, and ensuring that sales, support, and marketing teams are fully prepared for product launch.

- Well-defined success metrics, such as customer retention, engagement, and revenue growth, are critical for measuring the impact and value of new product features and enhancements.

- Strategic innovation that addresses unmet needs or disrupts industries helps build competitive differentiation, ensuring long-term relevance and growth in an ever-evolving market.

Multiple choice questions

1. **What is the primary purpose of a product roadmap?**
    a. To increase development speed without a clear strategy
    b. To outline the plan for developing and evolving a product over time
    c. To document all customer complaints
    d. To eliminate collaboration with external stakeholders

2. **Which type of roadmap is most useful for aligning product initiatives with business objectives?**
    a. Timeline-based roadmap
    b. Features-based roadmap
    c. Goal-based roadmap
    d. Dependency-based roadmap

3. **What is the first step in building a product roadmap?**
    a. Defining the product vision and customer needs
    b. Scheduling team meetings
    c. Creating a timeline for product launch
    d. Prioritizing marketing strategies

4. **How does a Features-based roadmap help a product team?**
    a. By focusing solely on long-term business goals
    b. By prioritizing and scheduling features-based on customer and business needs
    c. By ensuring strict adherence to project timelines
    d. By avoiding any dependency analysis

5. **Why are investment criteria important in roadmap development?**
    a. They help prioritize initiatives that align with business objectives and market demands
    b. They ensure all product ideas are approved without evaluation
    c. They simplify product development by excluding user feedback
    d. They reduce the need for collaboration between teams

6. **Who are the primary users of a product roadmap?**
    a. Only the PM and developers
    b. Internal and external stakeholders, including customers, partners, and investors
    c. Marketing and customer support teams exclusively
    d. Engineers and UX/UI designers

7. **What is a critical activity during pre-launch planning?**

   a. Waiting for the product to be fully built before involving stakeholders

   b. Conducting usability testing and aligning with marketing strategies

   c. Avoiding updates to stakeholders until the launch day

   d. Focusing only on deployment readiness

8. **How does Instagram's roadmap exemplify evolution over time?**

   a. By maintaining the same features since its launch

   b. By continuously innovating with features like Reels, Shopping, and Instagram Stories

   c. By avoiding market trends and focusing on internal objectives

   d. By limiting its offerings to a single functionality

9. **Which factor is most important when determining metrics for roadmap success?**

   a. Selecting metrics unrelated to product objectives

   b. Focusing on customer satisfaction and business objectives

   c. Ignoring data analytics and user engagement

   d. Relying only on revenue generation

10. **What is the key focus of pre-launch activities?**

    a. Ensuring marketing teams are the only stakeholders informed

    b. Preparing the product, aligning stakeholders, and ensuring a successful launch

    c. Delaying customer support training until after the launch

    d. Skipping legal and compliance reviews to save time

Answers

1	b
2	c
3	a
4	b
5	a
6	b
7	b
8	b
9	b
10	b

CHAPTER 6
Customer Centric Design

Introduction

This chapter covers one of the most important ingredients of a successful product, customer centric design. While earlier chapters laid the groundwork with strategy, planning, and execution, this one zooms in on the real driving force behind any great product: the people who use it. Because at the end of the day, no matter how well-designed or technically sound a product is, it only works if it genuinely solves a problem for the customer.

Customer centric design challenges **product managers** (**PMs**) to shift their perspective from building what the team wants to creating what users truly need. Even the most innovative features or well-structured roadmaps can fall short if they fail to resonate with real user problems and their underlying frustrations. At its core, this approach demands empathy, a deep understanding of user behavior, and a commitment to aligning product decisions with both user expectations and business outcomes.

This chapter will cover the principles, tools, and best practices that bring customer centricity to life. It examines how to discover user needs, write effective user stories, prioritize features, and leverage usability testing within an iterative design process. Readers will learn how to translate user insight into impactful product experiences, ensuring that what gets built not only solves the right problems but also delivers lasting value.

Structure

This chapter includes the following topics:

- Mastering customer centric approach
- A tale of two strategies from Amazon and BlackBerry
- User requirements
- User stories
- Product feature prioritization
- Usability testing and iterative design process

Objectives

This chapter provides readers with the essential mindset, tools, and techniques to adopt a customer centric approach in product development. It moves beyond theoretical understanding to practical application, enabling PMs to build products that are aligned with genuine user needs. Readers will learn how to effectively identify and interpret user requirements through targeted user research methods and how to translate these insights into well-crafted user stories that guide cross-functional teams. The chapter also introduces structured frameworks for prioritizing product features, helping readers balance user value with business objectives and technical feasibility.

Furthermore, it emphasizes the importance of usability testing and iterative design, highlighting how to validate assumptions and continuously improve the product through real-world user feedback. These skills prepare PMs to move from delivering isolated features to crafting cohesive, user-focused experiences.

By the end of the chapter, readers will be equipped to apply customer centric design principles in real-world scenarios, such as defining **minimum viable products** (**MVPs**), aligning stakeholders around user goals, and adapting quickly to changing market demands. This foundation sets the stage for the next chapter, which explores how data-driven decision-making enhances user-centricity through evidence-based insights.

Mastering customer centric approach

Before exploring the technical elements of user requirements, feature prioritization, and usability testing, it is essential to establish the mindset that underpins customer centric product design. Central to this approach is empathy—the ability to understand and internalize users' experiences, challenges, and motivations. Empathy enables product teams to uncover not only explicit needs but also latent issues that users may not even be aware of—often referred to as **aha moments**. In product management, empathy goes beyond user understanding; it involves forming a deep connection with user pain points and translating that insight into meaningful solutions.

To ground this concept, consider a brief reflective exercise. Think about your favorite app: *Is it unique in its category? What influenced your choice over competing alternatives? What features make it stand out? Could any scenario prompt you to switch, and why?*

Building on this reflection, ask further:

- *How does the app simplify your tasks or solve a specific problem?*
- *What emotions does it evoke—joy, convenience, achievement?*
- *Has it introduced features that have become indispensable?*
- *Would you recommend it to others, and for what reasons?*

While answers may vary, this introspection mirrors the choices users make daily in a competitive digital environment. Today's consumers demand intuitive design, real-time responsiveness, and personalization. A customer centric mindset is no longer optional; it is a fundamental driver of competitive advantage.

One of the best ways to ground your design decisions in empathy is by mapping the customer journey. This is not just about outlining the steps users take with your product; it is about understanding the emotional and psychological stages they go through as they interact with it. Every click, every screen, and every moment is an opportunity to either delight or frustrate them. By mapping these touchpoints, you uncover critical moments where your product must deliver value. This approach allows you to anticipate where users may experience friction and proactively design solutions that smooth their journey. The foundation of user stories and requirements lies in understanding these key moments and building features that address them effectively.

Of course, customer centricity does not mean blindly following every user request or suggestion. There is always a delicate balance between what users want and what is realistic or beneficial for the business. It is here where PMs must navigate the tension between user needs and business goals. While users might want an all-in-one solution with endless features, your job is to prioritize the most valuable and feasible ones. This delicate balancing act is an art in itself, deciding which features to develop based on how well they align with both user value and business objectives. This sets the stage for the prioritization process, which will help you ensure that you are building what matters most without losing sight of business goals.

Your product must evolve as user needs change, as new insights emerge, and as the market shifts. Adopting an iterative mindset allows you to embrace this reality, understanding that the first version of your product will likely not be perfect. But that is the beauty of it; each iteration, informed by usability testing and feedback, brings you closer to a product that truly resonates with users. It is this constant cycle of learning, refining, and adapting that ensures your product remains relevant and valuable in the long-term.

With this perspective in mind, the following case study illustrates a success story about how a company evolved and another that is nowhere to be seen. The story of *Amazon* and *Blackberry*.

A tale of two strategies from Amazon and BlackBerry

Customer centricity is often discussed as a guiding principle, but it is how companies put this principle into action that determines long-term success or failure. Understanding and responding to evolving customer needs is not a one-time exercise; it is a continuous, strategic commitment that shapes how products are built, refined, and delivered. Companies that embrace this mindset do not just react to customer feedback—they anticipate it, translating both expressed and unspoken needs into meaningful product experiences.

The following case study compares two well-known companies—Amazon and BlackBerry—that took drastically different approaches to customer understanding. While one continuously innovated by deeply embedding the customer journey into every decision, the other struggled to adapt and ultimately lost relevance in a fast-changing market. These contrasting stories highlight the real-world impact of customer centric design and provide valuable insights for PMs seeking to build not just functional products, but solutions that truly resonate with users.

Amazon as a masterclass in customer centric design

Amazon's journey to becoming a global e-commerce leader exemplifies the power of customer centric design. By focusing on deeply understanding its customers' needs, even before those needs were fully articulated, Amazon revolutionized the online shopping experience.

Aha moment

In the early days of e-commerce, shopping online was often cumbersome, plagued by long delivery times and clunky interfaces. Amazon recognized that what customers truly valued was convenience and time-saving, even if they could not explicitly express it. By empathizing with their customers' frustrations and examining their shopping journeys, Amazon identified pain points that customers themselves might not have been able to articulate, such as the annoyance of repeatedly entering payment details or waiting weeks for deliveries.

This customer-focused approach led to the following groundbreaking innovations:

- **One-click purchasing:** Amazon simplified the checkout process, addressing customers' need for speed and convenience by eliminating repetitive steps. This feature reduced cart abandonment and became a hallmark of seamless online shopping.

- **Amazon Prime:** By introducing Prime, Amazon transformed logistics into a competitive advantage. Customers gained access to faster shipping, exclusive deals, and premium content, creating an all-encompassing, value-driven shopping ecosystem.

Continuous listening and iteration

Amazon's commitment to understanding and acting on customer feedback became a core pillar of its strategy. Through active listening and analysis, Amazon consistently optimized its website's user interface, refined its logistics network, and developed personalized recommendation algorithms. These advancements addressed not only explicit customer requests but also unspoken desires for a tailored, frictionless shopping experience.

Building loyalty through anticipation

Amazon's ability to anticipate customer needs transformed shopping into a seamless, almost intuitive experience. By solving problems that customers had not fully articulated, such as the demand for integrated shopping and streaming services, Amazon fostered deep loyalty. Prime members, for instance, not only enjoyed faster shipping but also access to entertainment, further embedding Amazon into their daily lives.

Outcome

Amazon's relentless focus on the customer allowed it to dominate the e-commerce space, turning previously frustrated online shoppers into loyal advocates. This customer centric mindset, combined with a commitment to execution, helped Amazon evolve from a bookseller into a global marketplace, setting new standards for what customers expect from digital experiences.

BlackBerry and the cost of ignoring the customer journey

BlackBerry's rise and fall in the mobile phone industry illustrate the consequences of failing to adapt to customers' evolving needs. Once a market leader, BlackBerry's inability to adopt a customer centric mindset ultimately led to its downfall.

Initial success

In the early 2000s, BlackBerry revolutionized mobile communication with its physical keyboard and email functionality, catering primarily to professionals who valued productivity and secure communication. This focus on business users cemented BlackBerry's dominance, making it the go-to device for companies and governments.

Missed signals in a changing landscape

As the smartphone era emerged, customers' expectations began to shift. People increasingly sought devices that were not just tools for productivity but also versatile companions for entertainment, communication, and everyday tasks. Sleek touchscreen interfaces, app ecosystems, and high-speed internet connectivity became non-negotiable features.

However, BlackBerry remained entrenched in its belief that customers only needed physical keyboards and secure email. The company failed to understand the deeper evolution in customer behavior:

- **Unspoken needs:** BlackBerry did not recognize that customers wanted more than a work tool; they desired a flexible, user-friendly device capable of seamless multimedia experiences.
- **Lack of adaptation:** Despite early signals, BlackBerry continued to focus on its existing strengths, missing the aha moment that would have aligned its products with emerging customer demands.

Consequences of stagnation

As competitors like *Apple* and *Samsung* innovated with intuitive interfaces, robust app ecosystems, and sleek designs, BlackBerry clung to its existing formula. Its devices became outdated, unable to compete with the holistic experiences offered by modern smartphones.

Even when BlackBerry attempted to pivot, introducing touchscreen models and an app store, it was too late. The execution was poor, and customers had already moved on to competitors who had more effectively addressed their needs.

Outcome

By failing to step into its customers' shoes and adapting to their evolving journeys, BlackBerry lost its position as an industry leader. This lack of foresight and customer centricity serves as a powerful reminder of the importance of listening to customers, not just for what they say they need but for the unspoken desires that drive their choices.

Lessons learned

These two contrasting stories highlight the pivotal role of customer centric design as follows:

- **Amazon:** Demonstrates the power of understanding and anticipating customer needs to build loyalty and sustain growth.
- **BlackBerry:** Shows how ignoring evolving customer preferences can lead to irrelevance, even for a market leader.

For PMs, these examples underscore the importance of stepping into the customer's shoes, listening actively, and staying Agile in the face of changing expectations.

User requirements

As the focus shifts to the practical aspects of customer centric design, it becomes essential to explore user requirements, i.e., the critical insights that guide what a product should deliver to meet user needs effectively. Understanding these requirements forms the foundation for creating solutions that resonate with the target audience. A general understanding of customer centricity is not sufficient; it must be translated into actionable steps that inform the development process.

This section discusses how to gather user requirements, the importance of user stories, and best practices for ensuring that the product aligns with customer needs. Embracing these principles equips teams to create features that meet user expectations while contributing to the product's success in a constantly evolving marketplace.

User requirements, in simple terms, refer to the specific needs or conditions a product must meet to provide real value to users. They define the functionalities, features, and qualities that users expect from the product, serving as a clear guide for development efforts.

User requirements can be divided into the following two categories:

- **Explicit requirements:** These are the needs directly communicated by users. For example, if a user says, *I want to be able to save my favorite items*, that is an explicit requirement.

- **Implicit requirements:** These are the needs that users might not state directly but can be inferred from their behaviors and contexts. For instance, if you notice that users frequently abandon their shopping carts, it might imply a need for a more intuitive navigation system or a simpler checkout process.

The importance of understanding user requirements is considered the basic core principle, as they serve several critical purposes in the product development process:

- **Guiding development:** Think of user requirements as a North Star in the product development process. They are what keep the entire team: Designers, developers, marketers, everyone, aligned and working toward the same goal. Without the North Star requirements, it would mean that PMs are essentially building in the dark, hoping for the best. On the other hand, when PMs know what users need, it is like having a clear map that guides every decision.

  - **Example:** Take *Slack*, for example. Before it became the go-to tool for workplace communication, its founders spent a considerable amount of time talking to potential users. They asked thoughtful questions and, more importantly, listened closely to the answers. What they uncovered was a clear frustration—people were struggling with clunky, disjointed communication tools. Users wanted something intuitive, centralized, and compatible with the apps they already relied on. Armed with this insight, the Slack team set out to build exactly what was needed: Channel-based messaging, seamless file sharing, and robust third-party integrations. That deep focus on user needs is what ultimately turned Slack into a game-changer.

- **Ensuring user satisfaction:** A product's success is closely tied to user satisfaction. Prioritizing user requirements goes beyond simply fulfilling a checklist; it involves creating a product that users genuinely want to engage with, one that effectively solves their problems and enhances their lives. When users are satisfied, they are more likely to return, recommend the product to others, and remain loyal, contributing to long-term success and growth.

  o **Example:** Consider Apple's iPhone. From its inception, Apple understood that consumers were not just looking for a phone but an experience. Users wanted a device that was intuitive, visually appealing, and multifunctional, all within a sleek design. Apple successfully delivered on these expectations, resulting in a product that resonated deeply with its audience. This user-centric approach is evident in the iPhone's enduring popularity and the strong loyalty of its user base, reflecting a company that prioritized and addressed its customers' needs.

- **Risk mitigation:** Developing a product is a significant investment, and misaligned efforts can result in wasted resources. Clearly defined user requirements act as a safeguard, ensuring that teams remain focused on what truly matters to their audience. Prioritizing these requirements minimizes the risk of building unnecessary features or launching products that fail to meet user needs.

  o **Example:** A notable example of this misstep is *Google Wave*. Despite being packed with innovative features, Wave failed to resonate with users. The product's development overlooked the importance of understanding user needs and preferences. Without clear insight into whether users desired or required such a tool, the launch led to confusion rather than enthusiasm. Instead of solving a problem, Wave inadvertently created one. Had Google conducted more thorough user research, the company might have identified this gap early, preventing the costly failure. This serves as a reminder that user-centered design is essential for product success.

Ways to gather user requirements

Collecting user requirements goes beyond merely inquiring about what the users want; it entails a comprehensive understanding of their underlying needs, preferences, and challenges. To effectively gather user requirements, consider employing a variety of methods that can provide rich insights and foster meaningful engagement with your users. The following section discusses various approaches that can be considered.

User interviews

Conduct one-on-one interviews with potential users to explore their experiences, frustrations, and needs. Prepare open-ended questions to facilitate a deeper discussion.

Note: **The following are tips that can be taken into consideration:**

- **Start with broad questions and gradually narrow down to specific topics.**
- **Encourage users to share stories about their experiences with similar products.**

Consider an example of conducting an effective customer interview. *Alex*, a PM at a leading transportation company, is tasked with developing a real-time communication tool for coordinators and drivers. To gather insights, he visits the transportation office and conducts an interview with one of the coordinators.

Initial interview

In his initial interviews, Alex's primary focus was on gathering feedback, specifically about the proposed real-time communication feature, assuming it would be a game-changer for coordinators. He prepared a structured set of questions such as; *do you think a real-time chat tool would help you communicate better with drivers?* and *how often do you need to contact drivers while they are on the road?* While these questions yielded some responses, the feedback was superficial. Most coordinators provided simple *yes* or *no* answers, offering minimal insight into their actual experiences.

Alex soon realized that his line of questioning was too narrow, limiting the opportunity for coordinators to share their real-world communication challenges. As a result, he missed valuable details about the types of messages coordinators typically send, the urgency of their communications, and the specific pain points they encounter when communication is delayed or ineffective.

Mistakes made

Listed as follows are common observations from a user interview session that illustrate common pitfalls in approach and questioning style:

- The questions were overly focused on the proposed feature rather than exploring the coordinator's broader communication experience.

- The lack of open-ended questions prevented deeper insights and hindered the discovery of underlying challenges.

- Alex failed to explore the context in which communication issues arose, missing opportunities to uncover unexpected pain points or needs.

This example highlights the importance of approaching customer interviews with curiosity and flexibility. Rather than focusing solely on validating a pre-existing idea, effective interviews should prioritize understanding the user's day-to-day experiences and challenges.

Follow-up interviews

In his next round of interviews, Alex revises his approach to better understand the communication challenges coordinators face in their daily roles. Rather than leading with questions about the proposed feature, he begins by asking, *can you walk me through a recent situation where you had to communicate with a driver?* This open-ended question prompts coordinators to recount specific experiences, providing Alex with deeper insights into the context of their communication needs.

As coordinators share their stories, Alex listens attentively and follows-up with questions, such as, *what made that communication challenging?* And *how did you resolve the issue?* This conversational approach helps him uncover real frustrations, including delays in receiving updates and miscommunications about pickup times.

By allowing the conversation to flow naturally, Alex identifies common themes. Coordinators frequently struggle with coordinating schedules and require immediate updates when drivers are running late. These insights inform Alex's understanding of how a real-time communication tool could address these pain points. He refined the product concept to include features such as automated delay notifications and a simple interface for quick updates, ensuring the tool directly addresses the users' needs.

This approach demonstrates the value of focusing on **user experiences** (**UXs**) rather than solely validating a feature. By encouraging storytelling and exploring real-life scenarios, Alex gains actionable insights that contribute to developing a more effective and user-friendly communication tool.

The next section discusses additional methods that can be considered for gathering user requirements.

Additional methods for gathering user requirements

Beyond one-on-one interviews, PMs can benefit from a broader toolkit of research methods to capture both qualitative and quantitative insights. To deepen his understanding of user needs and validate key assumptions, Alex explores several complementary approaches. These methods help paint a more holistic picture of the UX, identify gaps in current solutions, and support the development of a product that is both intuitive and impactful. The following are the additional strategies Alex uses to gather meaningful user requirements:

- **Surveys and questionnaires:** Surveys are an efficient way to gather quantitative data from a larger audience. To maximize meaningful responses, Alex designs a balanced mix of multiple choice and open-ended questions. This structure captures both statistical trends and valuable qualitative feedback. Additionally, he keeps the survey concise to minimize fatigue and encourage participation.

- **Focus groups:** For a more interactive form of feedback, Alex facilitates focus groups by bringing together a diverse group of transportation coordinators. These discussions foster dynamic conversations, often surfacing insights that might not emerge in individual interviews. Coordinators share experiences, compare challenges, and suggest potential solutions, helping Alex refine the product vision further.

- **User observation and contextual inquiry:** To gain first-hand knowledge of how coordinators work, Alex conducts user observation sessions. By watching coordinators interact with existing scheduling software, he identifies workflow challenges and inefficient processes. Contextual inquiry takes this further; Alex visits coordinators in their work environments to observe real-time interactions and capture the nuances of their communication needs. Equipped with flexible goals, he remains open to unexpected insights.

- **Competitive analysis:** Conducting competitive analysis is another key step in Alex's process. He evaluates rival transportation products to identify well-received features and gaps in the market. By gathering feedback from users of these competing products, Alex uncovers common frustrations and opportunities to differentiate his product.

- **Usability testing:** Once a prototype is ready, Alex conducts usability testing to observe how coordinators interact with the product. By analyzing real-time user feedback, he identifies areas for improvement and ensures the tool is both intuitive and functional. This iterative approach allows the team to refine the product before the final launch.

- **Collaboration with customer support:** Alex also collaborates with the customer support team to gather insights from past user complaints and feature requests. Reviewing recurring themes in support tickets helps him pinpoint areas where the current communication process fails and guides further product improvements.

- **Continuous and iterative process:** Gathering user requirements is not a one-time task. It is an ongoing, iterative process that requires active listening, empathy, and adaptability. By combining various research methods, Alex ensures he gains a comprehensive understanding of user needs. This customer centric approach enables him to create a product that addresses real problems and provides a seamless, valuable UX.

In the next section, the focus will shift to translating these gathered user requirements into actionable user stories. This step will guide the product development process and ensure that the final product remains aligned with user expectations.

User stories

User stories play a crucial role in bridging the gap between user requirements and the development process. They serve as a communication tool that enables PMs, designers, and developers to collaborate effectively, ensuring the product aligns with user expectations.

Typically, PMs are responsible for crafting user stories, often working closely with designers, developers, and, most importantly, actual users. By involving diverse stakeholders, user stories capture multiple perspectives and provide a well-rounded representation of user needs. This collaborative approach ensures that the development process remains focused on delivering value.

While user stories are most commonly used in Agile development environments, they are equally valuable in other product management approaches. They serve as a key component of the product backlog, offering clear guidance on what the product should achieve from the user's perspective. Additionally, user stories assist in prioritizing work during sprints, helping teams stay aligned with project goals and maintain a user-centered focus throughout the product development lifecycle.

Now, it is essential to understand the structure of user stories. At their core, user stories follow a straightforward template as follows:

As a [type of user], I want [some goal] so that [some reason].

This structure keeps the focus squarely on the user and highlights the value behind the feature. For instance, let us say that Alex is still working on a real-time communication tool for transportation coordinators. A poorly constructed user story might look like this:

As a user, I want a chat feature.

At first glance, this seems clear enough, but it is vague and lacks context. *Who is the user? What specific need does this chat feature address? Why do they want it?* Without these details, the team might struggle to understand the purpose behind the feature or its importance.

Now, consider the following sample user story:

As a transportation coordinator, I want a real-time chat feature so that I can quickly communicate with drivers when they are running late, ensuring timely pickups and reducing customer complaints.

This revised user story provides clarity and context. We know who the user is, what they want, and why it matters to them. Specifying the challenges the coordinators face helps the development team grasp the importance of the feature, ultimately leading to a more targeted solution. Along with the user story, it is also important to mention the acceptance criteria to add clarity on the expectation, which will ensure that both the product and engineering team know what is expected, what should be tested, and when it will be considered as done.

The following are a couple of examples of acceptance criteria:

- **Successful message delivery:**
    - Given the transportation coordinator has access to the real-time chat feature
    - When they send a message to a driver
    - Then the driver should receive the message instantly with a notification

- **Read receipt confirmation:**

  o   Given the coordinator sends a message to a driver

  o   When the driver reads the message

  o   Then the coordinator should see a read receipt indicating the message was read

The following are some best practices for writing user stories that resonate:

- **Keep it simple:** User stories should be concise and easily understandable. Avoid jargon or overly complex language.

- **Focus on the user:** Always frame your stories from the user's perspective. This keeps the focus on delivering value.

- **Include acceptance criteria:** Define what success looks like for each user story. This ensures everyone knows when a story is complete.

- **Prioritize stories:** Not all user stories hold the same weight. Prioritize them based on user value, business impact, and technical feasibility.

- **Engage users in the process:** Involve real users in the story-writing process to ensure their needs are accurately captured.

- **Iterate and refine:** User stories are not set in stone. As you gather more feedback and insights, revisit and revise them accordingly.

By adhering to these best practices, product teams can create user stories that effectively guide the development process and ensure the product remains aligned with user needs.

User stories are typically housed in a product backlog, which serves as a prioritized list of features, enhancements, and fixes that require attention. As the product evolves and user needs shift, the backlog remains a dynamic, living document. Whether managed using digital tools like Jira, Trello, or Asana or maintained in a simple spreadsheet, it is essential to keep the backlog organized and accessible to the entire team to facilitate collaboration and maintain clarity.

Product feature prioritization

With a solid understanding of user stories and how they serve as a roadmap for product development, it is time to explore the critical process of prioritizing product features. This step is crucial because not all features are equally valuable, and determining which ones to address first can significantly influence the success of your product.

Reasons to prioritize features

The prioritization of features in product development is essential for effective resource allocation and strategic decision-making. While it may appear that all features addressing user pain points warrant immediate attention, especially within a customer centric framework, such an approach is rarely practical. Prioritization ensures that teams focus on delivering the highest value features first, aligning product development efforts with both user needs and business objectives.

When we prioritize, we focus on the features that provide the most value and impact on UX. This process involves assessing user needs and market trends and aligning these insights with business objectives. By dedicating resources to the most important features first, we can ensure that we address users' core issues, ultimately enhancing their overall satisfaction.

Moreover, prioritization helps streamline the development process, reducing time-to-market for crucial features. This not only drives user engagement but also positions the product competitively within the market. By delivering features that truly matter to users, businesses can foster loyalty and improve retention rates, leading to long-term success. Therefore, a strategic approach to feature prioritization is vital for achieving both user satisfaction and business goals.

Key stakeholders in feature prioritization

Feature prioritization is a critical and multifaceted process that involves close collaboration among various groups, including PMs, designers, developers, and key stakeholders. Each participant brings a unique perspective to the table, which is crucial for ensuring that the final prioritization effectively balances user needs, technical feasibility, and overarching business goals.

As the process unfolds, the team engages in discussions that help to identify and evaluate potential features, using criteria such as user feedback, market trends, and technical constraints to inform their decisions. A systematic approach, often facilitated by frameworks like the **must have, should have, could have, and will not have (MoSCoW)** method or the Kano Model, helps categorize and rank features-based on urgency and impact.

Importantly, this prioritization process is driven by clear business requirements that align with the company's strategic objectives. Business leadership plays a pivotal role by providing final approval on the prioritized list, ensuring that the selected features support the organization's vision and goals.

This collaborative approach not only enhances the sense of ownership among team members but also encourages cross-functional alignment, making it easier to rally support for the chosen features. In turn, this can lead to more effective product development cycles, reduced time-to-market, and ultimately, increased customer satisfaction and business performance.

Best practices for prioritization

Determining the right timing for this process is crucial for maintaining an efficient and effective product development cycle.

The best practice is to begin prioritizing the product backlog at least three months before the start of each year. This timeline allows product teams to solidify high-level priorities for the upcoming year. From there, it is recommended to start refining product requirement documents and consolidating the list of features about two months before each quarter. This proactive approach provides ample time for teams to review user stories, evaluate their alignment with business objectives, and engage in thoughtful discussions about each feature's importance.

During this phase, it is equally essential to collaborate closely with the engineering team to assess the level of effort required for each feature. Gaining alignment on technical feasibility and resource needs ensures a more accurate and realistic prioritization process.

Once the prioritization is finalized, the product backlog can be translated into a sprint backlog at the start of the quarter. This systematic approach keeps the development process on track, maintains cross-functional alignment, and ensures that the most impactful features are delivered efficiently.

Methods to prioritize features

Several methods prioritize product features, each with its strengths. The following are a few effective approaches:

- **MoSCoW method:** This technique categorizes features into four groups: must have, should have, could have, and will not have. This helps clarify which features are essential for launch and which can be deferred for later releases.

- **Kano Model:** This model evaluates features-based on user satisfaction. Features are classified as basic, performance, or excitement factors. Understanding how features impact user satisfaction can guide you toward the most valuable enhancements.

- **Value vs. effort matrix:** In this approach, you plot features on a two-axis grid based on their perceived value to users and the effort required to implement them. This visual representation makes it easy to identify quick wins and features that may require more resources but provide significant benefits.

- **RICE scoring: Reach, impact, confidence, and effort** (RICE) this method assigns a score to each feature-based on these four criteria, allowing you to quantify and compare the potential value of different features systematically.

- **Weighted scoring:** This method involves assigning weights to various criteria (such as user demand, alignment with business goals, and technical feasibility) and scoring features against those criteria. This helps you quantitatively assess which features should take priority.

The following table shows a sample feature prioritization list for the preceding user story, using a value vs. effort matrix:

Feature	Value (impact)	Effort (t-shirt sizing)	Priority
Automated delay notifications	High	**Medium (M)**	1
Real-time chat tool for coordinators and drivers	High	**Large (L)**	2
Driver location tracking	High	**Medium (M)**	3
Scheduling calendar for pickups	Medium	**Small (S)**	4
Customizable driver profiles	Medium	**Small (S)**	5
Feedback collection tool for users	Low	**Extra-small (XS)**	6
In-app training resources for drivers	Low	**Small (S)**	7

Table 6.1: Value vs. effort matrix template

Explanation of the columns is as follows:

- **Feature:** The specific functionality being considered for development.
- **Value (impact):** The estimated positive effect on user satisfaction or business goals. Categories can include high, medium, or low.
- **Effort (t-shirt size):** The level of effort required to implement the feature represented in t-shirt sizing (XS, S, M, L, XL).
- **Priority:** The order in which features should be developed, based on a combination of their value and effort required.

Insights from the prioritization

In this prioritization list, automated delay notifications rank as the highest priority due to their high-value and S effort, making them a quick win that can significantly enhance UX. Following closely are the real-time chat tool and driver location tracking, both classified as high-value but with a M effort, indicating they require more resources but also promise significant impact.

Conversely, features like in-app training resources and offline access have low value but a S and M effort, respectively. These features are lower on the priority list because their implementation may not yield a substantial return on investment compared to other options.

This effort value matrix provides a clear framework for your product development journey, guiding your team to focus on the features that will deliver the most value with the least effort while ensuring alignment with business requirements.

Usability testing and iterative design process

As we move forward with prioritization and finalize the features that gain priority for development, it is vital to highlight the significance of usability testing and the iterative design process. Usability testing involves actively evaluating how real users will interact with your product, identifying any challenges or frustrations they might encounter. This feedback is invaluable for refining the product to better meet user needs.

Furthermore, the iterative design process allows for continuous improvement. By gathering insights from usability tests, teams can make informed adjustments to the design, features, and functionality. This cycle of testing, feedback, and refinement ensures that the final product not only aligns with user requirements but also creates an engaging and delightful experience. Ultimately, prioritizing these practices fosters user satisfaction and loyalty, key elements for a successful product in today's competitive market.

Usability testing is an essential phase in the product development process, typically carried out by a collaborative team consisting of UX designers, PMs, and, at times, researchers. PMs will work in close collaboration with the UX designers. They are particularly vital to this process, as they possess a deep understanding of user behavior patterns and are adept at translating those insights into effective design elements.

During usability testing, UX designers create detailed prototype mockup designs, visual representations of the user interface that serve as the foundation for the testing phase. These mockups are not just static images; they often incorporate interactive elements using tools like Figma, InVision, and Balsamiq, closely resembling the final product. By allowing real users to interact with these prototypes, the team can gather valuable feedback on usability, functionality, and overall UX before actual feature development begins.

The participants in the testing are randomly selected and should reflect a diverse group. It is important not to guide the users or provide explanations during the process; instead, they should be encouraged to think aloud as they navigate each step of the testing. This iterative approach helps identify potential issues early on, enabling the team to refine designs based on real user interactions and preferences. Ultimately, this leads to a more user-friendly final product.

The ideal setting for usability testing is often in the user's work environment. Conducting tests in the natural habitat of your users allows you to observe their authentic interactions with your product. It provides valuable context about their workflows, pain points, and how they might use your feature in real-life situations. For instance, if you are testing the real-time communication tool for transportation coordinators, observing them in their office or on-site while they manage drivers can uncover nuances that a controlled environment might miss.

Role of UX designers and product managers

UX designers are responsible for crafting intuitive and user-friendly designs. They utilize UX mockups or prototypes to simulate how the product will function. These prototypes allow users to engage with the design, providing critical feedback on usability and functionality before developers invest time in coding.

PMs serve as the intermediaries between UX designers and stakeholders. They ensure that user insights gathered from usability testing are communicated effectively to both the design and development teams. They play a crucial role in prioritizing feedback based on business objectives and user impact, aligning everyone toward a common goal.

Best practices for usability testing

To maximize the effectiveness of usability testing, consider the following best practices:

- **Recruit a diverse participant pool:** Select a representative group of users who match your target audience. This ensures that the feedback you gather is relevant and comprehensive.

- **Prepare realistic scenarios:** Develop tasks that reflect genuine user interactions with your product. For instance, ask coordinators to simulate sending a message to a driver about a last-minute schedule change.

- **Conduct tests in the user's environment:** Whenever possible, conduct usability tests where users typically work. This allows you to observe their authentic interactions and behaviors.

- **Utilize UX mock designs:** Use prototypes and mock designs during usability tests. This allows users to interact with a simulated version of the product, enabling you to gather feedback on its usability and design before development begins.

- **Actively observe without interfering:** Allow users to express their thoughts and frustrations as they navigate the product, encouraging them to think out loud. Resist the urge to guide them; their genuine reactions will provide the most valuable insights.

- **Record sessions for analysis:** With user permission, record the testing sessions. This allows you to revisit specific moments for deeper analysis and discussion with your team later.

- **Iterate based on feedback:** After conducting usability tests, prioritize user feedback and implement changes in the design. Continuously iterate on the product based on user insights to ensure it meets their needs effectively.

Combining usability testing with an iterative design process creates a powerful framework for product development. When you seek user feedback and refine your product, you ensure that it evolves in alignment with user needs and expectations. This leads to a more successful product and fosters a culture of user-centricity within your team.

Conclusion

This chapter emphasized the importance of customer centric design in building products that meet and exceed user expectations. By focusing on understanding user needs through methods such as interviews, surveys, and usability testing, PMs can ensure that products are both functional and meaningful. Translating these insights into clear user stories, prioritizing features effectively, and continuously iterating based on feedback are key steps in delivering a successful product. The contrasting experiences of Amazon and BlackBerry further illustrate how a customer-first approach can drive growth, while neglecting user needs can lead to decline.

However, understanding customer needs is only part of the equation. In the next *Chapter 7, Data-driven Decision-making*, the focus shifts to how PMs can leverage data to make informed decisions. The next chapter will demonstrate how applying a data-driven mindset ensures product strategies remain aligned with user needs and business objectives, driving continuous improvement and long-term growth.

Points to remember

- The heart of product management lies in understanding and serving the customer, making customer centric design crucial for success.
- Cultivating empathy helps PMs to deeply understand user pain points, motivations, and behaviors, which informs better design decisions.
- Effective methods, such as user interviews, surveys, focus groups, and contextual inquiries, are vital for understanding user needs beyond surface-level feedback.
- User stories translate user requirements into actionable items for development, providing clarity and a shared understanding among teams.
- Embracing an iterative mindset allows product teams to continuously learn from user feedback and refine their products for optimal usability.
- Conducting usability testing, ideally in the user's work environment, helps identify usability issues and validate design choices before full-scale development.
- Collaboration between UX designers and PMs is essential; UX designers focus on UX, while PMs align feedback with business goals.
- Prioritizing product features-based on user value, business objectives, and technical feasibility is a critical balancing act that informs the product roadmap.
- Regularly prioritize the backlog two months before each quarter, ensuring alignment with the engineering team and securing buy-in on the level of effort estimates.
- The journey does not end with the product launch; ongoing usability testing and feedback are necessary to adapt and improve the product over time, ensuring it remains relevant to users.

Multiple choice questions

1. **What is the primary focus of customer centric design?**
   a. Building products based on what the company wants
   b. Prioritizing features that are easiest to develop
   c. Ensuring that user needs and experiences are at the core of all decisions
   d. Adopting the latest technological trends regardless of user feedback

2. **What is an essential mindset for adopting customer centric design?**
   a. Developing technical skills to build features faster
   b. Cultivating empathy to understand user pain points and behaviors
   c. Focusing on reducing development costs
   d. Avoiding all user feedback to stay innovative

3. **Which of the following demonstrates an effective application of customer journey mapping?**
   a. Outlining only the technical specifications of a product
   b. Designing features that address user frustrations and reduce friction points
   c. Creating a product that focuses solely on profitability
   d. Mapping the competitors' strategies

4. **What critical mistake did BlackBerry make that contributed to its downfall?**
   a. It focused on secure email functionality and ignored emerging user needs.
   b. It prioritized user feedback over profitability.
   c. It anticipated user needs before they were expressed.
   d. It embraced customer centric design too aggressively.

5. **What is one advantage of usability testing in the product design process?**
   a. It eliminates the need for iterative design.
   b. It allows teams to skip prototype development.
   c. It provides real-time feedback on product interactions.
   d. It only evaluates the business value of a product.

6. **In a user story, what is the purpose of the so that section?**
   a. To outline the technical requirements of a feature
   b. To explain why the user needs the feature and its value
   c. To provide a timeline for development
   d. To describe the acceptance criteria for the feature

7. **Which feature prioritization method categorizes features into must have, should have, could have, and will not have?**
   a. RICE scoring
   b. MoSCoW method
   c. Kano Model
   d. Value vs. effort matrix

8. **What does the Kano Model help identify in feature prioritization?**
   a. The effort required to implement features
   b. Features that excite users and impact satisfaction levels
   c. Features that align strictly with business goals
   d. Technically complex features

9. **What is the role of UX designers in usability testing?**
   a. Writing user stories for the backlog
   b. Developing prototypes and mock designs for testing
   c. Prioritizing features-based on technical feasibility
   d. Conducting market research for competitive analysis

10. **Why is it important to iterate after usability testing?**
    a. To reduce development costs
    b. To finalize the product without further changes
    c. To refine the product based on user feedback and insights
    d. To eliminate the need for user stories

Answers

1	c
2	b
3	b
4	a
5	c
6	b
7	b
8	b
9	b
10	c

Join our Discord space

Join our Discord workspace for latest updates, offers, tech happenings around the world, new releases, and sessions with the authors:

https://discord.bpbonline.com

CHAPTER 7

Data-driven Decision-making

Introduction

Product managers (**PMs**) live and breathe data in every decision they make. It helps to prioritize features, identify areas of strength and weaknesses, or areas needing improvement, and these decisions, if backed by data, weaknesses or needing improvement and these decisions if backed by data will carry weight during implementation. Not all decisions will be data-driven, as some are made from past experience, intuition, and an idea the PM feels strongly and is passionate about.

Innovation is not necessarily data-driven; it is an idea borne by real-life experience, gut instinct, and a creative mindset to fill a gap. Customer interviews, discovery sessions, and a keen eye on the market help drive innovative ideas. These ideas then lead to **minimum viable product** (**MVP**) that helps teams to fail fast and hone them into a better product. The data collected from this exercise provides clarity in formulating the final product.

Structure

This chapter covers the following topics:

- The power of data-driven product strategy
- Meta's data-led transformation of Oculus Quest
- Role of data in product decisions

- Data Value Pyramid framework
- Types of data
- Getting started with data analysis
- Importance of clean data
- Spotify and the data-driven product innovation
- PDM/PLM/PIM

Objectives

This chapter tells us about the importance of using data as a foundational tool in product decision-making. It highlights how PMs can transform raw data into actionable insights, reduce risk, and refine strategy throughout the product lifecycle. Readers will learn how to categorize and interpret data, apply analytics to optimize decisions, and ensure accuracy through clean and consistent data practices. Through real-world examples, such as *Oculus* and *Spotify*, the chapter demonstrates how leading companies use data to drive innovation, improve **user experience** (**UX**), and create scalable, high-performing products. The chapter also covers key tools and systems like **product data management** (**PDM**), **product lifecycle management** (**PLM**), and **product information management** (**PIM**) that support end-to-end PDM.

Data goes far beyond just the numbers on a dashboard or graphs in a presentation. Data is the foundation of our understanding of how users engage with our products, what they truly need, and how our offerings perform in the real-world. Data shows us patterns, highlights pain points, and brings objectivity to what could otherwise be subjective guesses. It allows us to see users in all their complexity, not just what they tell us in feedback, but what they do within the product. Every behavior within the product can be tracked, especially since we are talking about digital products. Track the response time, user behavior, crashes, feedback, etc.

Using data effectively can do more than validate or disprove our assumptions. We can prioritize features-based on usage insights, refining our strategies to align with user needs and overarching business goals. Data allows us to zoom in on what users value most and where they are getting stuck, helping us make informed choices that maximize product impact.

The power of data-driven product strategy

Data provides an objective lens through which teams can evaluate product performance, user behavior, and market dynamics. It minimizes reliance on assumptions by validating hypotheses with real-world evidence. Whether determining which features to build, identifying pain points, or measuring success post-launch, data empowers teams to act with purpose and measurable outcomes in mind. Throughout this chapter, we will examine how data can help de-risk decisions by surfacing what is working well and where opportunities for improvement exist. We will also discuss why intuition alone can fall short, especially when dealing with scale or complexity, and how structured data analysis can guide decisions at every stage of the product lifecycle from discovery to delivery and beyond.

Ultimately, leveraging data enables PMs to reduce user friction, increase retention, drive engagement, and optimize **return on investment** (**ROI**). When used effectively, data transforms not just how we make decisions, but also how we build, iterate, and grow products that are not only functional but truly user-centered and scalable.

Meta's data-led transformation of Oculus Quest

A compelling example of data's transformative power in product development is *Meta's Oculus Quest*. Unlike many **virtual reality** (**VR**) systems that require large physical spaces, Oculus brought immersive VR into the comfort of users' homes, with high-quality visuals, a wide range of games, and seamless online interaction.

What truly set Oculus apart, however, was Meta's commitment to leveraging data to continuously improve the product experience. During the development of the Oculus Quest, Meta closely analyzed how users engaged with the device, tracking preferences, behaviors, and pain points. These insights played a critical role in informing both hardware design enhancements and software updates, resulting in a more intuitive, accessible, and satisfying VR experience.

For instance, by analyzing user engagement and activity data, Meta was able to identify features that VR users found challenging, such as controller functionality and navigation within VR environments. This analysis led to continuous updates, including more intuitive hand-tracking technology and interface improvements, making VR experiences more accessible and enjoyable. Meta also uses data insights to understand which types of games and apps resonate with users, guiding content partnerships and feature enhancements.

Meta's approach with *Quest 3* and *Quest 3S* exemplifies the transformative power of data in product evolution. Through analyzing user feedback and behavioral data, Meta identified critical areas for improvement, transforming the original Quest model into a device that better serves a wide array of user needs. For instance, Meta recognized that many users were uncomfortable removing their glasses to use the headset, leading to the inclusion of a glass spacer in the Quest 3S packaging. They even offer custom prescription lenses, making VR experiences accessible to a broader user base.

Another key insight from user data was that VR was increasingly used for streaming media, not just gaming. This inspired the creation of theater mode, a feature that turns any space into a personal theater, dimming the surroundings and letting users anchor a virtual screen in their preferred position. This feature, tailored for movie lovers, enables

Meta to appeal to new user groups and enhance satisfaction by making VR more versatile in everyday contexts.

Battery life and comfort were also highlighted in data analysis as critical user pain points, leading Meta to introduce the Elite strap with Battery accessory. This add-on provides not only added comfort but also up to two additional hours of usage, addressing user complaints about VR sessions being too short or uncomfortable.

Meta's data-driven design refinements in Quest 3 and 3S showcase how they have leveraged insights to significantly improve user satisfaction, accessibility, and immersion, effectively broadening VR's appeal and usability. This iterative approach, informed by data at every step, illustrates the crucial role that data plays in optimizing product features and meeting evolving user needs.

Role of data in product decisions

Understanding the value of data in product management goes beyond simply acknowledging its importance. Data plays a critical role in shaping strategic decisions, guiding product improvements, and ensuring alignment with both user expectations and business objectives. It empowers PMs to move from assumptions to evidence-based decisions, helping teams reduce risk and optimize outcomes.

How exactly does data create this kind of value? To answer that, let us break down the progression of how data evolves, from raw numbers into meaningful insights that fuel smarter product strategies. Each step in this journey builds upon the last, ultimately enabling PMs to uncover patterns, anticipate behavior, and unlock opportunities for growth.

Here is how data delivers value at each stage of the product decision-making process:

- **Provides information:** The starting point of data's value is simple: It provides information. This information might come from various sources, like user activity logs, surveys, or customer feedback, and covers metrics and trends that reveal user interaction patterns, product performance, and emerging preferences. However, raw information alone has limited value. Its power comes alive when we interpret and analyze it, which leads us to the next step.

- **Information provides insights into user and buyer behavior:** Once we analyze the data, it transforms from simple information into insights. These insights are the key to understanding both user and buyer behavior. For example, data might reveal that users engage more frequently with certain features or spend longer time in specific areas of the app. Recognizing these patterns helps us understand what users enjoy, what frustrates them, and what they seek from the product.

  Insights into buyer behavior can also reveal purchasing preferences and pain points, helping tailor product offers or pricing models to different market segments. By identifying these behaviors, PMs can shape user journeys and craft a product that truly aligns with customer expectations.

- **Behavior leads to understanding product strengths and weaknesses:** As we dig deeper into user and buyer behavior, we can start to map out the product's strengths and weaknesses more clearly. This understanding is powerful for several reasons:

  o **Overcoming weaknesses can unclog the revenue stream:** Weaknesses often become roadblocks in the user journey, reducing satisfaction and even leading to churn. By identifying and addressing these weaknesses, you not only improve the UX but also remove barriers that may be hindering revenue flow. This could mean simplifying complex workflows, improving product stability, or enhancing usability, all of which contribute to smoother interactions and more consistent engagement.

  o **Strengths can lead to adjacencies:** Data can reveal which aspects of the product resonate most with users, pointing to its core strengths. Recognizing these strengths allows PMs to explore adjacent opportunities, new features, or services that complement what users already appreciate. For example, a popular social feature could lead to the development of more community-focused tools, creating new avenues for user engagement.

  o **Understanding loyalty and stickiness:** Loyalty is an invaluable asset for any product because it generates stickiness, or a user's tendency to stay engaged over the long-term. Data-driven insights reveal what builds loyalty, such as trusted functionality, responsive customer support, or unique features that users cannot find elsewhere. Loyalty does more than retain customers; it increases lifetime value, boosts word-of-mouth promotion, and solidifies a competitive edge. In a sense, loyal users form the backbone of a product's sustainability and growth.

Data Value framework

The Data Value framework illustrates how raw data evolves into strategic insights that drive informed decision-making. It is made of four key stages, helping PMs understand the increasing value each step contributes toward building smarter, data-informed strategies:

To fully appreciate the role of data in decision-making, it is important to understand how it evolves from raw inputs into strategic insights. The following list breaks down this transformation into four progressive stages, each building upon the last to unlock deeper understanding and more effective action:

- **Raw data (unprocessed and unorganized data):** At the foundation is the data in its rawest form. This is the unprocessed, unorganized set of inputs gathered from various sources like user logs, click-throughs, sales figures, and feedback forms. Raw data is the fundamental layer that captures the details of every interaction and activity, but lacks inherent meaning or context. For instance, numbers showing website visits or app usage times are basic data points. While valuable, they cannot provide direct insights on their own.

- **Informed data (organized data):** The next level up is informed data, where data begins to take on structure and meaning. Here, data is processed, sorted, and organized into a form that highlights patterns and relationships. By contextualizing the data, we convert it into information that offers more practical insight. For example, arranging website traffic data by pages visited, user demographics, and time of day reveals when users are most active and which content resonates with them. This structure gives meaning to raw data and allows PMs to begin analyzing trends and drawing preliminary conclusions.

- **Skilled data (contextualized, relevant information):** Once we have relevant information, the next step is transforming it into comprehension. Comprehension emerges when we interpret information within the context of specific objectives, goals, or challenges. It involves understanding why certain patterns exist and what they indicate about user needs, market conditions, or product performance. In practice, this might involve recognizing that high traffic on a particular page correlates with seasonal interest, such as a spike in fitness app usage in January due to New Year's resolutions. Once the why behind the what is understood, it allows the PMs to create strategies based on informed understanding.

- **Actionable data (actionable insights for strategic decisions):** Actionable data is the pinnacle of data value. Intelligence is achieved when actionable data is applied to make effective, strategic decisions that impact product development, user satisfaction, and business outcomes. It represents not only understanding patterns and trends but also knowing how to act on them. In our fitness app example, wisdom might lead the product team to launch a January promotion or introduce new workout plans based on observed user patterns. Wisdom is actionable, bridging the gap between insight and impact by guiding decisions that address real-world needs.

Bringing it all together

The Data Value framework, moving from raw data to actionable data, serves as a guide for PMs like you to maximize the value of your product's data. Each step builds upon the last to deepen understanding and refine decision-making:

- Data captures the essentials, but without organization.
- The informed data provides structure and reveals trends.
- Skilled data adds context, transforming data into insight.
- Actionable data empowers action, turning insights into effective strategies.

By navigating through each level of the data, you can harness the full potential of data, making choices that are not just informed but strategically impactful for your product's success.

Types of data

Data is typically divided into two main categories: Internal data and external data. Each plays a distinct role in shaping strategic decisions and originates from different sources within or outside the organization. To illustrate this concept simply, imagine running a small grocery store from your home.

Internal data includes everything you track inside your household, such as how much milk, bread, or eggs are left in the fridge, how many items you have sold, and the income you have generated. You might log this in a notebook or phone to help determine when to restock or evaluate how well your store is performing.

External data, on the other hand, comes from beyond your home. This could be a neighbor mentioning a new supermarket opening nearby or reading online that milk prices are expected to rise. These outside signals provide a broader view of market dynamics and help you adjust your strategy, like rethinking pricing or deciding to buy certain items in bulk.

In essence, internal data reflects what you already know from within your environment, while external data adds valuable context from the outside world. Both are essential for making well-informed, effective decisions, whether you are managing a home-based business or overseeing a complex product portfolio.

Internal data

Internal data is data generated within the organization, collected from various operational processes and customer interactions. It offers insights into how the company's products are performing and how well internal processes are functioning. Internal data typically resides in enterprise systems such as *SAP*, *Salesforce*, or *HomeGrown Solutions*, and it plays a vital role in driving strategic decisions across departments.

Examples of internal data include:

- **Production data:** Details about product manufacturing, timelines, production costs, and inventory levels. This data helps to monitor and improve the efficiency of production processes, ensuring timely delivery and cost-effective production.

- **Quality data:** Information on defects, quality control processes, product recalls, and metrics on product improvements. This data is crucial for identifying areas of concern within product quality and optimizing the manufacturing or development process to prevent future issues.

- **Sales data:** Records of first-time purchases, renewals, customer lifetime value, and sales performance by product or region. This data helps in identifying revenue trends, understanding customer preferences, and forecasting future sales.

- **Aftermarket data:** Insights into which additional features, accessories, or bells and whistles customers are purchasing post-product acquisition. This data allows companies to optimize upselling opportunities and identify popular add-ons or services to offer.

- **Operations data:** Data generated from internal processes that support day-to-day business activities, such as supply chain management, logistics, human resources, and financial transactions. This data is essential for understanding operational efficiency and ensuring that the company is running smoothly.

- **Customer support data:** Information collected from customer service interactions, support tickets, and issue resolutions. This data highlights common customer pain points, support team performance, and product satisfaction, which can guide improvements to both product and customer experience.

- **Marketing data:** Insights from marketing campaigns, customer engagement metrics (such as email open rates, click-through rates, and conversion rates), and advertising performance. This helps PMs understand which marketing efforts are driving customer interest and can influence product positioning and messaging.

- **Financial data:** Profit and loss statements, cost analysis, revenue forecasts, and other financial indicators. This data helps track the financial health of the product and the company, guiding pricing strategies, budget allocation, and resource investment decisions.

Internal data is typically housed across a variety of enterprise systems such as **enterprise resource planning** (**ERP**) tools, **customer relationship management** (**CRM**) platforms, internal databases, or even custom-built solutions. To ensure this data is usable and accessible, organizations often rely on APIs and integration tools to consolidate information from these disparate systems into a centralized view.

As a PM, collaborating with analytics teams becomes essential. These stakeholders can help pull relevant data into visual dashboards that offer real-time insights for both you and your business counterparts. Having this information readily available supports ongoing monitoring, alignment, and more informed decision-making across teams.

External data

External data, on the other hand, is gathered from outside the organization, including sources like social media, market research, industry reports, and customer reviews. This type of data provides insights into the broader market landscape, including competitor actions and customer perceptions. A common application of external data is brand sentiment analysis, which helps companies understand public perception and customer attitudes toward their brand and products. Sentiment analysis involves analyzing text from social media, customer reviews, and online forums to assess how customers feel about the brand. Combining this sentiment data with other external sources, such as geolocation data, customer preference insights, and contextual text analytics, enables companies to understand not only what people think of their brand but also how this perception compares to competitors and influences customer behavior.

External data and brand sentiment analysis

In addition to internal metrics, PMs must also pay close attention to what is happening outside their organization. External data offers valuable context, helping you understand how your product is perceived in the broader market and how customer expectations are evolving. One of the most powerful ways to tap into this external perspective is through sentiment analysis.

By analyzing public conversations, social media activity, and third-party feedback, sentiment analysis allows product teams to assess brand perception, competitive positioning, and emerging industry trends. These insights complement internal performance data, giving a more holistic view of both the product and the market it serves.

The following are some of the key insights that sentiment analysis can uncover:

- **Market share of voice:** Identifies which brands in the industry are most discussed on social media.
- **Consumer conversations:** Reveals what customers and prospects are saying about the industry, the brand, and competitors.
- **Industry buzz:** Highlights trending topics within the industry that generate the most conversation.
- **Influencer engagement:** Tracks which influencers are talking about the brand and competitors, highlighting opportunities for partnerships.

While internal data is typically housed within company systems like CRMs, ERPs, and analytics dashboards, external data often comes from a wider ecosystem. So, *how can PMs access and work with this valuable information?*

External data is usually aggregated in data warehouses or specialized analytics platforms that pull from a variety of outside sources, such as social media, market research reports, online reviews, and public datasets. APIs are instrumental in this process, enabling seamless integration between external sources and internal tools, and helping create a unified view of both market dynamics and brand perception.

Understanding how to combine both internal and external data sources is essential. Internal data provides insight into product performance, user engagement, and operational metrics. External data, on the other hand, helps you understand how your brand is perceived in a broader landscape and how your offering stacks up against competitors.

Together, these perspectives empower PMs to build well-rounded strategies, prioritize the right features, refine marketing efforts, and deliver products that not only meet internal goals but also resonate deeply with users in an ever-changing market.

Getting started with data analysis

Data analysis, in its most basic form, starts very early in life, long before you might think. As early as elementary school, we begin learning how to count, perform basic operations, and understand quantities. These early lessons in numbers and basic arithmetic are the foundation of data analysis. As we progress through school, we start working with more complex concepts: Geometry helps us understand shapes and space, algebra teaches us about patterns and relationships, trigonometry deals with angles and measurements, and calculus introduces us to rates of change. Each of these subjects builds on the idea of analyzing and interpreting numbers to make sense of the world around us.

As we grew, our tools and skills became more advanced. We move beyond traditional paper-and-pencil calculations and start using spreadsheets like Excel. With Excel, you can quickly analyze data, make calculations, create charts, and visualize patterns. Power users of Excel can go a step further, employing more advanced functions like pivot tables, macros, and complex formulas to manage and interpret large datasets. Then, as technology evolves, so do the tools we use, enter **business intelligence** (**BI**) tools and analytics platforms that allow us to dig deeper into data, create dashboards, and generate reports.

For those looking to go even further, data analysis can involve using programming languages like Python and R or even getting into **machine learning** (**ML**) for predictive analysis. These tools enable you to analyze massive datasets, uncover trends, and accurately predict future outcomes.

In product management, data analysis is not a one-time event. It is a continuous, ongoing process that evolves along with the product. From the earliest stages of gathering user feedback to tracking product performance, every phase involves analysis to refine the product and align it more closely with user needs and business goals. You must leverage data from multiple sources to make informed decisions, whether that is prioritizing features, improving UX, or fine-tuning marketing strategies.

Like how your math skills progress from essential addition to advanced calculus, the methods used in product data analysis also mature over time. Whether using spreadsheets or ML algorithms, the ability to analyze data effectively is critical to making smarter decisions and driving product success. Therefore, it is not just about understanding data but also about continuously leveraging it to improve and refine a product throughout its lifecycle.

Importance of clean data

Up to this point, we have explored the importance of data in driving product decisions. However, the true value of data lies not just in having access to it, but in ensuring it is clean, accurate, and reliable. In many organizations, data is often viewed as a hidden cost, where poor-quality data leads to inefficiencies, errors, and misinformed decisions. Clean data, on the other hand, reduces those costs by enhancing accuracy, minimizing rework, and enabling smarter, faster decision-making. Ultimately, it saves valuable time, resources, and budget.

Why clean data matters

When working as a PM or aspiring to become one, you must be ready to face challenges and adapt to rapid changes, customer preferences evolve, market conditions shift, and new competitors emerge. When you base decisions on incorrect or incomplete data, you risk misguided decisions that can negatively impact revenue, growth, and overall product success. For example, imagine you launch a marketing campaign based on faulty customer segmentation data. The campaign might fail if the data inaccurately classifies customer needs or demographics, leading to a wasted budget and missed opportunities.

Clean data also plays a crucial role in improving process efficiency and productivity. When your data is accurate, it empowers teams to work more effectively, whether it is development, sales, marketing, or customer support. Teams can rely on data-driven insights to streamline operations, optimize workflows, and avoid rework caused by poor data. This reduces costs and increases the likelihood of successful outcomes.

Consistency across multiple datasets

Another key advantage of clean data is consistency. In any organization, data comes from multiple sources: CRM systems, databases, spreadsheets, and more. When this data is clean and standardized, it ensures that all teams and systems use the same high-quality information. Consistency leads to more precise insights and better decision-making. On the other hand, if your data is inconsistent or messy, it can lead to confusion, misinterpretation, and, ultimately, incorrect inferences.

For example, if sales data from one department does not align with the numbers in the financial system, you may draw incorrect conclusions about revenue trends. Likewise, in product development, inconsistent data about user feedback could result in prioritizing the wrong features, causing the product to fall short of user expectations.

Data analytics value chart

Clean data is not only crucial for operational efficiency; it also becomes increasingly valuable when applied across different levels of analytics. As PMs seek to extract meaning from data, it is important to understand how analytics transforms raw numbers into actionable insights that guide strategic decisions.

Analytics can be broadly classified into four progressive levels, each answering a distinct type of question. From understanding past behavior to prescribing future actions. The effectiveness of each level, however, depends on the accuracy and reliability of the underlying data.

There are typically four types of analytics done to increase the value of data. Following is a breakdown of the four categories and how clean data plays a critical role at each stage:

- **Descriptive analytics:** This is the foundational level of analytics. Descriptive analytics tells you the history, whether it is sales performance, user behavior, or product usage. For example, you might look at how many customers clicked on a specific feature in the app last month. Clean data ensures these historical insights are accurate, so you can confidently assess past performance.
- **Diagnostic analytics:** Once you know the history, diagnostic analytics help you answer the reason behind it. For example, if sales dropped in a specific region,

diagnostic analytics might help you identify issues like a new competitor entering the market or changing customer preferences. Clean data is essential here because inconsistencies or errors can lead to incorrect conclusions about the root cause.

- **Predictive analytics:** Predictive analytics uses historical data to forecast future outcomes. Clean data enables more accurate predictions if you want to predict how many units of a product will be sold next quarter. Predictive models rely on consistent and accurate data to generate reliable forecasts that guide decision-making.

- **Prescriptive analytics:** The highest level of prescriptive analytics answers how to take action to achieve a desired outcome. For example, based on predictive analytics, you might identify that a product will have increased demand, and prescriptive analytics helps you determine how to optimize production and marketing efforts to meet that demand. Clean data is crucial at this stage to ensure that any recommendations or decisions made based on the data are sound and practical.

Spotify's data-driven product innovation

[1]An inspiring example of data-driven decision-making in action can be seen in Spotify, a platform that many interact with daily. Its success is rooted in its ability to leverage data not just to serve music, but to personalize every user's experience in a way that feels remarkably intuitive. From song suggestions to mood-based playlists, Spotify has turned data into a strategic differentiator.

Take *Discover Weekly*, for instance. This personalized playlist, updated every Monday, quickly became a flagship feature. When Spotify recognized that users loved discovering new music but often found exploration overwhelming, it responded by developing a data-driven solution. The platform began analyzing listening habits, identifying which songs users repeated, skipped, or saved, and blending that with the behavior of users with similar preferences. It further enriched the recommendation engine by diving into song metadata and audio attributes like tempo and energy levels. The result was a playlist that felt uniquely crafted for each user, driving billions of streams in its first year.

Another standout feature is *Spotify Wrapped*, a year-end summary that has evolved into a cultural phenomenon. Rather than offering a basic data report, Wrapped creates a celebratory reflection of each user's musical journey, highlighting top tracks, genres, and listening stats in an engaging format. This experience not only enhances user satisfaction but also serves as an ingenious marketing campaign. Millions of users share their Wrapped stats across social media, turning personal engagement into viral brand advocacy each December.

---

1 Stacy.Goldrick@groupsjr.com. (2023, November 30). Here is what is in store for your 2023 Wrapped — Spotify. Spotify. **https://newsroom.spotify.com/2023-11-29/wrapped-user-experience-2023/**
B3 Marketing. (n.d.). **https://www.b3.marketing/post/spotify-wrapped-a-masterclass-in-data-driven-marketing**

Spotify's innovation does not stop there. Recognizing that musical preferences shift with time, activity, and emotion, the company introduced context-aware playlists like daily mix, workout, and mood-based collections. By analyzing when and where users listened, alongside broader behavior trends, Spotify curated playlists that adapted to different moments in the user's day. For example, morning listeners often preferred upbeat tracks, while those exercising favored high-energy music. This attention to context kept Spotify relevant in diverse use cases throughout the day.

Behind the scenes, Spotify continuously optimizes its UX through A/B testing and behavioral analysis. User clicks, navigation paths, and friction points are mapped using heatmaps and interaction studies. These insights have driven thoughtful design enhancements, such as the persistent now-playing bar, which enables users to browse freely while keeping control over current playback, and small refinements that significantly improve overall usability.

Spotify's podcast strategy further illustrates the power of data. As consumption trends shifted toward spoken content, the company quickly adapted by analyzing podcast completion rates, skip behavior, and audience demographics. This data informed the development of exclusive shows and original content tailored to specific listener segments, positioning Spotify as a leader not only in music but also in audio storytelling.

Even seemingly minor changes have been data-informed. Spotify addressed concerns about audio quality and expanded accessibility by offering high-quality streaming and features tailored to users with disabilities. These decisions, although less visible, reflect a deep commitment to inclusivity and a seamless experience for all.

What sets Spotify apart is its relentless focus on listening to user behavior, not just through feedback, but through patterns of actual engagement. It does not release features blindly. Instead, it iterates continuously, applying what it learns to enhance every user interaction. This approach has helped the platform evolve from a streaming service into a digital companion that anticipates and responds to user needs in real-time.

Spotify's journey illustrates how mastering data can drive not only product innovation but also emotional connection. By anticipating needs, delighting users with relevant features, and constantly refining its experience, Spotify exemplifies the power of data-informed, user-centric design. PMs across industries can draw lessons from this model to build products that resonate deeply with their users.

PDM/PLM/PIM

Understanding the distinctions and interconnected roles of PDM, PLM, and PIM is vital for anyone working in the digital product development and delivery space. While these frameworks may initially appear similar, they operate at different stages of a product's journey and address specific needs, ensuring seamless collaboration and data management from ideation to customer delivery.

Let us begin with PDM, which focuses on managing and organizing product-related data during the design and development phases. It is the foundation for technical assets like source code, wireframes, or user flows, centralizing them in a version-controlled repository. For example, software development teams might use GitHub or Bitbucket as their PDM system to store and track changes to their codebase. This ensures that all team members, engineers, quality assurance testers, or designers, are working on the latest version of the product, avoiding duplication or errors, much like its role in manufacturing (e.g., managing **computer aided-design** (**CAD**) files and **Bill of Materials** (**BOMs**), PDM in digital products ensures granular details are accessible and up-to-date.

Building on this, PLM offers a more holistic perspective, managing the entire lifecycle of a product from ideation to eventual retirement. This means overseeing workflows, sprint planning, feature updates, and release cycles for digital products. Imagine a **software as a service** (**SaaS**) product; PLM ensures that as user needs evolve, updates are released efficiently, and all teams, development, marketing, and customer support, are aligned in their objectives. While PDM feeds technical data into the PLM system, PLM orchestrates the broader strategy, ensuring seamless collaboration across teams. PLM might track a smartphone's journey in manufacturing, from design tweaks to supplier changes. For digital products, it ensures feature updates, bug fixes, and UX improvements are executed effectively.

Finally, PIM becomes crucial when the product is ready for customers. This system manages customer-facing information such as product descriptions, pricing, release notes, and **frequently asked questions** (**FAQs**). For digital products like mobile apps or SaaS platforms, PIM ensures that app store listings, websites, and marketing materials reflect accurate and consistent information. Consider an e-commerce platform: a PIM system ensures that every product page, no matter the channel, includes up-to-date and trustworthy details like dimensions, features, and pricing. This consistency builds user trust and enhances the overall customer experience.

The above three are interconnected; each playing a unique yet complementary role. PDM manages the intricate details of a product's design or codebase, which flow into PLM for lifecycle oversight and coordination. When the product is market-ready, PLM data feeds into PIM, ensuring accurate and compelling customer-facing materials. Take the example of a smartwatch development cycle: Engineers use PDM to refine CAD files or code, PLM ensures that design and production teams collaborate effectively, and PIM guarantees consistent and appealing listings for e-commerce platforms. PDM stores the assets, PLM orchestrates the development journey, and PIM ensures customers understand and trust what they receive. By embracing these frameworks, businesses can streamline processes, reduce inefficiencies, and deliver superior digital experiences.

Conclusion

Data is not just about numbers on a dashboard; it is how product teams uncover what users really want, where they are getting stuck, and what to build next. In this chapter, we explored how data shapes better decisions, helps reduce risk, and fuels real product innovation. We looked at the full journey, from raw data to actionable insights, and saw how clean, reliable information helps teams stay focused and aligned.

Through examples like Meta's Oculus Quest and Spotify's personalized features, we saw how data can do more than just validate ideas; it can completely reshape a product's trajectory. We also dug into the tools and frameworks that support a strong data practice, like the Data Value Pyramid, analytics models, and the differences between internal and external data.

As you head into the next chapter, we will shift gears from data to the processes that bring products to life. In *Chapter 8, Product Development Methodology,* you will learn how different approaches, like Agile, Waterfall, and hybrid models, can guide your team through building and launching products. Whether you are iterating on a new feature or managing a full roadmap, *Chapter 8, Product Development Methodology,* will help you choose the right framework and make your execution as strong as your strategy.

Points to remember

- Data is foundational for product management, helping validate assumptions, guide priorities, and align strategies with business goals and user needs.

- The Data Value Pyramid progresses from raw data to actionable wisdom, emphasizing contextualizing and applying insights.

- Data is categorized into internal (e.g., production, quality, sales) and external (e.g., sentiment analysis, market trends), each serving unique functions in decision-making.

- Clean data reduces costs, improves efficiency, and ensures consistency, while unclean data can lead to costly errors and misinformed decisions.

- Analytics spans descriptive, diagnostic, predictive, and prescriptive methods, transforming raw information into actionable strategies.

- PDM, PLM, and PIM systems streamline the lifecycle of digital and physical products by centralizing data management and ensuring cross-functional alignment.

- Effective use of sentiment analysis combines external data sources to predict customer behaviors and market trends, enhancing brand strategy.

- Data analysis is an ongoing process that starts with essential tools like spreadsheets and progresses to advanced techniques like Python, R, and ML for deeper insights.

- Combining data sources through APIs enables efficient internal and external data sharing, fostering better decision-making across systems.

- Understanding and leveraging data empowers product teams to improve UX, optimize processes, and make informed, strategic decisions.

Multiple choice questions

1. **How does Spotify use data to personalize UXs?**
   a. By asking users directly about their preferences.
   b. By analyzing listening habits, playlists, and contextual data.
   c. By following trends in the broader music industry.
   d. By surveying artists for recommendations.

2. **What is Discover Weekly?**
   a. A curated playlist updated annually.
   b. A data-driven, personalized weekly playlist for users.
   c. A promotional campaign for new artists.
   d. A report on music industry trends.

3. **Why is Wrapped an effective campaign for Spotify?**
   a. It offers music discounts to premium users.
   b. It compiles users' listening stats, creating engagement and viral social media sharing.
   c. It provides an annual report for Spotify's investors.
   d. It serves as a tool for artists to gain more listeners.

4. **How does Spotify leverage external data to refine recommendations?**
   a. By analyzing competitor strategies.
   b. By tracking global music sales trends.
   c. By incorporating data like location, weather, and time of day.
   d. By monitoring user complaints.

5. **What role does A/B testing play at Spotify?**
   a. It ensures that only popular features are implemented.
   b. It tests how design changes impact user engagement.
   c. It surveys artists for playlist suggestions.
   d. It decides the prices for Spotify's subscription tiers.

Answers

1	b
2	b
3	b
4	c
5	b

CHAPTER 8

Product Development Methodology

Introduction

While many facets of product development have been explored, transforming an idea into a successful product demands more than innovation alone. It necessitates a structured, methodical approach that bridges concept and execution while simultaneously addressing customer needs, market trends, and technical feasibility. This structured approach is known as **product development methodology**, a framework that directs how teams conceptualize, design, build, and iterate on products to ensure value delivery and strategic alignment.

Structure

This chapter covers the following topics:

- Product development methodologies
- Understanding Waterfall model
- Agile product management
- Introduction to sprint
- Preparing prioritized backlog

Objectives

The objective of this chapter is to equip readers with a clear understanding of product development methodologies and how they directly influence the way teams bring ideas to life. As product development moves from concept to execution, adopting the right methodology is critical for ensuring that customer needs, market conditions, and technical capabilities are properly aligned.

This chapter explores the two most prominent methodologies, that is, Waterfall and Agile, highlighting their unique strengths, limitations, and contextual apps. Readers will gain insights into when each methodology is appropriate, and how factors like project complexity, industry regulations, and user feedback cycles shape this decision. Agile, in particular, is explored in depth through its ceremonies, sprint cycles, and iterative delivery model, enabling teams to deliver continuous value and respond to change effectively.

Beyond methodology, this chapter emphasizes the practical tools that bring structure to product execution, including **product requirement documents** (**PRDs**), sprint planning, and quarterly goal alignment. By mastering these techniques, readers will be able to foster cross-functional collaboration, reduce execution risks, and drive consistent product improvement. Whether you are operating in a startup or a large enterprise, this chapter provides the foundational knowledge and tactical guidance to adopt a methodology that supports innovation, speed, and user value.

Product development methodologies

There are various methodologies, each tailored to different types of projects and organizational needs. Some teams rely on Waterfall, a linear approach that emphasizes meticulous planning and sequential execution. Others thrive on Agile, a flexible and iterative framework that emphasizes collaboration, adaptability, and continuous delivery. Between these extremes lie hybrid models, blending elements of two, suited to specific contexts.

Understanding and selecting the right methodology is critical because it shapes how teams collaborate, make decisions, and deliver value. For example, developing software for a highly regulated industry like healthcare may require Waterfall's rigidity for compliance, while creating a consumer-facing mobile app may benefit from Agile's iterative approach to innovation.

No matter the methodology, the ultimate goal remains the same: deliver a product that solves problems, meets user expectations, and aligns with business objectives. Throughout this chapter, we will explore methodologies in depth, focusing on Agile, a dominant choice for modern product teams, and detailing the practical tools and practices that drive successful product development.

Understanding Waterfall model

The Waterfall model is one of the earliest software development methodologies, introduced by *Dr. Winston W. Royce* in a paper published in 1970. While Royce initially presented it as a flawed approach that required enhancements, the model gained traction as a linear and structured way of developing software. The Waterfall model divides the development process into distinct, sequential phases, where the completion of one phase is a prerequisite for the beginning of the next one. The key phases typically include requirements gathering, design, implementation, testing, deployment, and maintenance.

In its time, the Waterfall model became popular because of its simplicity and its alignment with traditional engineering processes, where linear progress was often essential for physical projects like construction or manufacturing. For example, just as one cannot build the roof of a house before laying the foundation, Waterfall assumes that certain phases of a project must be completed in a specific order.

Present relevance of Waterfall methodology

Most companies and product teams today fall into the Agile-dominated software development environment. The Waterfall model has significantly declined in popularity, particularly for digital product development. However, it is not entirely obsolete. The model remains useful in certain industries where strict compliance, rigorous documentation, and predictable timelines are critical. For instance, aerospace, healthcare, and government sectors often use Waterfall for projects involving safety-critical systems, as these require exhaustive upfront planning and minimal scope for iterative changes.

Despite its niche apps, most modern tech companies prefer Agile methodologies due to their flexibility and adaptability. Agile's ability to incorporate feedback and adjust mid-project aligns better with dynamic market demands and user-centric design approaches. Waterfall is more suited to projects where requirements are unlikely to change after the initial stages.

Advantages of Waterfall model

The Waterfall model offers several benefits, particularly in contexts where a highly structured and predictable process is required.

Following are some of the advantages:

- **Clear structure and simplicity:** The model's linear and sequential nature makes it easy to understand and implement, especially for teams unfamiliar with more iterative or dynamic methodologies. Each phase has clear deliverables and milestones, which helps with maintaining order.

- **Detailed documentation:** Waterfall emphasizes comprehensive documentation at each stage. This is particularly valuable in regulated industries where thorough records are necessary for compliance or when transitioning projects between teams.

- **Well-suited for fixed requirements:** In projects where requirements are clearly defined and unlikely to change, such as in government or military contracts, Waterfall ensures that these are fully understood before development begins.

- **Predictability:** The model provides a straightforward timeline with well-defined stages, making it easier to estimate costs and schedules. This predictability is useful for projects with rigid deadlines or budgets.

- **Focus on quality control:** Since testing is a distinct phase, there is often a stronger focus on ensuring the system functions correctly before deployment.

Disadvantages of Waterfall model

While the Waterfall model's structured approach can be advantageous, it has significant drawbacks, particularly for modern product development.

Some of the commonly identified disadvantages are as follows:

- **Lack of flexibility:** One of the most significant limitations of Waterfall is its rigidity. Once a phase is completed, revisiting it is challenging and costly. This becomes problematic in environments where user needs or market conditions can change rapidly.

- **Delayed testing and feedback:** Testing occurs only after implementation, meaning that errors or misunderstandings in earlier phases may not surface until late in the project. Fixing these issues can be expensive and time-consuming.

- **Unsuitability for dynamic requirements:** Modern software development often involves evolving requirements driven by user feedback, market trends, or emerging technologies. Waterfall's reliance on fixed requirements makes it will-suited for such projects.

- **High risk of project failure:** If any phase, particularly the requirements or design phase is flawed, it can cascade into subsequent phases, leading to incomplete or unsatisfactory results. There is little room for course correction mid-project.

- **Inefficiency for iterative improvements:** Waterfall does not accommodate iterative feedback loops or incremental product enhancements, which are central to user-centric design and Agile methodologies.

Agile product management

Agile product management is one of the most impactful approaches shaping how modern teams build and deliver products. Unlike traditional frameworks like Waterfall, which follow a rigid, step-by-step process, Agile embraces change. It allows teams to stay flexible, respond quickly to user needs, and continuously deliver value throughout the development cycle. The approach was formalized in 2001 through the Agile Manifesto, that are a set of principles created by a group of software developers who recognized the need for a more collaborative, iterative way of working. Their focus was on shortening feedback loops, delivering working solutions quickly, and adapting to change rather than sticking to a fixed long-term plan. What began with software has since expanded into other industries like healthcare, education, and entertainment.

The basis of Agile is incremental delivery. Teams work in short development cycles called **sprints**, typically one to four weeks long, each focused on delivering a small, usable part of the product. Whether it is a feature update, design improvement, or bug fix, every sprint ends with something tangible that can be tested, reviewed, and improved. This ensures teams are constantly learning, staying aligned with users, and moving toward meaningful outcomes with each iteration.

One of the most compelling strengths of Agile is how it brings every function in a team together. Whether you are a **product manager** (**PM**), designer, engineer, or stakeholder, Agile thrives on cross-functional collaboration. Through structured ceremonies such as daily stand-ups, sprint planning sessions, and retrospectives, Agile ensures continuous alignment and communication. This regular interaction fosters transparency, shared ownership, and a collaborative culture that supports innovation and accountability.

Agile is especially well-suited to industries where speed and adaptability are key. It has become the preferred approach in the tech space because it enables teams to respond quickly to shifting user expectations, market dynamics, and emerging technologies. Whether you are an early-stage startup or an established global enterprise, Agile provides the structure and flexibility to deliver value at pace. That said, Agile is not without its complexities. Its adaptability can, if not managed properly, lead to scope creep, where a project expands beyond its original intent. Additionally, Agile demands consistent and meaningful communication. Without that, teams can lose focus or encounter friction. Agile also places high demands on team involvement, which may be challenging for smaller or resource-constrained organizations.

However, when Agile is implemented effectively, the results can be transformative. Spotify's Agile model is well published. Spotify's adoption of the Agile mindset rather than applying Agile by the book was the key. Spotify tailored it to fit its culture by creating autonomous squads, small, cross-functional teams that operate like startups within the organization. This structure enabled rapid experimentation and feature delivery, such as the now-iconic *Discover Weekly* playlist, which offers users a personalized listening experience driven by continuous feedback and data.

Spotify's success with Agile lies in its iterative mindset. New features are developed incrementally, tested early, and refined based on real-world usage. When something does not work, the team adapts, relying on regular retrospectives to assess what went well, what did not, and how they can improve. This emphasis on learning and adaptability is a cornerstone of Agile. At its core, Agile is more than just a development methodology; it is a mindset. It challenges the notion of perfection as a fixed outcome and instead views it as a continuous process of learning and improvement. Agile encourages teams to center their efforts around user needs, delivering solutions that are not only functional but deeply aligned with user expectations and values. Agile remains one of the most reliable approaches for building resilient, user-centric products. It is not about rigidly following a predefined process, but rather about embracing change, encouraging collaboration, and maintaining the flexibility to respond quickly and effectively. Teams that adopt Agile with intention and consistency are better positioned to meet the needs of their users and exceed them.

Advantages of Agile

Agile product development offers a range of benefits that make it particularly effective where speed is critical, in user-driven environments. By embracing iteration, collaboration, and responsiveness, Agile empowers teams to build and improve products more efficiently.

Following are some of the key advantages that highlight why Agile has become the preferred methodology for modern product teams:

- **Flexibility and adaptability:** Agile thrives on its ability to adapt to changing requirements, allowing teams to pivot quickly in response to market shifts or evolving customer needs without compromising the entire project.

- **Customer centric development:** Frequent iterations and feedback loops ensure that the product aligns closely with customer expectations, addressing their real-world needs effectively.

- **Faster time-to-market:** Agile delivers functional product increments in short cycles, enabling faster releases and providing immediate value to customers.

- **Improved collaboration:** Agile fosters strong teamwork and transparency through practices like daily stand-ups and sprint planning, keeping all stakeholders aligned and engaged.

- **Enhanced quality:** Continuous testing and feedback ensure early identification of issues, leading to a higher-quality product and fewer post-launch defects.

Disadvantages of Agile

While Agile offers numerous advantages, it also presents certain challenges that teams must be prepared to navigate. The following drawbacks are not inherent flaws but rather trade-offs that arise from the flexibility and iterative nature of the methodology. Understanding these potential disadvantages is essential for effectively managing Agile processes and setting realistic expectations:

- **Scope creep:** Agile's flexibility can result in uncontrolled expansion of project scope, straining timelines and resources if not managed carefully.

- **Resource-intensive:** Agile requires significant team involvement, frequent meetings, and active stakeholder participation, which can be challenging for smaller teams or resource-constrained organizations.

- **Less predictable:** Without detailed upfront planning, it can be difficult to predict project timelines, budgets, and final deliverables, posing challenges for stakeholders seeking clear commitments.

- **Incomplete documentation:** Agile prioritizes working solutions over documentation, which can create challenges for onboarding new team members or addressing long-term maintenance needs.

- **Requires experienced teams:** Agile's success depends on the team's ability to understand and execute its principles effectively, making it challenging for inexperienced teams or those without proper training.

Agile ceremonies

When implementing Agile, one of the most notable transitions is the adoption of its structured yet adaptable ceremonies. These ceremonies serve as the foundation of the Agile process, promoting alignment, transparency, and continuous improvement across the team. Each ceremony plays a distinct role in maintaining focus and ensuring consistent progress. The following section outlines the key Agile ceremonies detailing their timing, objectives, and participants, and illustrates how they function as recurring checkpoints to keep teams cohesive and product development on track.

Introduction to sprint

One of the foundational elements of Agile product management is the sprint, a focused, time-bound period during which a team works collaboratively to complete a defined set of tasks or deliverables. This approach breaks down complex product development into smaller, manageable increments, allowing for continuous value delivery rather than deferring outcomes until the end of a prolonged development cycle.

A sprint is characterized by its short duration, typically ranging from one to four weeks, with two weeks intervals being most commonly adopted. During this time, the team concentrates its efforts on achieving specific objectives, culminating in the delivery of a potentially shippable product increment. This output is functional and can be reviewed, tested, or even deployed to users, ensuring that progress is both measurable and aligned with user needs and business goals.

Benefits of sprint

Sprints are a core component of Agile methodology, reflecting the principles of adaptability, collaboration, and incremental delivery rather than investing months or even years into developing a product that may ultimately misalign with user needs, sprints enable teams to design, test, and refine features in shorter, iterative cycles. This structured approach ensures continuous alignment with both user expectations and overarching business objectives.

For example, consider the development of a new feature, such as a dark mode, for a mobile app. Instead of attempting to design, develop, and deploy the entire feature in a single phase, one sprint might focus solely on the foundational elements, such as crafting the user interface for the initial set of screens. Subsequent sprints would then address additional components, such as integration within the app's settings. Each sprint builds progressively on the last, resulting in incremental value delivery throughout the development process.

Sprint structure

A sprint is not just a random burst of work; it is a structured and well-organized cycle. It starts with sprint planning, where the team decides what they can realistically accomplish based on the prioritized backlog provided by the product owner. The sprint then progresses with daily stand-ups, where the team syncs up, addresses blockers, and adjusts their approach as needed.

The key deliverable of a sprint is the product increment work that is potentially shippable or demonstrable. At the end of the sprint, the team holds a sprint review, showcasing the increment to stakeholders and gathering feedback. This is followed by a retrospective, where the team reflects on their process and identifies ways to improve in the next sprint.

Sprint duration

Choosing the appropriate sprint length is a critical aspect of Agile planning, as it directly impacts a team's ability to deliver value consistently while remaining adaptable. A sprint should be long enough to produce meaningful and tangible progress, yet short enough to allow for frequent inspection, feedback, and course correction.

For many Agile teams, a two week sprint offers an optimal balance between focus and flexibility. It provides sufficient time to complete a cohesive set of tasks without allowing work to become overly drawn out or disconnected from shifting priorities. However, the ideal sprint duration is not one-size-fits-all. It should reflect the nature of the product, the team's workflow, and the broader organizational environment. For instance, a one week sprint may be more effective in a high-velocity startup environment where rapid iteration and quick releases are essential. In contrast, a four week sprint might be more appropriate for teams working on complex features, systems with multiple dependencies, or products that require extensive design and testing cycles.

Ultimately, the chosen sprint length should support continuous delivery while enabling teams to stay responsive to stakeholder input, evolving requirements, and market conditions. It is equally important to periodically reassess the effectiveness of the current sprint cadence and adjust as needed to ensure optimal team performance and product outcomes.

Impact of sprint

Understanding the significance of sprints is essential for any product team aiming to maintain momentum, stay aligned with objectives, and deliver consistent value. One of the primary benefits of working in sprints is the clarity and focus they provide. By narrowing the scope of work to a defined, achievable set of goals within a limited timeframe, teams can direct their energy toward specific priorities without becoming overwhelmed by the broader scope of the project. Sprints also foster a continuous feedback loop rather than waiting until the end of a lengthy development cycle to assess progress, teams can gather input regularly, both internally and from stakeholders or users, enabling timely course correction. This iterative process reduces the risk of building features that miss the mark and ensures the final product remains aligned with user needs and business goals.

Moreover, sprints contribute to team morale and motivation. Delivering a tangible output at the end of each sprint reinforces a sense of achievement and forward progress. These frequent milestones not only validate the team's effort but also create momentum and a shared sense of purpose. In essence, sprints create a rhythm for the team, one that promotes focus, encourages learning, and builds confidence through continuous delivery and reflection.

Sprints in action

To illustrate how sprints function in a real-world setting, consider the development of a new feature for an e-commerce platform, specifically, **Saved Items** section that allows users to bookmark products for future reference.

In the first sprint, the product and engineering teams may begin by focusing on the backend infrastructure. This includes designing the database schema, setting up API endpoints, and ensuring that saved item data can be securely stored and retrieved. Although this initial phase is not visible to users, it lays the critical groundwork for functionality. In the second sprint, the focus might shift to the frontend interface. Designers collaborate with developers to create a user-friendly and visually consistent experience that aligns with the platform's existing design system. This could include components such as **Save for Later** buttons, saved items icons, and a dedicated page for users to view their bookmarked products.

By the third sprint, integration takes place. The backend and frontend are connected, enabling the complete flow from a user saving an item to viewing it in their personal list. This sprint also includes testing for usability, responsiveness, and edge cases to ensure a seamless experience. Each sprint results in a functional increment that can be reviewed, tested, and improved. This approach not only distributes the workload evenly but also reduces risk by identifying issues early and maintaining consistent progress toward a fully developed, user-ready feature.

Sprint planning

Sprint planning marks the beginning of each sprint, setting the tone for the work ahead. This ceremony typically takes place a week before the sprint and is focused on defining what the team will accomplish during the upcoming sprint cycle, which usually lasts for two weeks, but can be different in each company as per their practices, which can range from one to four weeks.

The product owner leads the session by presenting the prioritized backlog, carefully crafted based on business needs and user feedback. If your team does not have a product owner in addition to the PM, then the PM takes the lead to refine the backlog, and the best practice recommended is to add all the stories prioritized for the upcoming sprint into Jira under the specific epic and bucketized into sprints. You can add future stories into different sprint buckets. Once this stage is complete, then contact your engineering manager and the individual engineers, if you know who might be working on the Jira ticket, to get the sizing estimation. Once all of this is completed, then the sprint planning session is conducted, maybe a minimum of three days prior to the sprint, where all the stories are groomed and prioritized in order and based on the resource capacity available.

Consider the following example of how an initiative or feature is broken into smaller parts of epics and stories.

Let us say a product team is working on a *Loyalty and Rewards Program* for a food delivery app. This initiative is aimed at boosting customer retention and increasing repeat orders. To execute this initiative, the team might break it down into multiple epics, each representing a major functional area or milestone:

- **Epic 1: User points system:**
  - o **User story 1**: *As a user, I want to earn points for every order I place so that I feel rewarded for using the app regularly.*
  - o **User story 2**: *As a user, I want to see my total points in my profile so I know how close I am to my next reward.*

- **Epic 2: Rewards redemption:**
  - o **User story 1**: *As a user, I want to redeem my points for discount coupons so I can save money on future orders.*
  - o **User story 2**: *As a user, I want to view a list of available rewards so I can choose how to use my points.*

- **Epic 3: Badges and milestones:**
  - o **User story 1**: *As a user, I want to earn badges for specific achievements (like ordering from five new restaurants) to make the experience fun and motivating.*
  - o **User story 2**: *As a user, I want to share my badges with friends so I can show off my achievements.*

- **Epic 4: Gamification dashboard:**
  - o **User story 1**: *As a user, I want a dashboard where I can track my rewards progress and badge collection so I stay engaged.*
  - o **User story 2**: *As a user, I want to get notified when I unlock a new badge or reward to keep me motivated.*

The above is just an example to illustrate sample epics with two stories each, but in real-world scenarios, each epic will have multiple stories depending on the stage and complexity of the product.

The team, comprising developers, testers, and designers, then collaborates to break down the top-priority items into actionable tasks. They discuss technical feasibility, clarify requirements, and estimate the effort involved, often using techniques like story points or t-shirt sizing. A key player in this process is the Scrum master, who facilitates the session, ensuring everyone stays focused and aligned with Agile principles. Again, if a Scrum master is not present, then the engineering team does it by internally collaborating with each other. By the end of sprint planning, the team commits to a specific set of goals and ensures everyone understands their role in achieving them. It is a collaborative effort to balance ambition with realism, ensuring the sprint is both challenging and achievable.

Daily stand-ups for sprint

Daily stand-ups are quick, 15 to 30-minute meetings held at the same time every day during the sprint. They are designed to provide a status update and keep the team synchronized. Imagine it as the team's morning coffee meeting, a chance to touch base and set the pace for the day.

Each team member answers three core questions, as follows:
- *What did I work on yesterday?*
- *What will I work on today?*
- *Are there any blockers preventing me from moving forward?*

The Scrum master facilitates, ensuring the meeting stays on track and does not spiral into lengthy discussions, but recently, there are not many Scrum masters in most companies, so it is the engineering manager who facilitates the daily stand-ups. This ceremony involves the entire development team and includes the product teams if they want to stay informed. The goal here is not to solve every problem on the spot but to identify challenges early and address them after the meeting, keeping the sprint on track. Also, this is an opportunity for the product team to provide engineering with their updates during the last few minutes, time permitting, when the engineering update is completed.

Sprint review

At the end of the sprint, the team gathers for a sprint review. This is the time to celebrate progress and demonstrate the completed work to stakeholders. Think of it as a mini product launch where the team showcases the new features, updates, or fixes they have accomplished during the sprint.

The product owner usually leads the session, presenting the increment to stakeholders, who might include business leaders, customers, or other teams. The development team explains what they worked on, answers questions, and collects feedback. This feedback loop is invaluable because it ensures the product stays aligned with business objectives and user needs. Sprint reviews are not just about showing off; they are about staying in sync with the broader goals of the organization.

Sprint retrospective

The retrospective is perhaps the most introspective of Agile ceremonies. It is held immediately after the sprint review. It focuses on examining how the team worked together during the sprint, identifying areas for improvement, and celebrating successes. It is the team's opportunity to reflect and grow.

The Scrum master/member of the engineering team facilitates this session, guiding the team through discussions that typically answer three questions:

- *What went well during the sprint?*
- *What did not go well?*
- *What can we improve in the next sprint?*

This ceremony involves only the Agile team, providing a safe space for honest feedback. Actionable takeaways are documented and implemented in the next sprint, ensuring continuous improvement. The retrospective is a testament to Agile's commitment to adaptability and learning.

Commonly used retrospective tools

To facilitate effective retrospectives, Agile teams often rely on purpose-built tools that support collaboration, structure, and continuous improvement. The right tool can significantly enhance the quality of feedback, promote team engagement, and streamline the process of capturing and tracking action items.

Following is a curated selection of widely adopted retrospective tools, each offering distinct features to support various team needs and preferences:

- **Miro:** Miro is an online whiteboard platform with numerous templates, including ones designed specifically for retrospectives. Teams can collaborate in real-time, organize feedback visually, and use voting features.

  Following are the key features:
  - Customizable retrospective templates.
  - Real-time collaboration with sticky notes and voting.
  - Integrations with tools like Jira and Trello.
- **FunRetro (EasyRetro):** A purpose-built retrospective tool that allows teams to organize feedback into predefined categories, such as what went well and what could be improved.

  Following are the key features:
  - Intuitive retrospective board with voting options.
  - Anonymous input for candid feedback.
  - Export options for reports.
- **Retrium:** Retrium is designed specifically for retrospectives, offering a variety of techniques like Start/Stop/Continue, **Liked, Learned, Lacked, Longed For (4Ls),** and more.

Following are the key features:

- o   Multiple retrospective formats
- o   Anonymous feedback and voting
- o   Action item tracking and reporting

Following is the pricing:

- o   No free version
- o   Best for Agile teams committed to frequent, structured retrospectives.

- **Parabol:** Parabol simplifies retrospectives with built-in guidance, team engagement tracking, and automated meeting summaries.

Following are the key features:

- o   Retrospective templates and customizable boards
- o   Built-in facilitation and automated action item tracking
- o   Slack and Jira integrations

- **Trello:** While not specifically a retrospective tool, Trello's customizable boards can be adapted for retrospectives by creating columns for feedback categories.

Following are the key features:

- o   Kanban-style boards with customizable columns.
- o   Integration with tools like Slack and Jira.
- o   Commenting, tagging, and voting features.

Note: **We are not endorsing or promoting any specific brand or tool mentioned in this list. These top 5 tools have been selected based on their popularity and widespread usage within Agile teams as commonly reported by industry professionals. The suitability of a tool may vary depending on your team's specific needs, and we encourage exploring various options to determine what works best for your unique workflows and budget.**

Backlog refinement

While not always considered a formal ceremony, backlog refinement, sometimes called **grooming**, is an essential activity that occurs regularly, often mid-sprint. The product owner leads this session with the development team, reviewing and updating the product backlog to ensure it is ready for the next sprint planning session.

During refinement, the team clarifies user stories, adjusts priorities, and estimates effort. The goal is to keep the backlog organized and detailed, reducing the risk of confusion or delays during sprint planning. This session involves collaboration between the product owner, developers, and testers, with the Scrum master occasionally stepping in to facilitate.

Each Agile ceremony plays a unique role, but together they form a cohesive system of communication, alignment, and improvement. Sprint planning sets the direction, daily stand-ups keep the momentum, sprint reviews provide feedback, retrospectives foster growth, giving opportunities to identify areas for improvement in the process, and backlog refinement ensures preparedness. These ceremonies are not just meetings; they are opportunities for the team to collaborate, align, and adapt. By embracing these rituals, teams can navigate the complexities of product development with clarity and purpose, ensuring every sprint brings them closer to delivering exceptional value to their users.

Product requirement documentation

Before any product or feature is built, a shared understanding across teams is essential to ensure alignment and clarity of purpose. A PRD serves as this critical foundation. It defines the scope, rationale, and intended impact of a product initiative, acting as a single source of truth that guides product development from initial concept through to launch. PRD brings structure to the discovery and planning process, enabling cross-functional collaboration and ensuring that all stakeholders, like engineering, design, marketing, and beyond, are aligned on what is being delivered and why.

It is worth noting that not all organizations follow the practice of maintaining a separate PRD. In many product companies, the business case and product requirements are often merged into a single document known as the **business requirement document (BRD)**. While this approach may streamline documentation, it can sometimes blur the lines between business goals and user-centric product specifications. By contrast, a well-crafted PRD offers dedicated focus on the user problem, proposed solution, and functional detail, making it a valuable tool for teams aiming for clarity, agility, and accountability in the product development process.

Overview of PRD

PRD is a detailed blueprint that outlines the purpose, scope, and functionality of a product or feature. It serves as a bridge between stakeholders, ensuring that everyone, from developers and designers to marketing and sales teams, has a shared understanding of what is being built, why it is being built, and how it should function. PRD helps align business objectives with user needs, defining the *what* and *why* of a product while leaving the *how* to the technical and design teams.

At its core, PRD answers the following fundamental questions:

- *What problem are we solving?*
- *Who are the users, and what are their needs?*
- *What are the key features and functionality?*
- *How do we measure success?*

Expanded components of PRD

This section outlines the fundamental components of an effective PRD, with a focus on ensuring clarity, cross-functional alignment, and actionable guidance.

Problem statement

The problem statement is the cornerstone of PRD. It defines the current situation, focusing on the pain points experienced by users and the challenges faced by the business. This section should paint a clear picture of why the product or feature is needed, supported by user research, feedback, or market analysis.

Following is an example:

Users of a fitness app currently cannot share their workout achievements with their social circles. This lack of sharing not only limits their motivation to work out regularly but also hinders organic app referrals. From a business perspective, this gap affects user engagement, retention, and the ability to attract new users.

Vision

The vision provides the aspirational why for the project. It explains the future state the business aims to achieve through the product or feature, connecting it to broader business objectives.

Following is an example:

The vision is to create a socially engaging fitness platform where users can seamlessly share their achievements, inspire others, and create a community-driven growth engine. This aligns with the business goal of increasing active users and driving referrals.

Proposal

The proposal outlines a concrete solution to the problem. It describes the features and functionality planned to address the identified pain points, offering a roadmap for implementation.

Following is an example:

The proposal is to introduce a social sharing feature that allows users to share their workout summaries directly to *Facebook* and *Instagram*. This feature will include options for customizing messages and controlling privacy settings, creating an effortless and appealing sharing experience.

Value

The value highlights the anticipated outcomes of implementing the proposal. Unlike the output, which focuses on deliverables, for example, the feature itself, the value measures the impact on users and the business.

Following is an example:

The social sharing feature is expected to boost user engagement by 20%, reduce churn by 15%, and generate a 10% increase in new app referrals within the first quarter of launch. It will also enhance brand visibility through organic social media exposure.

Scope and out of scope

This section sets boundaries for the project, clearly stating what is included and excluded to prevent scope creep and maintain focus.

Following is an example:

- **In scope:** Integration with Facebook and Instagram for image and text sharing.
- **Out of scope:** Video sharing or integration with *TikTok* and *Snapchat* for this release.

Dependencies

Dependencies identify external factors or teams that the project relies on, helping to anticipate risks and plan for smooth execution.

Following are some examples:

- Reliance on Facebook and Instagram APIs for integration.
- UI mockups from the design team.
- Marketing materials to promote the new feature.

Stakeholders and responsibilities

This section specifies who owns PRD and who is involved in bringing the product to life. It fosters accountability and alignment among teams.

Following is an example:

- **Owner:** PM
- **Contributors:** Engineering, design, **quality assurance (QA)**, marketing, **user experience (UX)**
- **Approvers:** Head of product, **chief technology officer (CTO)**

Key metrics

Key metrics provide measurable outcomes to evaluate whether the feature achieves its intended goals. If you ask, how do you know the success metrics, even before the app or feature is launched, you are mistaken. These metrics are a set of **key performance identifiers (KPI)** that you should define when you are working on your discovery phase and should be recorded in the PRD. These metrics will define your goal, or in other words, what success means to you as a PM and what you expect as an outcome after the launch. It can include metrics that matter to monitor the performance and success, and also, there can be a set of metrics that you can monitor to ensure you do not break other interrelated systems, like do not harm metrics.

Success metrics

Success metrics are measurable outcomes that determine if the product or feature achieves its intended goals. They are defined during the discovery phase and documented in the PRD, guiding the team toward clear objectives. Success metrics should align with the business and user goals, indicating a positive impact of the feature after its launch.

Following are the examples of success metrics:

- **Feature utilization:** Tracking how many users adopt the feature regularly, such as 20% of users utilize the sharing feature weekly.

- **Growth in engagement:** Evaluating increases in user interactions resulting from the feature, like a 10% increase in app referrals from shared content.

- **User retention:** Monitoring the effect of the feature on keeping users engaged, such as a 15% reduction in churn among socially active users.

Performance metrics

Performance metrics focus on the operational and technical efficiency of the feature. These metrics ensure the feature delivers a seamless user experience and supports the expected workload.

Following are the examples:

- **System responsiveness:** Measuring the speed at which the feature performs, such as 95% of sharing actions complete within 2 seconds.

- **Error rates:** Monitoring stability and identifying issues, like less than 0.1% failure rate in the sharing feature.

- **Load handling:** Assessing scalability, such as supporting up to 1000 concurrent shares without degradation.

Do not harm metrics

Do not harm metrics, ensure that the new feature does not negatively impact other critical aspects of the product or business. These safeguards against unintended consequences maintain overall system integrity.

Following are the examples:

- **Impact on core features:** Monitoring unrelated but critical functionalities, such as no drop-in checkout completion rates after introducing the sharing feature.

- **Infrastructure health:** Ensuring the new feature does not overburden systems, like server response times remain under 500ms despite increased traffic from the feature.

- **Customer satisfaction:** Watching for adverse effects, such as no increase in customer support tickets related to the sharing feature.

The three categories, that is, success, performance, and do not harm metrics, work together to provide a holistic understanding of a feature's impact, ensuring it delivers value without compromising the broader product experience.

Best practices for creating PRD

Creating PRD is both a structured and collaborative effort, requiring clarity, alignment, and adaptability throughout the process. It serves as a foundational document that brings cross-functional teams together around a shared understanding of what is being built and why.

To begin with, the problem statement should always be backed by evidence. If users are experiencing challenges, support your claims with data from user surveys, behavioral analytics, or support logs. Avoid assumptions; every point in PRD should be grounded in insights gathered during the discovery phase. Collaboration is essential. Engage engineers early to assess technical feasibility and include designers to ensure the proposed solution is user-friendly and aligned with overall experience goals. This not only improves product quality but also fosters team alignment from the outset.

Importantly, PRD is not a static document; it evolves. As you gather new feedback or identify shifting priorities, the document should be updated accordingly. While key components such as the problem statement, scope, success metrics, and dependencies remain core, teams are encouraged to adapt the format to suit their workflows. Many PMs also include UX wireframes, useful links, or go-to-market notes in their PRDs to keep everything in one place.

In terms of tools, there is no single best platform. Commonly used options include *Confluence, Notion, Google Docs,* and *Productboard,* all of which support version control and collaboration. However, if your organization does not use any of these or relies on internal tools, that is acceptable. Even a basic document, structured clearly and shared consistently, can serve the purpose effectively. The tool is only a means to organize and communicate. What truly matters is the clarity, depth, and usefulness of the content itself.

Ultimately, a well-crafted PRD should act as a living source of truth, whether hosted in a sophisticated system or shared as a simple document. The focus should remain on creating alignment and making sure the product delivers real value.

Common mistakes in PRD creation

Even seasoned PMs can fall into common pitfalls when creating PRDs.

Following are a few mistakes to avoid:

- **Vague problem statements:** A problem statement like users do not share enough is too broad. Instead, detail the specific behaviors and challenges, such as users being unable to share their workout achievements on social media, leading to low referral rates.

- **Overloading with irrelevant details:** While it is essential to be thorough, including overly technical jargon or unnecessary background information can confuse stakeholders. Focus on actionable insights.

- **Poor prioritization:** Attempting to include too many features in a single PRD dilutes focus and stretches resources thin. Identify the most impactful features and save the rest for future iterations.

- **Lack of stakeholder input:** PRD that does not involve cross-functional input risks missing critical details. Engage all relevant teams early to ensure the document reflects a holistic perspective.

- **Neglecting success metrics:** Without clear metrics, it is impossible to measure the feature's impact. Always include measurable goals tied to user engagement, retention, or revenue growth.

PRD users

While the PM is responsible for writing and maintaining the PRD, it is a collaborative document used by multiple stakeholders. Engineers rely on it for technical direction, designers for aligning the UX with user needs, marketers for go-to-market strategies, QA for validating acceptance criteria, and so on. In short, PRD is a shared roadmap that ensures everyone is aligned and working toward the same objectives.

Best time to finalize PRD

Timing plays a critical role in the effectiveness of PRD. It serves as the product's blueprint, a central reference point that aligns user needs, business objectives, and technical feasibility. Determining the appropriate time to draft and share this document can significantly influence the success of the development process. If introduced too late, it may lead to rushed estimations, missed dependencies, or misalignment across teams. To ensure maximum effectiveness, the PRD should be developed with foresight, reviewed thoroughly, and communicated early to all relevant stakeholders, most importantly, the engineering team. The optimal time to initiate the PRD is during the discovery phase of a product or feature. At this stage, the team has typically collected key insights, conducted necessary research, and clearly articulated the problem to be addressed. It is during this phase that PRD begins to take form, shaped by a comprehensive understanding of user needs and market dynamics.

Drafting PRD is not solely about timing; it also plays a crucial role in setting the team up for success. It is advisable to finalize PRD ahead of quarterly planning to allow all stakeholders, particularly the engineering team, sufficient time to review its contents and offer constructive feedback. Much like preparing for a significant trip, PRD should not be rushed. It requires adequate time to be reviewed, questioned, and aligned across teams.

Once the draft is complete, it should undergo a structured approval process. This step is not a formality but a vital checkpoint to ensure clarity and alignment. Stakeholders from design, engineering, and business leadership must review the document for feasibility and completeness. For high-impact projects, this review often includes executive-level sign-off to ensure that the proposed direction aligns with broader strategic objectives.

After approval, PRD should be shared with the engineering team well in advance, ideally three to four weeks prior to quarterly planning. Engineers require this time to thoroughly understand the scope and provide accurate **level of effort** (**LOE**) estimates. Early distribution of PRD also enables timely adjustments to priorities based on their input.

By the time planning begins, the engineering team will already be familiar with key priorities. With LOE estimates provided, scopes clarified, and cross-team dependencies identified, the team enters quarterly planning prepared, minimizing last-minute debates and ensuring a confident, well-aligned execution strategy.

Following is a recommended structure for organizing PRD timeline in alignment with quarterly planning cycles:

- **Discovery phase:** This is the stage where the PRD begins to take shape, typically during the research and ideation process. It is advisable to initiate this phase two to three months before the upcoming quarter.

- **Stakeholder review and approval:** During this stage, the draft PRD is circulated among key stakeholders for feedback and formal approval. This should ideally occur one to two months prior to the start of the quarter to allow adequate time for revisions and alignment.

- **Sharing with engineering:** The finalized PRD should be shared with the engineering team no later than three to four weeks before quarterly planning. This timeframe enables engineers to analyze the document, understand the scope, and provide accurate LOE estimates, ensuring thoughtful and effective planning.

- **Quarterly planning:** At this point, PRD has been thoroughly reviewed, discussed, and integrated into the roadmap priorities. With all stakeholders aligned, the team is well-prepared to proceed with execution.

Aligning PRD timeline with quarterly planning ensures clarity, preparedness, and a seamless transition from strategy to execution. PRD should not be viewed merely as a planning document, but rather as a strategic asset that bridges vision and implementation. Sharing it with the right stakeholders, including any cross-functional teams whose input or approval is necessary at the right time, enhances decision-making and facilitates efficient delivery.

Quarterly planning and sprint cycles

Effective preparation is fundamental to the successful execution of any product development cycle. Quarterly planning and sprint cycles serve as the critical juncture where strategic intent is translated into actionable work. Achieving alignment in these phases requires thoughtful coordination, transparent communication, and a well-structured process.

The following section outlines how teams can prepare efficiently to ensure they are well-positioned to meet objectives and deliver value in the upcoming quarter.

Quarterly planning overview

Quarterly planning is the process of aligning cross-functional teams around a common set of goals and priorities for the upcoming three months. It provides an essential opportunity to step back, assess the broader strategic landscape, and determine where to direct focus and resources. For PMs, this phase is crucial for synthesizing insights gathered from customer feedback, business objectives, and technical feasibility to develop a well-informed plan that drives meaningful value and measurable outcomes.

During quarterly planning, the primary goal of the PM is to answer three key questions:

- *What are the top priorities for the next quarter?*
- *What resources do we need to accomplish these priorities?*
- *How will we measure success?*

Steps to preparing for quarterly planning

Preparation for quarterly planning is not a task to be initiated just a week before the session, it is a continuous, proactive process that builds momentum over time. Effective planning requires thoughtful coordination and timely alignment across teams.

The following steps outline a structured approach to preparing for a successful quarterly planning cycle:

1. **Review the product roadmap:** The product roadmap serves as a strategic compass during quarterly planning. Begin by reviewing it to identify high-priority initiatives, key milestones, and existing or potential dependencies. Consider questions such as:

    a. Are the current initiatives aligned with the organization's strategic objectives?

    b. Have there been shifts in market conditions or user expectations that warrant adjustments?

2. **Gather insights:** Collect qualitative and quantitative data from a variety of sources—customer interviews, product analytics, support tickets, stakeholder discussions to identify patterns, user pain points, and emerging opportunities. These insights will form the foundation for prioritization and strategic alignment.

3. **Finalize PRDs:** As previously discussed, PRDs should be shared with engineering well in advance, ideally, a month prior to the start of the new quarter. This allows ample time for review and the estimation of LOE, ensuring that priorities are not only relevant but also feasible within the team's capacity.

4. **Align with cross-functional teams:** Quarterly planning is not solely the domain of product teams; it requires coordination across departments. Collaborate with design, engineering, marketing, sales, and customer support to account for interdependencies. For example:

a. The design team may require additional time for usability testing.

b. Marketing may need to align feature launches with promotional campaigns.

c. Sales teams might offer input on how proposed features address client objections or market gaps.

Preparing prioritized backlog

The product backlog acts as the tactical bridge between quarterly goals and sprint execution. Refine and prioritize items based on user impact, business value, and technical feasibility. Group initiatives into categories such as *must have, should haves*, and *nice-to-haves* to enable clearer discussions and informed trade-offs during the planning session.

Bridging quarterly planning and sprint cycles

Connecting the strategic vision of quarterly planning with the tactical execution of sprint cycles is where the magic of Agile product management happens. While quarterly planning defines the what, the overarching goals and priorities for the next three months, sprint cycles tackle the how, breaking those goals into actionable, incremental steps. The relationship between these two levels of planning ensures your team operates with both a clear direction and the flexibility to adapt as new information emerges.

Integrating quarterly planning with sprint cycles

Quarterly planning provides the strategic foundation for sprint cycles by establishing a clear roadmap that outlines key deliverables, milestones, and business priorities. In the absence of this high-level direction, sprint cycles may become reactive, fragmented, or misaligned with organizational goals.

Prioritizing objectives

A core function of quarterly planning is the effective prioritization of initiatives. PMs play a pivotal role in synthesizing a diverse range of inputs, such as user feedback, competitive trends, stakeholder expectations, and technical constraints, into a cohesive set of priorities. These priorities serve as the guiding framework for sprint planning, ensuring that every iteration is grounded in meaningful business and user outcomes. For instance, if the primary objective for the quarter is to improve user retention, sprint efforts might be directed toward reducing onboarding friction, introducing personalized content recommendations, or implementing proactive user engagement strategies. By aligning each sprint with broader quarterly objectives, teams maintain focus and ensure that incremental progress contributes to measurable impact.

Breaking down strategic initiatives

Quarterly planning often includes large-scale goals, sometimes referred to as **big rocks**, such as launching a major new feature, expanding into a new market, or hitting specific revenue or engagement targets. To translate these into actionable work, they must be decomposed into smaller, manageable components that can be addressed within the confines of individual sprints. This decomposition process ensures that high-level ambitions are pursued in a structured, iterative, and achievable manner.

For instance, launching a new feature might involve the following:

- Conducting user research and finalizing requirements in one sprint
- Developing and testing the core functionality in subsequent sprints
- Preparing marketing and sales materials for a later sprint

This decomposition ensures that large initiatives are approached methodically, allowing teams to deliver incremental progress while maintaining focus on the end goal. Aligning cross-functional teams quarterly planning provides the shared vision that aligns all teams—engineering, design, marketing, sales, and customer support. This alignment is crucial for sprint cycles to operate smoothly.

For example, if a quarterly objective involves launching a new product feature, the design team needs to create mockups in parallel with development, the marketing team must prepare launch campaigns, and the support team should draft knowledge base articles. Sprint cycles then become the mechanism for coordinating these efforts, ensuring each team delivers its piece of the puzzle on time.

Feedback loop between sprints and quarterly plans

While quarterly plans guide sprint cycles, sprint outcomes also feed back into the planning process, creating a dynamic feedback loop.

Following is how this iterative relationship unfolds:

- **Course correction:** As sprints progress, new information may emerge, unexpected user feedback, technical challenges, or shifting market conditions that require adjustments to the quarterly plan. Agile's iterative nature allows you to pivot as needed without derailing the overall strategy.

  For instance, let us say a feature prioritized during quarterly planning proves more complex to develop than anticipated. Instead of forcing it through, you might decide to deprioritize it for the current quarter and focus on a different initiative that delivers faster value. This flexibility ensures your team remains productive without compromising quality.

- **Measuring progress:** Sprints provide regular opportunities to assess how well the team is progressing toward quarterly objectives. By reviewing sprint outcomes in the context of the quarterly plan, you can identify whether the team is on track or if adjustments are needed. For example:

  o If user testing reveals that a new feature is not resonating as expected, you can shift focus to address usability issues.

- o If development is ahead of schedule, you might pull additional items into the sprint backlog.

- **Celebrating wins:** Sprint reviews offer the chance to celebrate incremental wins that contribute to quarterly goals. These moments of recognition are essential for maintaining team morale and momentum. By highlighting how sprint achievements align with the bigger picture, you reinforce the value of each team member's contributions.

Maintaining flexibility while staying focused

One of the biggest challenges in bridging quarterly planning and sprint cycles is balancing flexibility with focus. Quarterly plans provide a strategic anchor, ensuring your team works toward meaningful outcomes, but sprint cycles must remain adaptable to changing circumstances.

Following are some strategies to achieve this balance:

- **Set clear priorities but leave room for adjustment:** While quarterly planning should establish clear priorities, avoid overloading the roadmap. Instead, build in buffer time to accommodate unforeseen challenges or opportunities. For example, reserve 10-20% of sprint capacity for addressing technical debt, responding to user feedback, or seizing market trends.

- **Focus on outcomes, not outputs:** When bridging quarterly and sprint planning, it is easy to get caught up in the what of deliverables. Instead, emphasize the why, the outcomes you are trying to achieve. For instance, instead of targeting the completion of a new feature, measure its impact on key metrics like user engagement or revenue growth.

- **Encourage continuous communication:** Regular communication between product, design, and engineering teams is essential for maintaining alignment. While sprint ceremonies like planning and retrospectives (which we have covered earlier in this chapter) provide structured touchpoints, informal check-ins and updates help teams stay connected and resolve issues proactively.

From planning to execution

The handoff from quarterly planning to sprint execution is a critical step that sets the tone for the entire development cycle.

Following is how to ensure a smooth transition:

- **Share the vision:** Before the first sprint kicks off, take time to share the quarterly plan with the entire team. Explain the why behind each priority, connecting individual tasks to broader business goals. This context fosters a sense of ownership and purpose.

- **Collaborate on sprint backlogs:** Work closely with the engineering team to populate sprint backlogs with tasks that align with quarterly priorities. Ensure each task is clearly defined, scoped, and sequenced to minimize confusion or delays during execution.

- **Monitor progress:** Usage of tools like burndown charts, velocity metrics, and dashboards to track progress against quarterly goals. Regularly review these metrics with the team to identify risks, celebrate wins, and maintain focus.

Importance of continuous improvement

Bridging quarterly planning and sprint cycles is not a one-time exercise, it is an ongoing process of learning, adapting, and improving. By leveraging insights from past quarters and sprints, PMs can refine their approach, making each cycle more efficient and impactful. Whether it is through better prioritization, stronger alignment, or more effective communication, every iteration brings them closer to delivering products that delight users and drive business success.

Conclusion

Building great products is not just about ideation; it is about execution, and how you execute depends on the methodology you adopt. This chapter laid the groundwork for understanding two foundational approaches: Waterfall, with its linear predictability, and Agile, with its adaptive, user-centric flexibility. While Waterfall still has relevance in high-compliance industries, Agile has become the gold standard in dynamic environments where user needs and market conditions are constantly evolving.

You also learned about Agile ceremonies like sprint planning, daily stand-ups, reviews, and retrospectives that serve as pillars of team alignment and continuous delivery. We explored how structured documentation through PRDs ensures clarity, accountability, and shared understanding across cross-functional teams, and as priorities evolve, quarterly planning and sprint cycles bridge long-term strategy with short-term execution, helping teams stay focused without losing adaptability.

Ultimately, the most successful teams are not defined by the methodology they choose, but by how well they apply it to solve the right problems for the right users, repeatedly and consistently.

In the next chapter, we will explore how to take these products to market successfully, focusing on how business models, pricing, and go-to-market decisions impact a product's growth and long-term sustainability.

Points to remember

- Product development methodologies provide a systematic framework to transition from concept to completion, ensuring alignment with user needs, market trends, and technical feasibility.

- Quarterly planning sets the strategic direction for the next three months, enabling teams to align around clear goals and priorities while preparing for execution.

- Sprints serve as short, focused timeboxes within Agile methodologies, allowing teams to deliver incremental value while staying flexible to change.

- Agile methodologies emphasize iterative development, collaboration, and adaptability, making them well-suited for dynamic environments and evolving user needs.

- Waterfall methodologies, while less flexible, are still relevant for industries requiring strict compliance and predictable outcomes.

- PRDs act as the blueprint for development, ensuring alignment among stakeholders and detailing the what, why, and expected outcomes of a product or feature.

- Success metrics measure the effectiveness of features and their impact on business goals, while do not harm metrics safeguard other systems and functionalities from unintended disruptions.

- Collaboration between cross-functional teams like product, engineering, design, and marketing, is critical for smooth execution of both quarterly plans and sprint cycles.

- Continuous feedback loops between sprints and quarterly planning allow teams to adapt quickly, incorporate new insights, and course-correct as needed.

- Balancing flexibility and focus are essential in Agile; teams must remain adaptable to changes while staying aligned with overarching strategic goals.

Multiple choice questions

1. **What is the main purpose of product development methodologies?**

    a. To create rigid project plans

    b. To systematically guide teams from concept to product completion

    c. To focus only on user feedback

    d. To prioritize business objectives over user needs

2. **What is one key feature of Agile methodologies?**

    a. Fixed requirements throughout the project

    b. Linear and sequential development phases

    c. Iterative delivery of functional increments

    d. Focus on extensive documentation

3. **What is the primary output of quarterly planning?**

     a. Detailed technical specifications

     b. User interface designs

     c. High-level goals and priorities for the next three months

     d. Bug fixes and minor updates

4. **How does sprint planning support sprint cycles?**

     a. By determining the overall quarterly objectives

     b. By breaking down prioritized tasks into actionable items

     c. By reviewing team performance

     d. By creating new user personas

5. **Why are success metrics important in product development?**

     a. To evaluate team efficiency

     b. To measure whether a product meets its intended goals

     c. To track competitors' performance

     d. To document project constraints

6. **What is the primary advantage of Agile over Waterfall?**

     a. Emphasis on fixed timelines and requirements

     b. Ability to adapt to evolving user needs and market conditions

     c. Extensive documentation requirements

     d. Strictly linear progress

7. **What is the role of PRDs in product development?**

     a. To outline only technical requirements

     b. To provide a shared understanding of the product's purpose, scope, and functionality

     c. To focus exclusively on user stories

     d. To document marketing strategies

8. **What is a common challenge of Agile methodologies?**

     a. Overemphasis on documentation

     b. Inability to accommodate feedback

     c. Risk of scope creep due to flexibility

     d. Rigid and inflexible team structures

9. **When should PRDs ideally be finalized?**

    a. During the sprint review

    b. After quarterly planning

    c. Before quarterly planning, during the discovery phase

    d. During the retrospective phase

10. **What ensures alignment between quarterly planning and sprint cycles?**

    a. Eliminating team collaboration

    b. Defining success metrics before planning begins

    c. Breaking down quarterly goals into incremental sprint tasks

    d. Avoiding feedback during sprint reviews

Answers

1	b
2	c
3	c
4	b
5	b
6	b
7	b
8	c
9	c
10	c

Join our Discord space

Join our Discord workspace for latest updates, offers, tech happenings around the world, new releases, and sessions with the authors:

https://discord.bpbonline.com

CHAPTER 9
Product Sales Strategy

Introduction

Until now, we have explored the journey of building great products, from discovery and development to creating stickiness and user value. However, building a great product is only part of the equation. The real challenge, and success, lies in taking that product to market effectively, connecting it with the right audience, and creating a revenue stream that is scalable, sustainable, and strategically aligned.

A well-defined product sales strategy turns ideas into growth engines. It bridges the gap between product development and market success, shaping how businesses position their offerings, monetize value, and compete in fast-changing environments. For PMs, this means going beyond features and roadmaps and into understanding pricing models, business viability, and market dynamics.

This chapter introduces the essential components of a product sales strategy, covering various business models, the power of cloud-enabled scale, the role of **return on investment (ROI)** in decision-making, and the impact of aftermarket strategies. You will also explore how to build investor confidence through strong product pitches and understand emerging digital trends that influence modern product monetization.

Structure

This chapter covers the following topics:

- Different business models
- Cloud computing and business model innovation
- The return on investment imperative
- The J-curve effect to visualize growth over time
- Aftermarket strategy
- Pitching to venture capitalists
- Next focus for PMs

Objectives

The objective of this chapter is to equip readers with a clear understanding of the manner in which product sales strategy serves as a critical driver of long-term product success. Readers will explore how PMs play a vital role in defining the manner in which a product reaches the market, generates revenue, and adapts to customer and industry shifts. The chapter explores core business models, from traditional one-time purchases to modern subscription and usage-based models, demonstrating the way each aligns with different product types and market dynamics. Readers will learn to identify the signs that call for business model pivots and how cloud computing and strategic partnerships enhance a product's scalability and performance in the digital ecosystem.

By the end of this chapter, readers will be equipped with practical frameworks and insights to craft, evaluate, and evolve a product sales strategy that drives revenue, supports innovation, and sustains product market fit in competitive markets.

Different business models

As a PM, you must first understand how your product creates value. At the heart of this understanding lies the business model, the way a company makes money. While there are many variations, businesses generally operate within eight core business models. Each model has its own nuances, advantages, and optimization strategies. Listed in *Table 9.1* are the eight core business models, which are key for you to gain an understanding. Even if you are not working on all core business models, still knowing what they are and how they differentiate is important.

The following table outlines various common business models:

Business model	Product examples
One-time sale	Smart phones
Rent	Rental trucks
Subscription	OTT platforms
Pay per use	Cloud services, charging stations
Commission	App based services
Service	Marketplace
Marketing services	Advertising
Asset management	Banking

Table 9.1: Types of business models

To craft an effective product sales strategy, PMs must first understand the various ways in which businesses generate revenue. At the core of any go-to-market plan is the underlying business model, a structured approach to value creation and monetization. While the specifics may vary across industries, most organizations operate within one or more of the following foundational models. Each model comes with its own strengths, challenges, and data-driven levers for optimization. The following list gives an overview of the eight most common business models used in both traditional and digital product ecosystems:

- **One-time sale:** The most traditional business model begins with selling a product. In this model, a business designs, produces, and sells a tangible item or digital product for a one-time payment. A notable example is *Apple's iPhone*, a product that combines advanced technology, intuitive design, and premium branding to support its pricing strategy. For businesses engaged in physical product sales, success depends on optimizing unit economics, including reducing production costs, setting competitive prices, and achieving healthy profit margins.

  The iPhone exemplifies a successful product that integrates hardware and software to deliver a superior **user experience (UX)**. Apple continuously analyzes market data to understand consumer preferences, such as the demand for larger screens, enhanced cameras, or extended battery life. This data-driven approach enables the company to refine its offerings and maintain a leading position in the smartphone market.

- **Rent:** Not every product needs to be owned. The rent-a-thing model capitalizes on infrequent needs, where customers prefer to borrow rather than buy. Home Depot, Penske, and U-Haul are classic examples. Customers rent trucks or trailers for short-term use, saving money and avoiding the burden of ownership. This business model thrives on understanding consumption patterns, frequency of use, timing, and regions.

For digital PMs, renting also applies to subscription-based tools like cloud storage, where customers essentially rent digital space. Data analytics is crucial here. For example, U-Haul relies on geographic data to position trucks where demand is highest, ensuring availability while minimizing unused inventory.

- **Subscription:** Subscription models are a staple in the digital age as they provide many benefits, such as ease of payments, no upfront investment, and customers can upgrade to a higher tier once they get used to the product. This helps create stickiness. Whether it is *Netflix* or *Spotify* for music streaming, this model thrives when customers need a product regularly. The key to success lies in engagement, the frequency with which users interact with the product, and the value they derive from it.

  Take ChatGPT as an example. It offers a freemium model, where basic features are free, but advanced capabilities require a paid subscription. This approach allows users to experience the product's value before committing to it financially.

- **Pay per use:** Usage-based models, like **Amazon Web Services (AWS)**, **Microsoft Azure**, and **Google Cloud**, charge customers based on consumption. This is ideal for infrastructure services where usage fluctuates. These cloud computing resources, customers pay only for the storage, computing power, or bandwidth they consume.

  To optimize this model, the cloud service providers collect granular usage data. Customers receive dashboards that show their consumption patterns, enabling them to manage costs effectively. From a PM's perspective, this data can reveal how customers use specific features, where inefficiencies occur, and how pricing structures can be refined.

- **Commission:** Platform businesses, like *Airbnb* or *Uber*, embody this model. Instead of selling or renting a product, they act as intermediaries, connecting supply and demand while taking a percentage of every transaction. Airbnb, like Uber, does not own assets; it facilitates bookings and earns a commission. This model requires optimizing **gross merchandise value (GMV)**, the total value of transactions processed on the platform.

  Data-driven decision-making is the backbone of platform success. Uber and Airbnb analyze market conditions, pricing trends, and booking frequencies to improve their matching algorithms and optimize revenues. For example, by introducing *Smart Pricing*, Airbnb enabled hosts to adjust their prices based on market demand, increasing bookings and revenue for both parties.

- **Service:** Service-based businesses, such as consulting firms or IT solution providers, charge for expertise and hands-on help. For instance, *Total Solutions, Inc.* delivers tailored software solutions to businesses. Here, the focus shifts to optimizing skillsets and ensuring client satisfaction.

Service-based businesses rely heavily on qualitative and quantitative data. Feedback from clients, project timelines, and resource utilization metrics helps managers improve processes and allocate skills efficiently.

- **Marketing services:** Content platforms like *YouTube* rely on advertising to generate revenue. Instead of charging users, they monetize attention. YouTube collects vast amounts of data about user behaviors, preferences, and demographics to target ads effectively.

  The power of data is undeniable in this model. By analyzing user engagement metrics, such as click-through rates, impressions, and conversion rates, YouTube optimizes its ad algorithms to deliver results for advertisers while enhancing the UX.

- **Asset management:** Finally, financial firms like *Fidelity* and *Charles Schwab* among others operate on an **asset management** model. They charge clients a percentage of the assets they manage, aligning their success with the financial growth of their clients.

  Here, data helps portfolio managers make investment decisions. They analyze market trends, risk factors, and asset performance to optimize returns. For PMs in fintech, data is invaluable for building tools that monitor investments, automate insights, and provide actionable recommendations.

Identifying a business model shift

A business model is not inherently fixed. As markets evolve and competitive dynamics shift, organizations must remain adaptable to sustain their relevance. Recognizing when a business model has become ineffective requires ongoing vigilance and the ability to identify key indicators of change. One notable signal is the emergence of disruptive startups that begin capturing market share. For instance, *Netflix's* transformation of the entertainment industry through digital streaming rendered the traditional video rental model, exemplified by blockbuster, obsolete. Similarly, rising competition can lead to margin erosion and declining revenues, prompting the need for innovation.

Evolving consumer behavior serves as another critical indicator. The widespread adoption of e-commerce fundamentally altered retail, and companies that failed to respond, such as *Toys"R"Us*, suffered significant losses in market position. Regulatory developments also present risks, particularly in data-driven industries. For example, stricter data privacy laws have forced advertising platforms to reconsider how they collect and leverage consumer data. In some cases, organizations proactively disrupt their own models to maintain strategic advantage. Apple's decision to introduce the iPhone, effectively phasing out its own iPod line, demonstrates a forward-thinking approach to capturing emerging demand for multifunctional devices.

For PMs, early identification of such signals is essential. Leveraging data analytics to monitor market trends, uncover customer pain points, and evaluate new opportunities enables organizations to adapt strategically, ensuring continued competitiveness and resilience.

Cloud computing and business model innovation

As digital products increasingly dominate the marketplace, cloud computing has become a foundational component of many successful business models. It enables organizations to offload infrastructure, software, and platform management to third-party providers, who maintain and scale these resources remotely. The advantages of cloud computing, such as scalability, cost efficiency, and accelerated time-to-market, align seamlessly with the demands of digital-first strategies. Cloud computing fundamentally reshapes how businesses build, scale, and deliver their products. By eliminating the need for significant upfront investments in physical infrastructure or data centers, the cloud empowers startups and smaller companies to compete on more equal footing with larger enterprises. While it is not necessary for PMs to possess deep technical expertise equivalent to that of system architects, a working understanding of cloud concepts is increasingly valuable.

At its core, cloud computing delivers a suite of services, ranging from servers and storage to databases, networking, software, and analytics, over the internet. Rather than managing on-premises infrastructure, companies pay only for the resources they consume on a flexible, usage-based model. For digital PMs, this model offers the ability to accelerate innovation cycles, support cost-effective scaling, and streamline product deployment.

A prominent example is Netflix, whose global streaming platform operates on AWS. By leveraging the scalability and reliability of AWS, Netflix can efficiently manage massive volumes of traffic without the burden of maintaining its own physical servers.

The four major types of cloud computing models

To fully leverage the benefits of cloud computing, it is essential to understand the different service models that underpin modern digital infrastructure. These models offer unique capabilities that serve distinct business and technical needs. From delivering end user applications to providing foundational computing resources, these cloud models enable product teams to innovate faster, scale efficiently, and reduce operational overhead. The following breakdown provides an overview of each model, supported by real-world examples that illustrate how they are applied across various industries:

- **Software as a service (SaaS):** SaaS delivers software applications over the internet on a subscription basis. End user access the software via a browser without needing installations or updates. Everything is managed in the cloud by the service provider.

  The following are examples of companies effectively leveraging SaaS:

  o Figma, a collaborative design tool, operates on the SaaS model. Designers can access Figma's features on any device, collaborate in real-time, and avoid software installation hassles. This model enables consistent updates and improves UX.

o   Slack revolutionized team communication by offering its product as a SaaS. By focusing on UX, integrating with third-party tools, and using a freemium-to-paid model, *Slack* captured millions of users. Companies paid for advanced features, creating a highly scalable subscription revenue stream.

- **Platform as a service (PaaS):** PaaS provides a platform where developers can build, test, and deploy applications. It abstracts the underlying infrastructure, allowing teams to focus solely on coding and innovation.

  Consider the example of *Heroku*, a PaaS provider. Heroku allows developers to deploy applications without worrying about servers or configuration. Startups and small teams can scale applications quickly without infrastructure overhead. It works by simplifying the development process, PaaS accelerates time-to-market and lowers technical barriers. PMs can focus on features and value creation instead of technical complexities.

- **Infrastructure as a service (IaaS):** IaaS offers virtualized computing resources, like servers, storage, and networks, on a pay-per-use basis. Businesses have full control over their operating systems and applications while outsourcing hardware management to the cloud provider.

  A few examples are given as follows:

  o   AWS provides IaaS solutions, enabling businesses to rent **virtual machines (VMs)**, cloud storage, and networking capabilities. For companies like Airbnb, this means they can dynamically scale their server needs during high-demand periods without investing in costly physical infrastructure.

  o   Airbnb hosts millions of property listings and handles vast spikes in traffic during holidays or events. By leveraging AWS, Airbnb can scale server capacity up and down to match user demand, reducing costs while maintaining reliability and performance.

- **Function as a service (FaaS):** FaaS, also known as **serverless computing**, allows businesses to run code in response to events without managing servers. Developers deploy functions that execute only when needed, significantly reducing costs and complexity.

  Consider the example of AWS Lambda, which lets developers execute small code snippets in response to triggers, such as user uploads or database changes. The reason it matters is that FaaS is ideal for products requiring microservices, event-driven processing, and low-latency operations. It enables flexibility, scalability, and pay-for-use efficiency.

Partnership business models in the cloud ecosystem

Cloud computing has also paved the way for partnership business models, where companies collaborate to offer combined services. Partnerships allow businesses to expand their reach, integrate new capabilities, and accelerate growth.

Types of cloud partnerships

Having established the foundational models of cloud computing, i.e., SaaS, PaaS, IaaS, and FaaS, it is important to examine the way businesses can maximize their impact by engaging in strategic cloud partnerships. While each model provides powerful capabilities on its own, their full potential is realized when organizations collaborate with the right partners to enhance scalability, operational efficiency, and customer value. Cloud partnerships go beyond technical integration; they represent strategic alliances that allow companies to combine specialized expertise, share resources, and expand their market reach. Whether an organization is building a SaaS application, leveraging infrastructure through providers like AWS or Azure, or developing tailored solutions for niche markets, these collaborations can significantly amplify product impact and growth.

For PMs, understanding the landscape of cloud partnerships is essential to identifying strategic opportunities that align with product goals.

The following list explores four key types of cloud partnerships: Channel partners, service partners, platform partners, and function partners, explaining their roles, strategic importance, and how leading companies use them to drive success:

- **Channel partners:** Channel partners play a vital role in the distribution and commercialization of cloud-based products. These partners typically act as intermediaries between the cloud solution provider and the end customer, extending the provider's market reach by leveraging established sales networks, industry relationships, and regional market expertise. They may include **value-added resellers (VARs)**, system integrators, **managed service providers (MSPs)**, and telecom operators. In a channel partnership, the partner often resells, bundles, or customizes a provider's offering, whether SaaS, IaaS, or PaaS, to meet the specific needs of enterprise customers. For instance, *IBM* and *AT&T* are prominent examples of channel partners that have successfully distributed cloud infrastructure and software solutions at scale. IBM, through its vast global sales force and consulting capabilities, resells and implements third-party cloud technologies while adding strategic services such as integration and migration. AT&T, on the other hand, has partnered with leading cloud providers to offer businesses a seamless package of connectivity, infrastructure, and cloud services.

  The strategic importance of channel partnerships lies in their ability to accelerate customer acquisition and market penetration, especially in regions or industries where the cloud provider lacks a direct sales presence. Channel partners also add value by offering localized support, compliance expertise, implementation guidance, and tailored training, all of which contribute to a more seamless **customer experience (CX)**.

For PMs, working with channel partners presents both opportunities and responsibilities. On one hand, these partners can help bring products to new markets faster and at lower cost. On the other hand, PMs must ensure that partners are equipped with the right collateral, training, pricing structures, and support systems to represent the product effectively. This requires close coordination between product, sales, and partner enablement teams. A well-executed channel strategy not only expands reach but also builds long-term relationships with key enterprise clients.

- **Service partners:** Service partners play a critical role in helping businesses navigate the complexities of adopting and implementing cloud solutions. These partners offer consulting, implementation, customization, and ongoing support services to ensure that businesses can effectively leverage cloud platforms. Companies like *Capgemini* and *Infosys*, for example, work as service partners by bridging the gap between cloud technology and business operations. Their expertise lies in understanding the specific needs of an organization, aligning the cloud solution to fit those needs, and guiding clients through successful implementations. Whether it is migrating to a cloud-based infrastructure or deploying enterprise-level SaaS products, service partners enable companies to adopt cloud technologies efficiently while minimizing risk and operational disruptions.

  For instance, Capgemini worked closely with a large financial institution looking to migrate its legacy systems to a cloud environment. The company provided end-to-end consulting, ensuring a seamless migration strategy while mitigating risks associated with data security and downtime. Through tailored cloud solutions and dedicated support, the financial institution reduced operational costs and improved scalability, enabling it to better serve its growing customer base.

- **Platform partners:** Platform partners focus on providing robust cloud platforms that businesses can integrate with to scale their offerings. These partners offer foundational cloud services like infrastructure, development tools, and environments for hosting, processing, and deploying applications. Platform providers such as *Microsoft Azure* and *Google Cloud* collaborate with businesses to enable their products and services to thrive on these ecosystems. The partnership often involves integration, optimization, and co-development of cloud-based solutions to deliver enhanced value.

  For example, Microsoft Azure serves as a platform partner for *Microsoft Teams*. Teams leverages Azure's infrastructure to offer businesses a scalable and reliable platform for communication, collaboration, and productivity. By using Azure's vast capabilities, including data storage, **artificial intelligence (AI)** services, and real-time communication tools, Microsoft Teams has become one of the leading productivity platforms, providing businesses worldwide with an integrated digital workspace. This symbiotic relationship demonstrates how platform partners provide the backbone for businesses to develop innovative, cloud-based solutions.

- **Function partners:** Function partners specialize in helping businesses optimize specific areas of their operations by adopting cloud models, like FaaS or PaaS. These partners often bring deep expertise in business processes, regulatory compliance, and technical execution to ensure companies can extract the maximum value from their cloud investments. Consulting firms, such as *Deloitte* and *PwC*, act as function partners, guiding businesses through cloud transformation initiatives to streamline development, deployment, and operational processes.

  A notable example is Deloitte, which works with a global healthcare provider to adopt a FaaS model to improve their appointment booking system. By leveraging a serverless architecture on AWS Lambda, Deloitte helped the healthcare provider create a scalable and cost-efficient solution for managing high volumes of patient appointments. The cloud-based system dynamically scaled resources based on user demand, reducing infrastructure costs while enhancing the UX for patients and staff. Function partners like Deloitte provide targeted, strategic expertise to ensure cloud adoption, driving measurable value and operational efficiency.

To recap, partnerships play a key role in any product strategy as the PM can take advantage of the partner's expertise in crafting the best solution for the customer.

Evaluating the right time for cloud adoption

Recognizing the appropriate time to transition to cloud-based solutions is critical for maintaining competitiveness and operational efficiency. Many organizations reach a tipping point where traditional systems, tools, or infrastructure become insufficient to support scalable growth. Escalating infrastructure costs, inefficiencies in maintenance, and prolonged development cycles often signal the need for modernization. Cloud adoption addresses these challenges by shifting from capital-intensive, hardware-bound investments to flexible, pay-as-you-go models. This transition not only alleviates the financial and operational burdens associated with server management and hardware upgrades but also accelerates innovation and delivery. Organizations benefit from near-instant scalability, whether increasing storage capacity, processing power, or bandwidth, which empowers teams to focus on customer value rather than system limitations.

Additionally, competitive pressures often serve as a catalyst for change. As market dynamics evolve, businesses that rely on outdated infrastructures may struggle to keep pace with more Agile competitors. Cloud platforms, such as PaaS and FaaS, enable faster development cycles, rapid deployment, and iterative experimentation. These capabilities are especially valuable in high-velocity environments where time-to-market can define success or failure.

Another compelling driver for cloud adoption is the need for data-driven decision-making. As data volumes increase exponentially, businesses must be able to extract actionable insights efficiently. Cloud-based analytics tools provide real-time visibility into customer behavior, market trends, and operational performance. This capability is particularly impactful for product teams, who can use these insights to optimize offerings, tailor marketing strategies, and improve CXs. Ultimately, cloud adoption should not be viewed solely as a cost-saving initiative, but rather as a strategic move toward building long-term competitive advantage. Whether integrating SaaS for enhanced workflow or deploying IaaS to support scale, cloud technologies position organizations to innovate at speed and adapt to change more effectively than legacy systems allow.

The flexibility, agility, and scalability offered by cloud solutions are transformative, but only for those prepared to act decisively. In an industry where hesitation can result in lost momentum and market share, proactive adoption of cloud technology is often the difference between merely surviving and leading. Once changes are implemented, measuring their effectiveness becomes essential. Assessing ROI serves as a critical validation step to ensure that the chosen strategy delivers the intended outcomes. Organizations that evaluate success through well-defined financial and operational metrics will be better positioned to optimize their approach and sustain growth.

The return on investment imperative

ROI is the cornerstone of evaluating the success of any strategy, product, or initiative. At its core, ROI measures the profitability of an investment relative to its cost. The formula is as follows:

$$ROI = (Money\ gained - money\ spent) / money\ spent \times 100$$

This metric is powerful because it distills performance into a single percentage. For instance, if you invest $100,000 into a new feature that generates $150,000 in revenue, your ROI is 50%. However, ROI is not without limitations. It does not capture nonfinancial benefits, like customer satisfaction, brand loyalty, or long-term strategic value. It also does not directly reflect cash flow, which is critical for understanding a company's financial health.

To get a clearer picture, businesses often rely on annualized ROI, which measures profitability over time. This metric helps managers understand whether an investment remains viable as market conditions change.

Annualized return on investment

While ROI is an essential tool for measuring profitability, it is often static, capturing performance at a single point in time. To better understand the long-term value of an investment, businesses turn to annualized ROI, which measures profitability on a year-over-year basis. Imagine you have launched a subscription-based SaaS product with an initial investment of $1 million. In the first year, the product generates $500,000 in revenue. By the third year, however, revenue climbs to $2 million annually due to growing adoption and improved engagement strategies. Calculating ROI at each stage provides critical insights into the performance of the product and whether your business strategy needs adjustment.

Annualized ROI helps PMs identify trends, such as when profitability plateaus or begins to decline. For instance, a SaaS company may realize that its annualized ROI has dropped from 30% to 15%, signaling a need to refresh its value proposition, improve its retention strategy, or optimize customer acquisition costs.

For any business, a double-digit annualized ROI is often considered healthy. However, it is important to look beyond this single metric. Relying solely on ROI can mislead decision-making by ignoring non-monetary factors, like customer satisfaction, market positioning, or future growth potential. A high ROI today does not guarantee long-term sustainability unless supported by robust strategic plans.

The limitations of return on investment

ROI is undoubtedly useful, but it has limitations. One of the primary drawbacks is that it does not directly account for a company's cash flow. Positive ROI on a project does not necessarily mean the business is healthy; if cash flow is weak, the company may still face financial challenges. Consider a scenario where a digital platform invests in a product feature that boosts revenue significantly but also incurs substantial ongoing operational costs. While the short-term ROI looks impressive, the long-term strain on cash flow might undermine profitability.

Another limitation is that ROI does not capture nonfinancial benefits like improved user satisfaction, brand reputation, or customer loyalty. A redesign of a digital product may not immediately translate into increased revenue, but it may lead to lower churn rates or higher **net promoter score** (**NPS**). Over time, these intangible benefits create measurable value, even if ROI does not reflect them initially.

Furthermore, ROI does not offer a complete picture of business value. A product with a lower ROI might still be strategically valuable because it unlocks opportunities in adjacent markets or enhances the CX. For example, a freemium model might have low ROI initially, but as users upgrade to paid plans, the long-term value far outweighs the upfront costs.

To address these limitations, PMs should adopt a holistic approach to measuring performance, combining ROI with customer metrics, operational efficiency, and strategic alignment. By layering multiple perspectives, you gain a clearer understanding of your product's impact.

The return on investment spreadsheet

Calculating ROI, especially for complex projects, often requires a systematic approach. An ROI spreadsheet is a valuable tool for PMs to forecast, analyze, and evaluate investments. A sample image of an ROI spreadsheet is illustrated as follows:

Returns Summary	Total Return	Feb-23	Feb-24	Feb-25	Feb-26	Feb-27
Multiple of Invested Capital	2.04x	0.29x	0.64x	1.14x	1.58x	2.04x
XIRR=ROI	43.73%					

Operating Model	Jan-23	Feb-23	Feb-24	Feb-25	Feb-26	Feb-27
Total Revenue		$1,000,000.00	$1,070,000.00	$1,102,100.00	$1,135,163.00	$1,169,217.89
Costs						
Initial Investment	($400,000.00)					
Development Cost % of Revenue	($450,000.00)	($400,000.00)	($374,500.00)	($220,420.00)	($312,169.83)	($321,534.92)
Manufacturing Cost % of Revenue		($150,000.00)	($160,500.00)	($165,315.00)	($170,274.45)	($175,382.68)
Operating Cost % of Revenue		($40,000.00)	($42,800.00)	($44,084.00)	($45,406.52)	($46,768.72)
Sales & Mkting Cost % of Revenue		($25,000.00)	($26,750.00)	($27,552.50)	($28,379.08)	($29,230.45)
Aftermarket Cost % of Revenue		($25,000.00)	($26,750.00)	($27,552.50)	($28,379.08)	($29,230.45)
Transactin Costs (Gpay, Apple Pay etc) % of Revenue		($10,000.00)	($10,700.00)	($11,021.00)	($11,351.63)	($11,692.18)
Net Operating Income	($850,000.00)	$350,000.00	$428,000.00	$606,155.00	$539,202.43	$555,378.50
Less Taxes		($105,000.00)	($128,400.00)	($181,846.50)	($161,760.73)	($166,613.55)
Net Income	($850,000.00)	$245,000.00	$299,600.00	$424,308.50	$377,441.70	$388,764.95

Operating Model Inputs	Jan-23	Feb-23	Feb-24	Feb-25	Feb-26	Feb-27
Model Structure Inputs						
Revenue Start Date		2/19/2023				
Initial Investment $	$400,000.00					
Revenue						
Year 1 Revenue Assumption		$1,000,000.00				
Revenue Growth Rate			7%	3%	3%	3%
Costs						
Initial Development Cost $	$450,000.00					
Development Cost % of Revenue		40.0%	35.0%	20.0%	27.5%	27.5%
Manufacturing Cost % of Revenue		15.0%	15.0%	15.0%	15.0%	15.0%
Operating Cost % of Revenue		4.0%	4.0%	4.0%	4.0%	4.0%
Sales Cost % of Revenue		2.5%	2.5%	2.5%	2.5%	2.5%
Aftermarket Cost % of Revenue		2.5%	2.5%	2.5%	2.5%	2.5%
Transactin Costs % of Revenue		1.0%	1.0%	1.0%	1.0%	1.0%
Total Cost % of Revenue		65.0%	60.0%	45.0%	52.5%	52.5%
Tax Assumption	30.0%	30.0%	30.0%	30.0%	30.0%	30.0%

Figure 9.1: Sample ROI spreadsheet

PMs must approach ROI analysis with structure and precision, and a practical way to do this is by using a well-defined ROI spreadsheet that breaks down key financial components. The following steps outline the process to build and utilize this tool to forecast returns, assess viability, and support data-driven decision-making:

1. **Identify costs:** List all the expenses associated with the investment, including development, marketing, operations, and maintenance costs.

2. **Track returns:** Estimate expected revenue or benefits over time. These could include direct income, cost savings, or improved customer metrics like retention.

3. **Adjust for time:** Consider the time value of money; returns earned in later years are worth less than returns today. Discount future revenues to their present value using an appropriate rate.

4. **Calculate ROI:** Use the formula to calculate ROI for each period and annualize it if needed.

For example, a SaaS company investing in a new analytics dashboard might create a spreadsheet that forecasts revenue growth, calculates churn reduction, and estimates operational costs over a three year period. With clear data inputs and assumptions, the PM can evaluate whether the investment justifies the resources.

It is understood that PMs may not be part of the finance team; however, having a foundational understanding of how financial figures are derived and what outcomes they indicate is essential for evaluating strategic success. Without this knowledge, it becomes challenging to track performance metrics or engage in meaningful discussions with finance stakeholders. For those interested in exploring ROI in greater depth, please refer to the footnote[1].

The J-curve effect to visualize growth over time

The J-curve is a concept often used in business to describe the trajectory of an investment's returns. The following figure depicts the J-curve effect, where initially, returns may dip as upfront costs are incurred, but over time, the returns begin to rise, creating a *J* shape:

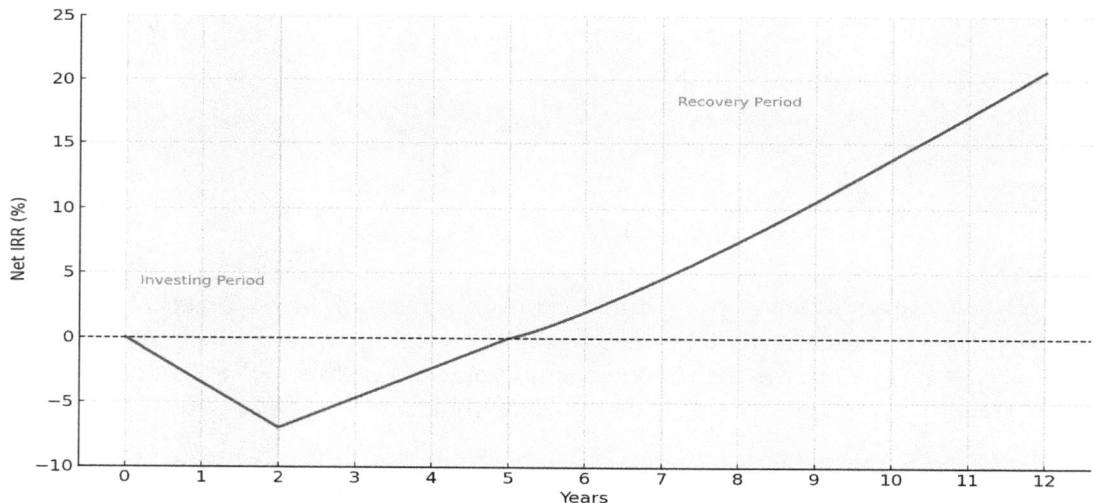

Figure 9.2: The J-curve effect

Consider a startup launching a subscription product. In the early months, marketing costs are high, user acquisition is slow, and revenue is minimal. The business appears to be

---

1 Read this first: **https://corporatefinanceinstitute.com/resources/valuation/internal-rate-return-irr/**
This second: **https://corporatefinanceinstitute.com/resources/excel/xirr-function/**

operating at a loss. However, as the product gains traction and customer acquisition costs decline, revenue begins to outpace expenses, leading to exponential growth.

The J-curve underscores the importance of patience and strategic investment. For digital PMs, understanding this curve is essential for setting expectations with stakeholders. Growth takes time, and short-term setbacks are often part of the journey toward long-term profitability.

Aftermarket strategy

While initial product sales drive revenue, the aftermarket presents a massive opportunity for sustained growth. The aftermarket refers to services, add-ons, and complementary products offered after the initial purchase. For digital products, this could include software updates, premium subscriptions, or integrations with other tools. Let us revisit the automotive industry as an example. Thirty years ago, car manufacturers focused primarily on selling vehicles. Today, aftermarket services, like software-controlled features, maintenance plans, and in-car subscriptions, are a significant revenue stream. *Tesla* exemplifies this shift by offering over-the-air software updates, unlocking new features for customers without requiring a physical visit to a dealership.

The aftermarket thrives because it targets an existing customer base, a captured audience. Customers who have already purchased a product are more likely to engage with related services, creating stickiness and driving recurring revenue. From a business perspective, aftermarket margins are often double those of initial product sales. Services like subscription renewals, premium support, or personalized features can significantly boost profitability without the high costs of acquiring new customers.

Digital transformation has revolutionized the aftermarket landscape. For every percentage point of growth in digital services, the growth rate increases exponentially. Take the example of *Ring's security systems*, which started as a video doorbell and evolved into a full-fledged security ecosystem. Customers now subscribe to 24/7 monitoring, cloud storage for video footage, and advanced AI-driven alerts. The key to aftermarket success lies in continuous value delivery. Digital PMs must ensure their products evolve over time, meeting new user needs and leveraging emerging technologies. For instance, *Amazon's Subscribe and Save* program uses data to predict when customers will need refills of household items. This recurring model not only enhances convenience for customers but also ensures steady revenue for Amazon.

Knowing when to pivot

Knowing when to pivot to a new business model is a skill that sets great PMs apart. If disruptive startups begin attracting your customers, increased competition shrinks your margins, or customer behaviors shift dramatically, it may be time to rethink your approach. Take Netflix, for example. Originally a mail-order DVD rental service, Netflix pivoted to a subscription-based streaming platform when it recognized the growing demand for on-demand digital content. By staying ahead of technological and behavioral trends, Netflix disrupted itself before competitors could.

As a PM, continuously monitor market trends, analyze customer data, and evaluate your product's performance. A data-driven approach ensures you are not caught off guard when it is time to pivot or innovate.

Product lifecycle and pricing strategies

To effectively implement after-market solutions, PMs must understand how pricing evolves throughout the product lifecycle. What is typically observed in the market is that when a product is introduced, the pricing has to be competitive for it to be recognized and for the sales to grow. Once its value is better understood by the consumers, the product then enjoys higher sales as it gains market share. In this period, the pricing can be higher as well, to improve the profit margin. As the product ages, the sales start to plateau and eventually reduce. While this cycle is not always hundred percent true, it is the typical pattern of any new product introduction.

Product pricing is not static; it evolves alongside the product itself. As a product progresses through its lifecycle, from introduction to eventual decline, pricing strategies must adapt to reflect changes in market demand, competition, and consumer behavior. Each phase of the lifecycle presents unique challenges and opportunities that require thoughtful pricing decisions to maximize value, drive adoption, and sustain profitability. The following list outlines how pricing approaches shift across four key stages, i.e., introduction, growth, maturity, and decline:

- **Market introduction phase:** When a product enters the market, the focus is on creating awareness and driving adoption. At this stage, companies often use cost-plus pricing or skimming, targeting early adopters willing to pay a premium for innovation. For example, Apple often launches its newest iPhone models at a high price to capitalize on early demand.

- **Market growth phase:** As the product gains traction, differentiation becomes critical. Companies emphasize value-based pricing and focus on building brand loyalty. Consider how premium features in SaaS platforms, like *Figma* or *Zoom*, attract businesses willing to pay for added functionality while maintaining competitive value.

- **Market maturity phase:** In mature markets, differentiation shrinks, and competitors flood the space. Pricing strategies shift to include discounting or bundling to maintain market share. For example, in cloud computing, platforms like AWS and Microsoft Azure often reduce prices or offer bundled services to retain customers and optimize consumption.

- **Sales decline phase:** When a product nears the end of its lifecycle, strategies focus on cost-cutting and value extraction. Discounts, loyalty incentives, or aftermarket services help extend the product's relevance. Take security software platforms that provide legacy support, ensuring businesses can continue to operate efficiently while transitioning to newer tools.

The importance of aftermarket service

The importance of the aftermarket extends well beyond profitability. First, the margins in aftermarket services are typically double those of initial product sales. Unlike new customer acquisition, the cost to engage and serve existing customers is significantly lower, making the aftermarket an efficient channel for growth. Additionally, aftermarket services set the stage for recurring revenue. Offering subscription-based upgrades, support plans, or new digital features encourages ongoing customer engagement. For instance, Amazon's Subscribe and Save model incentivizes repeat purchases, creating stickiness through convenience and cost savings. It saves customers money and time, while Amazon locks in predictable, repeat business. This program has been instrumental in creating stickiness; customers are more likely to remain loyal because the convenience is hard to replicate elsewhere.

Competitors like *Walmart* have taken note of this success and responded with their *Walmart+* program, which takes a slightly different approach but with similar goals. Walmart+ combines convenience with added value for customers. While *Amazon Prime* offers exclusive benefits like *Prime Video* for its subscribers, Walmart+ counters with its own entertainment perk: Access to *Paramount+* streaming services. This integration mirrors Amazon's strategy of bundling entertainment alongside its core retail offering, enhancing the value proposition of the subscription. However, Walmart adds another layer of differentiation by offering fuel discounts at *ExxonMobil, Murphy USA,* and *Walmart gas stations*. For frequent drivers, these savings can make a significant impact, providing tangible benefits that extend beyond digital content or retail shopping.

These competitive dynamic highlights an important lesson for PMs: Aftermarket services are not just about locking customers into recurring transactions; they are about creating comprehensive value that touches multiple aspects of a customer's life. Amazon succeeded by bundling retail savings with entertainment, and Walmart quickly recognized an opportunity to combine those strengths with real-world benefits like fuel savings.

This reveals that the aftermarket strategy works best when it is thoughtfully designed to meet customers where they are. It is not just about offering upgrades or subscriptions; it is about understanding how you can embed your product or service into the customer's daily habits and routines. Whether that means saving them money, time, or offering added value, aftermarket strategies like Subscribe and Save or Walmart+ succeed because they integrate deeply into customer lifestyles, making the decision to stay loyal an easy one.

The takeaway here is that recurring revenue and aftermarket success are not driven by the product alone. The surrounding ecosystem, the convenience it delivers, and the unique value-adds you offer can make all the difference. Whether adding a streaming service, loyalty benefits, or cost-saving incentives, aftermarket strategies must align with customer priorities to deliver real, sustained impact.

Digital impact on aftermarket growth

With technology enabling real-time feedback, predictive analytics, and remote monitoring, businesses can now provide aftermarket services that are smarter, faster, and more impactful. For example, in the industrial equipment sector, companies use **Internet of Things (IoT)** enabled sensors to monitor machinery performance. Predictive maintenance models analyze usage patterns and alert customers to potential issues before they escalate. This not only reduces downtime for customers but also opens a steady revenue stream for businesses through subscription-based maintenance services.

The same principles apply in product management, for instance, *Adobe Creative Cloud* transitioned its traditional licensing model to a cloud-based subscription, where software updates, feature enhancements, and troubleshooting support are delivered seamlessly. This ensures continuous engagement, recurring revenue, and improved customer satisfaction.

For every 1% increase in digital services, companies often see a 5% to 10% improvement in growth rates. By leveraging digital tools, PMs can unlock aftermarket opportunities that scale rapidly without significant manual intervention.

Pitching to venture capitalists

For digital PMs, pitching to **venture capitalists (VCs)** often becomes a defining moment in a product's journey. Whether launching a new product or scaling an existing one, a strong pitch can open the door to critical funding, partnerships, and long-term growth, it is not just a presentation, it is a chance to bring a vision to life, backed by the right financial support. A successful pitch does more than explain a product's features. It tells a compelling story about why the product matters, the problem it solves, the long-term strategic vision, and why the team behind it is best positioned to succeed. VCs are looking for ideas that are bold, scalable, and financially sound, but they also want to believe in the people executing them.

The reality is that most investors hear hundreds of pitches each month. Many ideas get lost simply because they were not delivered clearly or confidently enough. This is why how a pitch is delivered is just as important as what is being pitched. A good pitch grabs attention early, builds trust, and shows that the team not only understands the market but knows how to win in it.

PMs, in particular, need to showcase more than the product's potential. They need to show they have done the work, validated the market, built a thoughtful business model, and planned for scale. VCs want to see evidence: Traction, user interest, maybe even early revenue. However, more than anything, they want to know how the team can execute and adapt. It is worth noting that pitch meetings are usually brief, often no more than 10 or 15 minutes. That is not a lot of time to make a strong impression. Every slide, every word, and every moment counts. A solid pitch builds momentum, and for many PMs, it becomes the turning point that takes an idea from prototype to reality.

The importance of a great pitch

A well-prepared pitch can be transformative. It not only secures funding but also builds relationships, opens doors to strategic partnerships, and sets the stage for future opportunities. VCs are not just giving you money; they are buying into your vision and your team. A great pitch communicates that you have done your homework, validated your market, and thought through the challenges and opportunities ahead. It reflects not only the product's potential but also your leadership and ability to navigate complexity.

To deliver a winning pitch, clarity is key. Investors do not want to sift through jargon, unclear value propositions, or unproven claims. They want to see a well-structured narrative that includes the problem, the solution, the market opportunity, the competitive landscape, the financial projections, and, most importantly, the ROI. VCs are fundamentally driven by profitability and growth, so your pitch must demonstrate both short-term viability and long-term scalability.

The mindset behind a successful pitch

Before crafting your pitch, put yourself in the VC's shoes. They are not just investing in ideas; they are investing in returns. Every VC firm operates under pressure to deliver exceptional returns to its investors, which means they are searching for opportunities that offer substantial upside. For them, risk is inevitable, but the reward must be significant enough to justify the gamble.

This is why scalability is such a critical factor. Your pitch needs to communicate that your product is not just a good idea, it is a big idea that can capture market share, drive revenue, and grow exponentially. If you are working on a digital product, highlight its ability to scale quickly and efficiently, leveraging technology to expand its user base, reduce costs, and generate repeatable revenue. Investors want to see evidence of traction, such as early adopters, pilot results, or projections based on validated assumptions.

Let us look at the following example of an unsuccessful pitch:

We have built a really cool app that people are going to love. It is like Uber but for pets. There is nothing else like it, and we believe the market is huge. We have not done much testing yet, but we are confident it will go viral once we launch. We are looking for funding to hire more developers and maybe spend a bit on ads.

The aforementioned pitch does not work for the following reasons:

- Vague problem statement
- No market validation or data

- Lacks financial clarity
- Does not communicate why the team is capable
- No clear business model

Consider the following example of a successful pitch:

PawPorter is solving a growing challenge faced by over 20 million urban pet owners in the *United States*, access to safe, reliable pet transportation. Our mobile-first platform connects pet parents with verified, trained transport providers for vet visits, grooming appointments, and daycare drop-offs, eliminating missed appointments and improving overall pet care logistics. In a three month pilot across *NYC, Austin*, and *San Diego*, we completed 12,000 rides, achieved a 94% repeat booking rate, and helped reduce no-show rates by 32% for our clinic partners. Our North Star Metric is monthly completed rides, currently at 4,800 and growing 28% **month on month** (**MoM**). This early traction confirms product market fit and operational scalability.

The **total addressable market** (**TAM**) for pet mobility and adjacent services (like mobile grooming and pet supply delivery) exceeds $1.8 billion in the U.S., with untapped international potential. Our go-to-market strategy focuses on clinic partnerships, affiliate programs, and pet care influencers, offering both organic and scalable acquisition channels. We operate on a freemium model, monetizing through a 15% transaction fee and tiered monthly subscriptions for high-frequency users, such as multi-pet households and professional pet sitters.

We are now raising $1.2 million in seed funding to expand our team, optimize routing and dispatch technology, and launch in ten new metro markets over the next six months. Our founding team brings deep domain expertise, the former Uber logistics lead and a senior product leader from *Chewy*, and we are uniquely positioned to define and own the pet mobility-as-a-service category.

This is not just about transportation; it is about creating a seamless ecosystem for pet logistics, enhancing care access while building the infrastructure for a new vertical in the pet economy.

This pitch works due to the following reasons:

- **Clear value proposition:** Simple problem-solution framing with relevance to urban pet owners
- **Validated traction:** Hard metrics from a real pilot, not assumptions
- **Growth signals:** MoM growth, high retention, clinic impact
- **Market potential:** Large TAM and whitespace opportunity
- **Business model:** Freemium and transactional revenue
- **Execution readiness:** Go-to-market plan and an experienced founding team
- **Strategic vision:** Positioning PawPorter as a category leader

Template for pitching

To successfully capture the attention of investors, PMs must be able to tell a compelling, data-backed story in just a few minutes. A well-structured pitch clearly articulates the problem, solution, traction, and potential upside, while also demonstrating why your team is best suited to execute. The following template provides a practical framework that PMs or anyone pitching can customize to fit their product and stage, ensuring no critical element is missed during a pitch presentation:

- **Opening problem statement:** Clearly state the problem you are solving. *Why does it matter? Who is experiencing it?*

  We are solving a growing problem for [X million or billion users or customers] [clear, relatable problem]. Today, [brief context: what the audience does now and why it is broken].

- **Solution and product:** Introduce your product and how it solves the problem uniquely.

  Our product, [product name], is a [describe type of product: on-demand platform, SaaS, or marketplace, etc.] that enables [target audience] to [core value proposition or function]. It delivers [primary benefit] while removing the friction of [specific challenge].

- **Pilot or early traction:** Showcase evidence that your idea works.

  In a [duration] pilot across [markets or regions], we achieved [key usage or engagement metrics], such as [repeat rate, growth %, user satisfaction, etc.]. Based on this traction, our North Star Metric is [metric name], which currently stands at [value] and is growing at [MoM or **quarter over quarter** (QoQ) rate].

- **Market opportunity:** Define your TAM and the revenue potential.

  The TAM for [category or industry] is [$X billion] in [region or globally], with significant adjacent potential in [related categories or verticals].

- **Business model:** Explain how you make money and what drives growth.

  We use a [freemium, subscription, commission, or usage-based] model, generating revenue from [customers or transactions]. We also plan to expand into [future monetization avenues].

- **Go-to-market strategy:** Describe how you will acquire customers.

  We plan to expand to [X new markets] over the next [timeframe], leveraging [channels like B2B partnerships, influencers, organic growth, paid acquisition]. Our business model combines [e.g., transaction fees, subscriptions, SaaS pricing], designed for scalability and user retention.

- **The ask and funding:** Specify how much funding you are raising and what it will be used for.

We are raising [$X] to support [team hiring, product development, go-to-market execution, etc.]. Our team includes leadership experience from [companies, sectors, or relevant domain expertise], positioning us to execute at scale.

- **Vision or closing hook:** Provide your product tagline or closing statement.

    This is not just about [product category], it is about [broader mission or future category creation]. We are building the future of [industry transformation], and this is just the beginning.

Things to avoid in a pitch

One of the fastest ways to lose a VC's interest is by making the pitch unnecessarily complex. Overly technical explanations, dense jargon, or unclear messaging can distract from the core value of the product. Investors may not be familiar with the finer details of the underlying technology, and they should not have to work to understand the problem being solved. A strong pitch keeps the focus on the end user and the value being delivered. A useful test is to present the pitch to someone outside the industry, such as a family member. If they struggle to understand it, the pitch likely needs simplification.

Beyond clarity, a common pitfall is failing to clearly articulate the product's value proposition or underestimating the competitive landscape. Investors expect to see that the team has done its homework. Claiming that a product has no competition is often seen as a red flag, as it signals either a lack of market understanding or naivety. Instead, founders should acknowledge existing alternatives and emphasize how their solution is uniquely positioned, whether through differentiated technology, a more scalable business model, or superior UX.

Another frequent mistake is overpromising on projections. While ambition is important, exaggerated forecasts can damage credibility. Investors are drawn to confident, data-driven plans that strike the right balance between aspiration and realism. Transparency about potential risks, along with a plan to mitigate them, signals maturity and preparedness. Founders who combine optimism with thoughtful risk management build stronger trust with potential investors.

Storytelling also plays a crucial role in a pitch. A pitch is not just about presenting slides or numbers; it is about crafting a narrative that resonates emotionally. Investors need to see the passion behind the idea and understand the why that drives the team. Real-world anecdotes, testimonials, or pilot success stories make the pitch relatable, human, and memorable. It is this emotional connection, paired with rational validation, that often turns interest into investment.

Pitching to VCs is a skill that can be developed with preparation and practice. The most compelling pitches balance vision with validation; they inspire belief while grounding ambition in evidence. For digital PMs, it is an opportunity not just to showcase the product but also to demonstrate leadership, critical thinking, and readiness to execute.

Ultimately, a pitch is not just a plea for capital; it is the opening of a partnership. When done well, it communicates that the team has a sound strategy, understands the market deeply, and has the discipline to turn an idea into a scalable business. Clarity, authenticity, and adaptability are key to leaving a lasting impression.

In contrast to vague or overly technical pitches, consider the clarity and depth in PawPorter's approach. Rather than overwhelming investors with features, the pitch focuses on a real, growing need: reliable pet transportation for 20 million urban pet owners in the U.S. backed by a three month pilot across key cities with measurable results: 12,000 rides, 94% repeat bookings, and a 32% reduction in no-show clinic appointments, PawPorter demonstrates traction. The pitch also clearly states its North Star Metric (monthly completed rides), outlines its addressable market ($1.8 billion), and presents a thoughtful go-to-market and monetization strategy. Importantly, it closes by highlighting the team's experience in logistics and pet tech, reinforcing their capability to deliver on this vision. This blend of storytelling, data, and clarity is what sets apart a strong pitch from the rest.

Next focus for PMs

A PM's role is inherently dynamic, demanding the ability to juggle multiple priorities while anticipating future developments. In an era defined by rapid digitization and the rise of AI, staying ahead of the curve is no longer optional; it is essential. While delivering immediate value remains a key responsibility, looking toward the future ensures readiness to navigate shifting market conditions, adopt emerging technologies, and address evolving customer needs. This raises a critical question: *Which focus areas should PMs prioritize to ensure long-term product success?* The following list outlines some recommendations where PMs can invest their time and focus:

- **Emerging technologies and trends:** The pace of technological advancement is accelerating rapidly, making it essential for PMs to remain informed and adaptable. Emerging technologies, such as AI, **machine learning (ML)**, blockchain, **augmented reality (AR)**, and **virtual reality (VR)**, have moved beyond industry jargon. They now serve as powerful tools for building smarter, faster, and more innovative products. **Generative AI (GenAI)**, in particular, is reshaping multiple facets of digital product development, from automating customer support through AI-driven chatbots to streamlining product design with AI-assisted prototyping. Understanding where these technologies intersect with a product's functionality can uncover new opportunities to enhance UX, improve operational efficiency, and deliver greater value.

  For example, AI-powered analytics can help product teams decode user behavior and prioritize features more effectively, while the IoT enables real-time data collection from connected devices, offering insights that can inform more responsive and personalized experiences. By actively exploring and integrating such technologies, PMs can ensure their offerings remain competitive and future-ready.

- **Customer centric innovation:** In the pursuit of technological advancement, it is essential not to lose sight of the CX. The most effective PMs remain steadfast in their focus on solving real user problems and consistently delivering meaningful value. As personalization and user-centered design continue to shape modern digital products, placing customers at the heart of every decision has become a distinguishing factor in product success.

  To stay ahead, PMs must proactively identify emerging pain points and anticipate evolving user needs. This involves conducting regular user interviews, analyzing behavioral data, and systematically gathering feedback. These insights ensure that the product roadmap is not only reactive but also forward-looking. Tools such as NPS and **customer effort score (CES)** can further aid in measuring satisfaction and identifying areas for refinement, enabling continuous improvement and deeper customer connection.

- **The rise of super apps:** Super apps are reshaping markets by consolidating multiple services into a unified digital experience. For digital PMs, this trend presents a compelling opportunity to broaden their product's value proposition by addressing adjacent user needs. A strategic focus on ecosystem building becomes essential, which involves identifying areas where the product can expand, such as integrating features like digital payments, subscriptions, or e-commerce functionality.

  In doing so, PMs should also consider how strategic partnerships with third-party providers can enhance platform capabilities and increase user stickiness. For example, a productivity application might incorporate embedded video conferencing or project management tools to provide a more comprehensive solution and grow its user base. By proactively identifying such opportunities, product teams can scale their offerings beyond core functionalities and deliver a seamless, end-to-end experience that supports long-term user engagement and platform growth.

- **Sustainability and social responsibility:** Today's consumers demand more than great products; they expect companies to embrace sustainability and social impact. PMs have the power to make their products part of the solution by prioritizing sustainable development, reducing resource consumption, and addressing environmental concerns. Whether through eco-friendly packaging, energy-efficient systems, or fair labor practices, integrating sustainability into product strategy can boost customer loyalty and align with evolving global priorities.

  Brands such as Tesla have revolutionized electric vehicles, while companies like *Patagonia* demonstrate responsible manufacturing practices. These examples illustrate that sustainability is not merely a buzzword; it provides a genuine competitive advantage.

- **Leveraging data-driven decision-making:** Living in a data-rich world, and the ability to harness data, will define the success of a PM. As a PM, having focus on building a robust framework for data-driven decision-making and understanding which metrics matter most to the product, whether it is **monthly active users (MAUs)**, retention rates, or **customer lifetime value (CLV)** and using analytics to guide everything from feature prioritization to pricing strategy is not optional any more it is a core basic necessity.

Implementation of tools like *Google Analytics*, *Amplitude*, or *Mixpanel* can help to effectively track product usage and user journeys. Additionally, considering adopting predictive analytics to uncover patterns, forecast trends, for making smarter decisions on future strategic roadmaps will help in reinventing the scope of future deliverables.

- **PLG: Product-led growth (PLG)** is emerging as one of the most powerful strategies in digital markets. It focuses on using the product itself to drive acquisition, retention, and expansion. Successful PLG companies, like *Slack*, *Zoom*, and *Figma*, create products so intuitive and valuable that users become their best advocates. To embrace PLG, focus on improving onboarding experiences, removing friction points, and creating aha moments that showcase value immediately. Encourage viral growth by building shareable features, free trials, or freemium models that allow users to experience your product before committing.

- **Mastering go-to-market strategies:** Once the product is ready, a strong go-to-market strategy ensures it reaches the right audience and achieves rapid adoption. Aligning marketing, sales, and product teams to convey a cohesive story about the product's value is essential. Positioning and messaging should be refined to resonate deeply with customer pain points.

  Effective go-to-market strategies also require the ability to pivot based on market feedback. Whether entering a new market, launching a super app, or scaling within an exponential market, agility and alignment across teams are critical to sustained success.

- **Futureproofing with adaptability:** Finally, one of the most vital skills a PM must master is adaptability. As markets shift, technologies evolve, and customer behaviors change, PMs must remain flexible. A product that performs well today might require significant improvements tomorrow. Recognizing opportunities for pivots or innovations, and having the courage to execute them, can future-proof both products and careers.

  PMs should continuously monitor emerging trends, stay alert to disruptive competitors, and consistently ask *what is next?* Their ability to adapt, innovate, and embrace change will ensure their products remain ahead of the curve.

Exploring the future

As a PM, staying informed about emerging trends and technologies is critical to driving long-term growth and positioning your products for the future. Based on the current progress, the key areas you could focus on are responsible AI, the metaverse, edge computing, smart spaces, and the importance of ethical AI and tokenization. The technology is changing rapidly, and areas of focus should be periodically reviewed by the PM.

The following list highlights some of the key considerations for PMs responsible for building digital solutions:

- **Responsible AI for balancing innovation and accountability:** AI has become an essential driver of innovation across industries. From recommendation engines and predictive analytics to **natural language processing** (**NLP**) tools, like *ChatGPT*, AI enhances efficiency, decision-making, and UXs. However, with great power comes great responsibility. Responsible AI emphasizes ensuring that AI systems are ethical, transparent, and fair.

  For example, consider AI used in loan approvals or job recruitment systems. If the algorithms are trained on biased datasets, they can unfairly discriminate against specific demographics. Responsible AI focuses on mitigating such risks by introducing measures like bias detection, explainability, and continuous monitoring to ensure fairness and accountability.

  As a PM, incorporating responsible AI principles means working closely with data scientists, engineers, and ethicists to address the following issues:

  - **Data privacy:** Protecting user data and ensuring compliance with the following laws:

    - The *General Data Protection Regulation* (*GDPR*) is a legal framework that sets guidelines for the collection, processing, and storage of personal data of individuals within the *European Union* (*EU*) and the *European Economic Area* (*EEA*). Enforced on May 25, 2018, GDPR aims to protect user privacy and empower individuals to have greater control over how their personal information is used.

    - *California* has robust consumer data protection laws, including the *California Consumer Privacy Act* (*CCPA*) and its amendment, the *California Privacy Rights Act* (*CPRA*). These laws grant consumers rights to access, delete, and opt out of the sale of their personal data while requiring businesses to be transparent about data collection and usage. Additionally, laws like *California Online Privacy Protection Act* (*CalOPPA*) mandate privacy policies, and the *data breach notification law* requires timely disclosure of data breaches.

- **Bias and fairness:** Identifying and removing algorithmic bias to create inclusive solutions.

- **Transparency:** Making AI decisions interpretable and understandable to stakeholders.

  For example, companies like *Microsoft* have established AI principles to guide ethical AI use, ensuring their products align with fairness and privacy guidelines. By embracing responsible AI, you enhance trust, reduce risks, and create products that positively impact society.

- **The metaverse for a new era of immersive experiences:** The metaverse is no longer science fiction; it is a rapidly emerging digital frontier. Defined as a virtual space where people interact, work, play, and transact in immersive 3D environments, the metaverse holds transformative potential for businesses. Major players like *Meta* (formerly *Facebook*), *Microsoft*, and *Epic Games* are heavily investing in this space, making it critical for PMs to understand its implications.

  The metaverse combines technologies, like VR, AR, blockchain, and digital twins, to create seamless, interactive environments. Consider the following examples:

  o **Retail:** Virtual shopping experiences allow customers to browse and purchase products in immersive environments. Brands like *Nike* and *Gucci* are already creating metaverse stores to engage customers.

  o **Workplaces:** Remote collaboration tools like *Microsoft Mesh* enable teams to work in virtual spaces, improving engagement and productivity.

  o **Entertainment:** Platforms like *Fortnite* are evolving into social spaces where users attend virtual concerts and events, generating new revenue streams.

  For PMs like you, understanding the metaverse opens opportunities to design products that integrate with these immersive ecosystems. Whether it is enhancing virtual CXs or building tools that support the next generation of digital collaboration, the metaverse will shape the future of engagement.

- **Edge computing for faster, smarter, and more efficient analysis:** While cloud computing remains dominant, edge computing is gaining momentum as data generation increases. Edge computing involves processing data closer to its source, reducing latency, enhancing real-time analytics, and improving operational efficiency.

  Imagine a self-driving car analyzing traffic data in real-time; it cannot afford the latency caused by sending information back to a distant cloud server. Instead, edge computing enables faster decision-making by processing data locally on the vehicle.

  Key applications of edge computing are as follows:

  o **IoT devices**: Smart home devices and sensors that rely on real-time processing.

  o **Healthcare**: Wearable devices that monitor vitals and alert doctors to potential health risks instantly.

  o **Industrial automation**: Edge systems optimize machinery performance and reduce downtime in manufacturing.

  Edge computing offers an opportunity to build real-time, data-driven products that deliver unparalleled performance. It also complements IoT systems, creating intelligent ecosystems where devices communicate seamlessly with minimal delays.

- **Smart spaces for integrating technology into physical environments:** Smart spaces refer to environments where physical and digital systems seamlessly converge to enhance UXs. These spaces leverage IoT, AI, and edge computing to create interactive and optimized environments across industries.

  Some examples are as follows:

  o **Smart cities:** Integrated systems monitor traffic, energy consumption, and waste management to improve urban living. Cities like *Singapore* use IoT sensors and AI to reduce traffic congestion and enhance safety.

  o **Smart homes:** Platforms like *Amazon Alexa* and *Google Nest* integrate lighting, security, and entertainment, creating personalized home experiences.

  o **Workplaces:** Smart offices use sensors and AI to optimize space utilization, monitor energy consumption, and enhance employee productivity.

  You can leverage smart spaces to design products that integrate with these environments, focusing on user personalization, automation, and connectivity. Whether it is smart lighting systems or enterprise-level workspace tools, the demand for integrated digital ecosystems is growing rapidly.

- **Ethical AI for building trust through fair technology:** While AI brings tremendous value, its adoption raises concerns about ethics and unintended consequences. Ethical AI ensures that AI technologies align with principles of human rights, accountability, and fairness. As a PM, embedding ethical AI into your development process involves the following:

  o **Transparency:** Ensuring users understand how decisions are made by AI models.

  o **Accountability:** Defining processes to address AI errors and unintended impacts.

  o **Inclusivity:** Avoiding biased data that could marginalize specific user groups.

  For example, *IBM Watson* actively promotes ethical AI by focusing on fairness and transparency in its healthcare diagnostics tools. Implementing ethical AI not only reduces risks but also builds long-term trust with customers and regulators.

- **Tokenization for unlocking value with digital assets:** Tokenization refers to converting real-world assets, like real estate, art, or commodities, into digital tokens stored on a blockchain. These tokens can be securely transferred, divided, or traded, enabling greater accessibility and liquidity.

  Tokenization creates opportunities for businesses to do the following:

  o **Democratize ownership:** By splitting assets into digital tokens, even small investors can access high-value assets like real estate.

  o **Enhance transparency:** Blockchain ensures every transaction is traceable and secure.

    o   **Drive innovation**: Tokenized loyalty points, digital rewards, or in-app currencies can improve customer engagement.

For instance, real estate platforms now allow fractional ownership through blockchain-based tokens. PMs can explore tokenization to create new monetization models, streamline payments, or build customer centric reward systems. As a PM, the future holds immense opportunities to lead with innovation, responsibility, and strategic vision.

The top three key takeaways are as follows:

- **Stay curious:** Explore how emerging technologies like AI, the metaverse, edge computing, and tokenization can unlock value for your product.
- **Focus on ethics:** Build products responsibly, ensuring transparency, fairness, and inclusiveness.
- **Lead with innovation:** Future-proof your products by embracing new technologies and creating seamless, user-focused ecosystems.

By keeping a pulse on these trends and fostering a growth mindset, you will position yourself and your product to thrive in an increasingly digital and interconnected world. The tools are already here; it is your job to decide how to use them to create meaningful, lasting value.

Conclusion

A well-executed product sales strategy is essential for turning innovative products into sustainable business successes. It involves carefully selecting and optimizing the right business models, leveraging scalable solutions, such as cloud computing, and strategically evaluating financial metrics like ROI to ensure profitability and growth. PMs must stay vigilant, recognizing the critical moments that call for pivots or adaptations in their sales approach. Ultimately, mastering the elements outlined in this chapter, including aftermarket services, go-to-market alignment, and adaptability, positions PMs to not only meet immediate market demands but also anticipate future shifts, securing long-term competitive advantage.

In the next and final chapter, readers will explore additional critical skills PMs must develop, such as project management, negotiation, managing without direct authority, navigating legal discussions, and reviewing contracts, all of which are essential for holistic success in product management roles.

Points to remember

- A robust product sales strategy bridges product development and market success, driving sustainable revenue and customer engagement.

- Business models are fundamental to understanding how a product creates and delivers value. There are eight core models: Sell a thing, rent a thing, take a cut, charge a subscription, charge based on usage, sell a service, advertising, and percentage of assets.

- Cloud computing accelerates product innovation and growth through scalable infrastructure and strategic partnerships, including channel, service, platform, and function partners.

- Businesses should monitor signs like rising competition, consumer behavior changes, and declining margins to evaluate the need for a new business model.

- ROI and annualized ROI are key metrics for measuring product and strategy success, though ROI has limitations in reflecting cash flow and intangible benefits.

- The J-curve visualizes how investments initially dip in profitability before achieving exponential growth, requiring patience and strategic vision.

- Aftermarket strategies, like subscriptions or upgrades, generate recurring revenue and deepen customer loyalty, with margins often higher than initial product sales.

- Walmart+ and Amazon's Subscribe and Save highlight how aftermarket strategies can integrate convenience, digital content, and real-world benefits.

- A compelling pitch to VCs combines a clear problem-solution narrative, scalability, traction, and realistic ROI projections while avoiding overpromising or a lack of preparation.

- Slack's successful pitch focused on rapid user adoption, seamless integrations, and freemium-to-paid growth to secure exponential investment.

Multiple choice questions

1. **What is the primary goal of a product sales strategy?**

    a. To create viral marketing campaigns

    b. To ensure product visibility through SEO only

    c. To drive revenue, build sustainable customer engagement, and effectively position the product

    d. To reduce production costs at scale

2. **How does the take a cut business model work?**

    a. By charging a subscription fee to buyers and sellers separately

    b. By manufacturing and selling products directly to customers

    c. By acting as an intermediary and earning a commission on each transaction

    d. By offering free products and monetizing through ads

3. **What role does cloud computing play in scaling digital products?**

    a. It reduces customer acquisition costs through social media

    b. It provides physical retail spaces for digital products

    c. It enables scalability, flexibility, cost savings, and accelerates innovation by offering infrastructure over the internet

    d. It eliminates the need for user feedback

4. **Which option correctly matches the cloud computing models with their purpose?**

    a. SaaS: Hardware as a service | PaaS: Cloud storage | IaaS: Application deployment | FaaS: Streaming service

    b. SaaS: Software on subscription | PaaS: Platforms for app development | IaaS: Virtual infrastructure | FaaS: Serverless computing triggered by events

    c. SaaS: Pay-per-click ads | PaaS: Digital marketing | IaaS: Server manufacturing | FaaS: Video conferencing

    d. SaaS: Data warehouses | PaaS: Transportation logistics | IaaS: Insurance platforms | FaaS: Fitness apps

5. **What are key signs that a business might need to pivot to a new business model?**

    a. When profits are at an all-time high

    b. When competition is increasing, margins are shrinking, consumer behavior shifts, regulatory disruptions occur, or there is a proactive push for innovation

    c. When marketing campaigns fail after one attempt

    d. When a company's branding colors need refreshing

6. **What is ROI, and why is annualized ROI considered more insightful?**

    a. ROI is revenue divided by expenses; annualized ROI accounts for inflation rates.

    b. ROI is *(money gained – money spent) / money spent × 100*; annualized ROI measures profitability over time and better reflects long-term trends and viability.

    c. ROI tracks marketing performance; annualized ROI measures server uptime.

    d. ROI is calculated only by customer feedback; annualized ROI measures brand loyalty.

7. **How does the J-Curve illustrate the growth of a new product or investment?**

    a. It shows immediate exponential growth after launch

    b. It depicts slow and steady growth from day one

    c. It shows initial losses followed by exponential growth as adoption increases and efficiencies improve

    d. It reflects seasonal market fluctuations only

8. **Why are aftermarket services often more profitable than initial product sales?**

    a. They require heavy marketing investments upfront

    b. They generate recurring revenues from an already engaged customer base with typically higher margins

    c. They increase warehouse storage needs

    d. They help companies reduce their innovation cycles

9. **How do Amazon's Subscribe and Save and Walmart+ create customer stickiness through aftermarket strategies?**

    a. By offering product personalization for free

    b. By locking in recurring purchases through savings and bundling digital and real-world benefits

    c. By increasing prices slowly over time

    d. By offering one-time flash sales only

10. **What are key elements of a strong pitch to VCs, and what mistakes should PMs avoid?**

    a. Focus solely on product features without mentioning the market opportunity

    b. Clearly articulate the problem, solution, market size, business model, and ROI while avoiding complexity, unrealistic projections, poor competition analysis, and scalability gaps

    c. Promise maximum profits in six months without a plan

    d. Highlight internal HR practices over business growth potential

Answers

1	c
2	c
3	c
4	b
5	b
6	b
7	c
8	b
9	b
10	b

CHAPTER 10
Wearing Multiple Hats

Introduction

There is a great quote by *Deep Nishar*, *A great project manager (PM) has the brain of an engineer, the heart of a designer, and the speech of a diplomat.* Product management is thus not for the faint-hearted, as there are multiple hats to be worn. At its core, it involves bringing a vision to life, transforming ideas into products that solve real problems and deliver value to users. However, the reality is that a PM role often extends far beyond the confines of a typical job description. On any given day, a PM acts not only as a strategist but also as a negotiator, project manager, storyteller, and even a diplomat. They constantly shift between roles, adapting to the demands of a fast-paced, cross-functional environment.

This matters because a product's success hinges not just on its features or design, but on how effectively people, processes, and priorities are managed. In the absence of formal authority, a PM's ability to influence stakeholders, rally teams, and align efforts is their greatest asset. Excelling in this role requires a broad and diverse skill set that transcends technical know-how or market insight. It demands navigating organizational complexity, mastering collaboration, and maintaining a clear vision while staying attuned to the details. For anyone hesitant about cross-functional communication or stakeholder management, now is the time to embrace and practice these skills, because they are essential to truly mastering the craft of product management.

Structure

This chapter will cover the following sections:

- Project management basics
- Managing without authority
- Maximizing team utilization
- Managing contracts and legal considerations
- Negotiation
- Stakeholder management
- Art of storytelling

Objectives

This chapter explores the key skills essential for any PM aiming to succeed in a multifaceted role. From project management and effective team utilization to negotiation and stakeholder engagement, each section offers a high-level overview of these competencies and guidance on how to navigate them, even without being an expert in every area. Throughout the chapter, readers will encounter real-world stories, examples, and practical tips designed to help them embrace the challenges and opportunities that come with wearing multiple hats in product management.

Project management basics

The fundamentals of project management and its distinction from product management were covered in an earlier chapter, so this section will focus on a high-level overview of the essential areas PMs should be familiar with. While formal certifications or deep expertise in project management are not necessary, there are many scenarios, particularly in startups or smaller organizations, where a PM may need to step into a dual role due to the absence of a dedicated project or program manager. In such cases, a foundational understanding of project management becomes invaluable.

Project management is the discipline of planning, organizing, and overseeing the execution of tasks to meet specific objectives within defined constraints such as time, scope, and budget. For PMs, this is not just a peripheral skill; it often underpins the successful delivery of ideas. While product management focuses on defining the what and why, project management provides the how and when.

Understanding project management is especially critical in resource-constrained environments. For instance, in smaller teams or budget-limited projects, a PM may need to take charge of coordinating resources, managing timelines, and ensuring the smooth execution of the product roadmap. Without effective project management, even the best product ideas risk stagnation due to miscommunication, delays, or poor resource allocation.

PMs who can apply project management principles are better equipped to navigate cross-functional dynamics, align stakeholders with diverse priorities, and maintain executional momentum. Consider the example of launching a new app feature: the PM must ensure engineering has detailed specs, marketing is aligned on launch timelines, and customer support is prepared for post-release feedback. In such cases, project management is not optional—it is essential for delivering impact.

Core areas of project management

While PMs are not expected to be certified project management professionals, having a strong grasp of key project management principles is essential, especially in environments where roles often overlap or where dedicated project support may be limited or unavailable. Among the many facets of project management, the three core areas stand out as particularly critical for PMs: Time management and scheduling, risk management, and resource allocation. These elements form the foundation of successful execution. They ensure that product initiatives stay on track, adapt to change, and make the most of available resources. In the sections that follow, we will explore each of these areas through practical insights, examples, and strategies tailored to the unique demands of product management:

- **Time management and scheduling:** Time is one of the most limited and valuable resources in any project. For PMs, effective time management involves crafting schedules that strike a balance between speed and quality. Visual planning tools such as Gantt charts and Kanban boards can offer clarity, helping teams stay organized and aligned throughout the development process. Breaking down large initiatives into smaller, manageable milestones allows progress to be tracked more easily while enabling the early identification of potential delays. Some PMs enhance time management by integrating calendar tools directly into platforms like *Confluence*, where product requirement documents are maintained. By creating events with reminders, tagging stakeholders, and consolidating relevant information on a single page, these tools improve transparency and coordination. Even travel dates related to product launches can be added to the calendar, keeping teams informed and allowing for better planning.

  Consider an e-commerce platform preparing to launch a new recommendation engine. In this scenario, the PM must synchronize the efforts of data engineers, frontend developers, and **quality assurance (QA)** testers, ensuring that all components are completed in time for a high-traffic shopping season. Through effective scheduling, the team can avoid last-minute scrambles and capitalize on key business opportunities.

- **Risk management:** Every project carries a degree of uncertainty, but proactive risk management acts as a critical safety net, reducing the likelihood of disruptions and ensuring smoother execution. For PMs, managing risk goes beyond reacting to issues as they arise; it is about foreseeing potential challenges and preparing the team to address them effectively. This process begins with the early identification of risks, whether they originate from resource constraints, technical complexities, or interpersonal conflicts among stakeholders. By recognizing these risks in advance, PMs can implement contingency plans that help maintain project momentum. The following questions are an example of questions a PM should ask on every project, to identify, recognize, and mitigate risks:

- *What is not changing?* These typically are low-risk areas, so they can be lower in priority in risk mitigation, if any.

- *What is changing?* This question helps identify the areas needing change management, and then an appropriate mitigation plan can be crafted.

- *What project areas are at high risk and why?* This helps to be proactive and minimize schedule slippage.

Consider the example of an e-commerce application with a launch scheduled around a major holiday season. A PM might anticipate delays related to regulatory approvals or critical **system security plan (SSP)** testing. Rather than waiting for these obstacles to materialize, the PM initiates parallel workstreams, allowing other components, such as UI design and marketing assets, to progress uninterrupted. This forward-thinking approach ensures that, once the bottleneck is cleared, the team can seamlessly resume integrated development and remain on schedule.

Effective risk management also involves cultivating a culture of adaptability. Scenario planning, where teams explore potential *what-if* situations, helps minimize surprises. In the case of SSP delays, a PM might preemptively line up alternative vendors or allocate additional resources to expedite the process once it begins. Maintaining open lines of communication and conducting regular risk assessments further strengthens team resilience. This proactive mindset not only conserves time and resources but also fosters trust and confidence among stakeholders, essential components for successful product delivery.

- **Resource allocation:** Resource allocation is both a strategic discipline and a creative process, requiring thoughtful alignment of team capabilities, project timelines, and overarching goals. For PMs, this responsibility is particularly nuanced, as they must navigate competing priorities while sustaining team motivation and productivity. Effective resource allocation is not merely about distributing tasks—it involves aligning the right skills, tools, and budgets with key objectives to ensure meaningful progress and measurable outcomes.

Take, for example, an e-commerce application approaching its launch phase. If a delay occurs in securing SSP testing approval, a critical compliance milestone, it does not mean the entire project must come to a standstill. A PM who understands strategic resource allocation will examine the roadmap to identify areas that can progress independently. The **user interface/user experience (UI/UX)** team might focus on refining user flows or enhancing accessibility, while the marketing team can prepare launch campaigns, finalize content, and schedule promotions. Keeping these streams active minimizes downtime and enables the team to swiftly regain momentum once the approvals come through. Optimal resource allocation also involves matching tasks to individual team members' strengths. A senior developer, for instance, might be tasked with optimizing complex backend payment algorithms, while a junior developer works on modular frontend components. This kind of skill-based distribution reduces friction, speeds up development, and boosts overall efficiency.

In cases where internal capacity is limited, PMs may look outward for temporary support. Bringing in a freelance cybersecurity consultant to handle SSP-related issues can help maintain forward motion without overwhelming the in-house team. It is important to recognize that resource allocation is not a one-time event—it is an ongoing effort that adapts to changing conditions. Throughout this process, transparent communication is essential. PMs must clearly articulate how allocation decisions support the broader project goals, and they should make a point to celebrate incremental achievements. Recognizing small wins helps maintain morale and fosters a sense of progress, even amid delays or uncertainty.

Best practices in project management

Delivering successful products requires more than just a great idea—it demands disciplined execution grounded in best practices. For PMs, these practices serve as guiding principles that help navigate complexity, manage uncertainty, and drive alignment across teams. Whether defining clear objectives, making tough prioritization calls, or adopting flexible development frameworks, applying proven methods can significantly improve outcomes. The following section explores three best foundational practices: clear objectives and scope definition, prioritization techniques, and iterative development, which are essential to building products efficiently and effectively in dynamic environments.

Clear objectives and scope definition

Every project begins with defining clear objectives and scope. Vague goals or ambiguous deliverables can lead to scope creep, misaligned priorities, and wasted resources. A PM should establish a shared understanding of what success looks like among all stakeholders. For instance, if a team is building a **minimum viable product** (**MVP**), the PM must define what features are critical for launch and what can be deferred to later iterations.

Prioritization techniques

Not all tasks are equally important. Prioritization frameworks like **must have, should have, could have, will not have** (**MoSCoW**) or the **Eisenhower Matrix** can help teams focus on what truly matters. For PMs, this ensures that limited resources are directed toward high-impact work. Consider a scenario where a customer-facing app has several bugs and a pending feature release. Using prioritization, the PM might decide to fix critical bugs first to improve UX, deferring non-essential features to the next sprint.

Iterative development

Adopting iterative development methodologies, such as Agile, ensures that progress is incremental and that feedback is continuously incorporated. Sprints allow teams to focus on delivering small, tangible outcomes while maintaining flexibility to adapt to new insights.

Managing without authority

Managing without formal authority is one of the most complex and defining aspects of the product management role. Unlike traditional leadership positions, PMs rarely have direct control over the cross-functional teams they depend on; engineering, design, marketing, and sales often report to their own departmental leads, each with distinct priorities and roadmaps. Despite this, the PM remains accountable for driving the product forward, aligning diverse stakeholders, and ensuring successful delivery. The key to succeeding in this environment lies not in hierarchy but in influence, empathy, and strategic communication.

Influence begins with trust and alignment. Effective PMs recognize that most teams are operating under constraints and doing their best to meet their own objectives. Resistance to collaboration is rarely intentional; it often stems from overloaded schedules or misaligned perceptions of urgency. That is why successful PMs consistently focus on communicating the why behind their requests. By placing tasks within the broader context of shared goals, emphasizing how a particular deliverable contributes to the success of the product, the team, and the company, they foster greater understanding and buy-in. Involving stakeholders early in the product lifecycle is another proven strategy. When PMs engage cross-functional partners during the discovery phase, even if their involvement is not needed until much later, it creates a sense of ownership and shared responsibility. Early collaboration not only builds rapport but also helps surface potential constraints, making it easier to plan effectively and avoid last-minute bottlenecks.

Clear, empathetic communication is essential. When requesting support, successful PMs go beyond task lists; they articulate the value of each request and maintain transparency about timelines, trade-offs, and limitations. This approach fosters a sense of partnership rather than control, encouraging teams to contribute because they feel respected, informed, and aligned with the vision.

Flexibility and compromise are also central to managing without authority. Not every request will be met with enthusiasm, and adaptability is key. PMs who offer solutions instead of simply flagging problems tend to create more constructive dialogue. For example, if a team is stretched thin, reframing the conversation around a question like, *what is the least disruptive way we can achieve this together?* shifts the dynamic from tension to collaboration.

Ultimately, managing without authority is about creating a culture where people choose to engage, not because they have to, but because they trust the PM, believe in the vision, and feel like valued contributors. It is a continuous exercise in influence, communication, and relationship-building. The most meaningful moments often emerge when teams rally around a shared objective, without the need for formal mandates—these are the moments where the true impact of product management is felt.

Leading without authority as a PM

PMs operate at the crossroads of engineering, design, marketing, sales, and operations, all while holding little to no formal authority over these teams. Success in this role depends on the ability to build trust, communicate clearly, and align diverse stakeholders around a shared vision. The following best practices outline how PMs can strengthen their influence and drive outcomes in environments where persuasion matters more than position.

Collaborating without authority

Product management is inherently a collaborative function that sits at the intersection of multiple disciplines, each with distinct priorities, goals, and expertise. Without direct authority, PMs face the critical challenge of guiding these cross-functional teams toward a unified product vision. To succeed, they must rely on influence rather than command, and that begins with building credibility, communicating effectively, creating alignment, and managing resistance.

Establishing credibility

Credibility is the foundation of influence. Teams are far more likely to trust and follow a PM who demonstrates expertise, empathy, and consistency. Building credibility involves having deep product knowledge, understanding the product's technical architecture, user pain points, and business value is essential. When PMs can actively engage with engineering challenges or design proposals, they earn the respect of their peers. Following through on commitments builds trust. Delivering promised updates, reports, or decisions on time and with quality reinforces a PM's dependability.

For instance, during the development of a subscription feature for a **software as a service (SaaS)** product, a PM who clearly articulates how the feature boosts user engagement and drives revenue demonstrates strategic alignment, earning the team's confidence and commitment.

Clear communication

Effective communication is a cornerstone of collaboration, and PMs must consistently connect day-to-day decisions to the broader product vision. This involves storytelling and having the ability to use relatable narratives to highlight the why behind initiatives. For example, instead of stating, *we need to improve page load times*, framing it as *a faster page means fewer user drop-offs and better conversion rates* can resonate more strongly across teams.

Additionally, PMs should also be good active listeners, creating space for input and showing genuine attention to team feedback, which fosters a culture of respect and collaboration. Acknowledging different perspectives strengthens relationships and helps surface better solutions.

Creating alignment

Alignment is not about unanimous agreement—it is about shared understanding. Ensuring that all stakeholders know the goals, priorities, and their role in execution is critical. Some of the techniques to do this are through shared metrics; by using KPIs such as user satisfaction, adoption rates, or revenue growth, it provides a unified focus and encourages accountability across functions. Also, it is important to do regular check-ins, through recurring cross-functional meetings promote transparency, resolve blockers, and ensure alignment on progress and next steps.

For example, when launching a new e-commerce feature, a PM might unite the team around a shared goal of reducing cart abandonment by 10%. Engineering focuses on optimizing checkout flows, design improves interface clarity, and marketing tailors messaging, each function contributing toward a collective outcome.

Overcoming resistance

Resistance often stems from misaligned priorities, unclear goals, or a lack of trust. PMs can mitigate this by focusing on relationships and empowerment, by taking time to understand team dynamics and individual motivations, which helps build trust. For instance, a developer who is hesitant about a new framework might be more receptive after understanding how it enhances efficiency or reduces long-term maintenance. Providing autonomy while offering support enables teams to take ownership of their work. Empowered individuals are more engaged, proactive, and collaborative.

Consider a situation where a marketing team resists postponing a campaign for technical improvements. A PM who listens to their concerns, clearly communicates the benefits of the delay, and involves them in the decision-making process is far more likely to gain their buy-in.

Best practices for managing without authority

Managing without authority remains one of the most transformative challenges in the journey of a PM. Early in their career, many PMs come to realize that success does not stem from issuing directives or asserting control, it comes from creating an environment where teams feel supported, heard, and empowered to do their best work. This realization often leads to the adoption of a servant leadership mindset: approaching collaboration not with demands, but with questions like, *what do we need to succeed?*

This shift in perspective fosters openness and collaboration. When PMs position themselves as enablers rather than commanders, trust grows organically. Teams begin to share roadblocks, propose creative ideas, and work together more fluidly, knowing they are operating in a supportive environment. However, trust alone is not always enough to resolve the inevitable disagreements that arise, particularly when team priorities clash. In such moments, data becomes a critical tool. Objective evidence helps depersonalize discussions and bring clarity to complex decisions. Effective PMs ground their requests in solid data, clearly articulating both the value of pursuing a particular course of action and the cost of inaction. When hard data is not available, other credible sources such as customer feedback, user interviews, or usability studies can be used to strengthen the case. Crafting a compelling, evidence-based narrative turns a request into a story stakeholders can understand and rally behind.

Another often-overlooked aspect of managing without authority is the importance of celebrating wins. In the fast-paced world of product development, it is easy to jump from one milestone to the next without acknowledging the effort and collaboration that made success possible. Recognizing team achievements, whether through a quick shoutout or a more structured celebration, not only boosts morale but reinforces a culture of appreciation and shared accomplishment.

At the core of all this lies relationship-building. Investing time in listening, understanding, and genuinely connecting with colleagues yields benefits that no roadmap or metric can replicate. When teams feel seen and valued as individuals, not just as resources, they become more invested in the PM's vision. They contribute more willingly, go the extra mile, and become true partners in the journey.

Maximizing team utilization

Team utilization is one of the most nuanced and strategic aspects of product management. It extends far beyond assigning tasks or keeping individuals busy. Instead, it revolves around understanding each team member's unique strengths and aligning those capabilities with the needs of the project. When done effectively, team utilization transforms a group of professionals into a cohesive, high-performing unit, where each person contributes meaningfully to a streamlined and productive workflow. However, mastering team utilization is far more of an art than a science.

In high-stakes projects with tight timelines, PMs may be tempted to drive all teams at full speed. Yet experience shows that optimal results come not from uniform intensity, but from thoughtful alignment of skills. For example, developers who excel at rapid prototyping can focus on building proofs of concept, while those with a keen eye for detail may be better suited to refining the final product. UX researchers can focus on user interviews, while visual designers craft the required assets. This tailored approach maximizes impact while minimizing burnout—an essential consideration in sustaining team momentum.

Workload management plays a crucial role in team utilization. Burnout is not just detrimental to morale—it can derail timelines, compromise quality, and reduce long-term team effectiveness. Regular check-ins with the team lead help PMs assess not only progress but team capacity and well-being. When workloads become imbalanced, responsibilities can be redistributed, or lower-priority tasks can be deferred. The goal is not to push harder but to work smarter.

Team utilization also extends beyond core product and engineering teams, especially in large-scale initiatives involving multiple stakeholders. In such cases, early and transparent communication becomes critical. PMs who proactively inform stakeholder teams about upcoming expectations give those teams time to prepare, increasing alignment and reducing friction. This foresight is especially valuable when working across departments, such as marketing, operations, legal, or finance.

Cross-functional collaboration is a cornerstone of successful utilization. PMs serve as the connective tissue between discipline engineering, design, marketing, customer success, and more. Unifying these groups under shared objectives enhances cohesion and drives results. Clear goals, such as reducing churn or launching a new feature, transform fragmented contributions into coordinated efforts. When teams understand the collective mission, they are more likely to contribute proactively, seeing their work as essential to a greater outcome.

Resource constraints are a constant in product management. Whether it is limited headcount, tight budgets, or shared engineering bandwidth across multiple product teams, prioritization becomes essential. Effective PMs approach this challenge like triage: Focus on what is most critical, allocate resources to high-impact areas, and defer less urgent tasks. Preparation is key. Maintaining updated product requirement documents one or two quarters in advance, securing alignment with business stakeholders, and obtaining financial validation for high-value features can make a compelling case when it is time to negotiate for limited resources. In some cases, stakeholder advocacy becomes the differentiator that helps a feature move to the top of the priority list. Transparency is another foundational principle. When teams understand the reasoning behind certain decisions, why one feature is prioritized while another is delayed, they are more likely to support those choices. Clear, open communication builds trust. PMs who explain the rationale behind trade-offs, welcome feedback, and remain flexible in their decision-making foster a culture of mutual respect. When it is time to advocate for critical deployments, trust ensures the message is taken seriously because the team knows not every request is treated as urgent by default.

Long-term success in team utilization also depends on nurturing growth. PMs who invest in the professional development of their team members not only strengthen current execution but build future capability. Giving junior developers leadership opportunities or encouraging designers to experiment with new tools fosters ownership, skill-building, and team engagement. These growth moments compound over time, benefiting both the individual and the broader organization.

Ultimately, team utilization is a continuous, dynamic process that demands strategic thinking, emotional intelligence, and a deep awareness of team dynamics. By aligning strengths with responsibilities, managing workloads, fostering cross-functional collaboration, and embracing transparency, PMs can unlock extraordinary performance. The result is not just the successful delivery of a product, but the formation of a resilient, motivated, and high-functioning team.

Streamlining team utilization

Several templates can help streamline team utilization and ensure effective collaboration and resource management. Below are a few that are commonly used by PMs, along with how you can adapt them to your workflow:

- **Sprint planning: A shared vision for the next sprint:** Sprint planning is the starting line for any productive development cycle. It is a collaborative effort where the team comes together to decide what work can be accomplished in the next sprint. As a PM, your role is to provide the what and the why. This means presenting the prioritized backlog, outlining business goals, and defining the sprint's success criteria. But you do not do this in isolation. The **engineering manager** (**EM**) works alongside you to assess the technical feasibility of tasks, guide the team through effort estimations, and balance the workload across developers.

    A well-structured sprint planning board is essential. It should not only showcase tasks but also highlight vacations, PTOs, and other commitments. Overlooking these details can lead to unrealistic sprint goals and eventual team frustration. For instance, if two key engineers are on leave for half the sprint, the EM must help adjust the scope or reassign tasks without compromising quality. The goal is not just to fill the board with as many tasks as possible; it is about setting the team up for sustainable success.

    One of the challenges in sprint planning is dealing with carryover work or technical debt. Here, the collaboration between the PM and EM is vital. While the PM advocates delivering value to the customer, the EM ensures that the foundation of the product remains robust. Together, you might allocate 20% of the sprint to addressing technical debt, ensuring the team does not become bogged down by accumulating issues over time. This balance between immediate priorities and long-term health is where the PM-EM partnership truly shines.

- **Daily stand-ups: A pulse check for the team:** Daily stand-ups are the cornerstone of Agile methodologies. These short, usually 15 to 30 minutes, focused meetings provide the team with an opportunity to align on progress, share blockers, and plan the day ahead. In organizations without a Scrum master, the EM often takes on the role of facilitator. It is not about micromanaging; it is about fostering an environment where the team feels empowered to share updates and raise concerns.

    As a PM, your role is to listen actively and address external blockers, whether they are stakeholder approvals or delays from dependent teams. For instance, if a backend API from a parent system is delayed, your immediate focus should be on collaborating with the EM to reprioritize work. Look for opportunities to work on frontend features in parallel or work on the tasks in the backlog, if any, instead of waiting. These types of decisions need to be made swiftly and should be well coordinated to avoid losing time.

The EM's role in stand-ups complements yours. They provide technical guidance, ensuring the team stays on track with implementation details. If there are recurring blockers, the EM might suggest a deeper technical discussion after the stand-up to avoid derailing the team's momentum. Both of you must be attuned to the nuances of team dynamics, celebrating wins, and addressing frustrations before they escalate.

A common pitfall to avoid in stand-ups is turning them into status update meetings for leadership. The purpose of the stand-up is for the team to align, not for you to gather metrics for a report. Keep the meeting short, focused, and team-centric. Encourage team members to share their challenges openly, knowing that you and the EM are there to support them.

- **Resource allocation: Balancing capacity and priorities:** Efficient resource allocation is the invisible thread that holds a team's productivity together. Without dedicated Scrum masters, the responsibility of balancing workloads often shifts to the PM and EM. While the PM ensures that the team is working on the most impactful tasks, the EM ensures that the workload is evenly distributed based on individual capacity and expertise.

  Consider a scenario where an engineering team is tasked with delivering a new feature alongside resolving a critical bug. The PM's priority is clear—delivering customer value. However, the EM understands the technical implications of ignoring the bug. Together, you strategize. Junior engineers might be allocated to less complex tasks, while senior engineers handle the critical bugs and the more challenging aspects of the feature. This division ensures that progress continues without overburdening anyone.

  One key factor in resource allocation is planning for production post-launch support, absences, PTOs, vacations, and even unexpected leaves must be accounted for in sprint planning. If a key engineer is scheduled to be out, you might decide to prioritize tasks that do not depend on their expertise. Tools like resource planning boards can help visualize team availability, making it easier to set realistic goals.

  Resource allocation also involves addressing carryover work and engineering debt. As a PM, you might advocate for new features, while the EM emphasizes the importance of maintaining system health. This balance requires open communication and mutual respect. Together, you can allocate a portion of each sprint to resolving technical debt, ensuring the product remains scalable and maintainable.

  Ultimately, effective team utilization is a collaborative dance between the PM and EM. Both roles bring unique perspectives to the table, but their shared goal is the same: To enable the team to deliver high-quality work without burnout.

By fostering open communication, leveraging data, and planning proactively, you can ensure that your team remains engaged, productive, and aligned with the product's vision.

- **Building team morale: Celebrating contributions:** Effective team utilization is not just about tasks, it is about people. Acknowledging individual and team achievements boosts morale and fosters a culture of trust. Celebrate milestones, whether it is completing a challenging sprint, resolving a long-standing bug, or delivering a feature ahead of schedule. As a PM, a simple thank you or a team lunch can go a long way in building goodwill.

Remember, a well-utilized team is not overworked or under-challenged—it is engaged, motivated, and aligned with the product vision. By focusing on clear communication, prioritization, and adaptability, you ensure your team's potential is maximized, paving the way for product success.

Managing contracts and legal considerations

Contracts often represent one of the lesser explored, yet critically important, aspects of product management. For many PMs, the first encounter with a legal agreement can feel overwhelming, an unfamiliar landscape filled with complex terminology and formal language. It is not uncommon to sit silently through legal discussions, unsure of what to ask or how to contribute. However, contracts are far more than dense legal documents, they form the backbone of partnerships, vendor relationships, and cross-functional commitments that enable a product to succeed.

The challenge lies in the fact that PMs are not trained legal professionals. They do not spend their days drafting agreements or interpreting clauses. Still, their role is essential in ensuring that contracts accurately reflect the product's capabilities, limitations, and operational realities. While legal teams bring deep expertise in compliance and regulation, PMs serve as the subject matter experts on the product itself. Bridging this gap requires collaboration, not deference.

PMs must recognize that their input is crucial during contract reviews. Legal advisors may not have insight into how a product handles data, what it technically can or cannot do, or what features are still in development. That is where product leadership becomes vital. By translating product functionality into clear, actionable terms, the PM ensures that the terms outlined in the contract are realistic, relevant, and aligned with the product roadmap. For instance, consider a case where a product only processed anonymized, aggregated data and did not store or collect personally identifiable information. In such a scenario, standard *General Data Protection Regulation (GDPR)* clauses designed for sensitive data would not apply. Yet, without clarification, such clauses may still find their way into a contract. PMs who take the time to clearly articulate the product's data practices can prevent unnecessary legal obligations, reduce friction, and streamline execution.

Ultimately, understanding contracts is not about becoming fluent in legal language; it is about becoming an effective partner in the legal process. PMs who take ownership of their role in contract discussions ensure that what is agreed upon on paper is both technically feasible and strategically sound. This proactive approach not only protects the product but also strengthens cross-functional collaboration and contributes to smoother, more successful partnerships.

Building a relationship with legal teams

One of the most valuable lessons in product management is understanding that the legal team can be one of the PM's strongest allies, if engaged early and communicated with clearly. Legal teams are, by design, risk-averse. Their role is to protect the organization from potential liabilities. However, this well-intentioned caution can sometimes result in contracts that are overly broad or misaligned with the actual functionality of the product.

To prevent such misalignment, it is essential for PMs to proactively educate their legal counterparts about the product. It should never be assumed that the legal team is familiar with the technical nuances, operational flow, or data handling practices of a product. Providing this context can make a significant difference in how contracts are structured. Key areas to highlight include data collection methods, privacy implications, and regulatory compliance measures. Whether through a live demo, annotated screenshots, or detailed documentation, PMs should aim to clearly convey what information the product collects, processes, and stores. This level of clarity enables legal teams to tailor contract language more precisely to the product's real-world behavior, thereby reducing unnecessary clauses and potential confusion.

By investing time upfront in this cross-functional collaboration, PMs not only contribute to more accurate and relevant agreements but also help accelerate the contract review process. With fewer rounds of revision and less ambiguity, the team benefits from improved efficiency and stronger alignment between legal protections and product realities.

Negotiating contracts

While negotiating contracts may initially seem daunting, it is fundamentally about achieving clarity and fairness between parties. Contracts define critical elements such as scope of work, delivery timelines, payment terms, **intellectual property** (IP) rights, and liability. PMs are often best positioned to contribute meaningfully to these negotiations, as they possess deep insight into the product's requirements, technical roadmap, and business objectives. When engaging with external vendors, for instance, PMs play a vital role in aligning contractual terms with product timelines and strategic goals. Ensuring that deliverables promised by the vendor match key milestones on the product roadmap is essential to avoid delays or misalignment. Additionally, attention must be paid to IP clauses, particularly when third-party vendors are involved in writing code or building features for the product.

In such cases, it is crucial to confirm that the contract clearly states the company's ownership of all work produced. This prevents future disputes and safeguards the organization's proprietary assets. By advocating for precise, product aligned terms, PMs help protect the integrity of the product while fostering transparent, effective partnerships.

Regulatory compliance

Regulatory compliance is one of the more complex and often daunting aspects of contract management in product development. Legislation such as the GDPR and the *California Consumer Privacy Act (CCPA)* imposes strict requirements on how user data is collected, stored, processed, and shared. In response, legal teams frequently include broad, catch-all compliance clauses in contracts to mitigate risk. While well-intentioned, these clauses may either exceed what is necessary or fail to address the specific realities of the product.

It is the PM's responsibility to ensure that these compliance provisions accurately reflect the product's functionality and data practices. If the product does not collect or process personal data, there is no need to include extensive requirements around encryption protocols or consent mechanisms. Conversely, if sensitive data is involved, the contract should explicitly outline the methods by which the product meets regulatory standards.

By clearly articulating how the product operates and interacts with user data, PMs help legal teams tailor contracts that are both compliant and practical. This proactive clarity reduces the risk of misalignment, avoids unnecessary obligations, and minimizes the likelihood of future legal or operational issues.

Managing risks and expectations

Every contract carries inherent risks, but the way those risks are addressed can significantly influence a product's success. Liability clauses, for example, determine accountability in the event of service disruptions or failures. Consider a scenario where a product integrates with a payment processor that experiences an outage—*who bears responsibility for the resulting revenue loss?* Contracts must clearly define such scenarios to eliminate ambiguity during critical moments. However, effective risk management extends beyond contractual language. It also involves setting realistic expectations with internal teams. If a contract includes aggressive timelines or stringent **service level agreements** (**SLAs**), it is essential to ensure that the team has the necessary resources and capacity to meet those obligations. Overcommitting in a contract can lead to burnout, compromised quality, and reputational damage.

One of the most effective ways to manage contract risk is to engage the legal team early and consistently. Waiting until the final stages of negotiation to involve legal experts often results in delays and missed deadlines. Maintaining detailed records of discussions, decisions, and changes throughout the negotiation process helps prevent miscommunication and ensures clarity about the terms agreed upon.

It is also critical to recognize the division of expertise between legal and product functions. Legal professionals are authorities in compliance and liability, but they may not fully understand the technical or strategic nuances of a product. The more context and information PMs can provide, whether related to architecture, user data handling, or market constraints, the better equipped the legal team will be to draft precise, relevant contracts.

Rushing through contract reviews is another common pitfall. While looming deadlines may tempt teams to expedite the process, the cost of overlooking unclear or unfavorable terms can be far greater than a delayed release. Every clause should be reviewed thoroughly, and questions should be raised when terms seem vague or misaligned with the product's operations. Ultimately, managing contracts and legal obligations is about more than checking boxes—it is about protecting the product, advocating for fair and achievable terms, and ensuring alignment between legal frameworks and product realities. Though it may not be the most visible aspect of product management, it is one of the most impactful. With a proactive and collaborative approach, PMs can confidently navigate the complexities of contracts and lay the foundation for strong, sustainable partnerships.

Checklist for preparing for legal discussions

When collaborating with the legal team, it is essential to understand where PMs need to inform the legal team and where explicit alignment or approval is required. The following, while not exhaustive, is a revised checklist highlighting both aspects:

- **General product overview:**
  - **Inform legal**:
    - Describe the product in simple terms: What does it do?
    - Who are the end users (e.g., consumers, businesses, developers)?
    - Where will the product be available (specific regions or countries)?
- **Data collection and processing:**
  - **Inform legal**: Provide a clear summary of the data your product collects, including:
    - Types of data (e.g., personal, behavioral, financial).
    - How the data is processed and stored.
    - Where the data is transmitted (e.g., third-party integrations).
    - Highlight any new data collection features in the roadmap.
  - **Alignment needed**:
    - Ensure the data collection and processing practices comply with relevant regulations (e.g., GDPR, CCPA).
    - Validate that storage and retention policies meet legal requirements.

- **Regulatory considerations:**
  - **Inform legal:**
    - Share the regions where your product operates or plans to expand.
    - Describe the types of users (e.g., children, healthcare professionals) if special regulatory considerations apply.
  - **Alignment needed:**
    - Confirm that product features adhere to regional laws and industry-specific regulations (e.g., *Health Insurance Portability and Accountability Act* (*HIPAA*) for healthcare).
    - Verify jurisdictional requirements for contracts, such as cross-border data transfers or export compliance.
- **Existing contracts and agreements:**
  - **Inform legal:**
    - Highlight any dependencies on third-party vendors or services.
    - Provide details of existing contracts affecting product operations.
  - **Alignment needed:**
    - Review existing agreements to ensure they:
      - Address liability appropriately.
      - Include necessary data-sharing permissions.
      - Meet compliance responsibilities between parties.
- **User consent and communication**
  - **Inform legal:**
    - Share how user consent will be obtained (e.g., opt-ins, cookie banners).
    - Present drafts of privacy policies, terms of service, and other user-facing communications.
  - **Alignment needed:**
    - Validate that the consent mechanism and policies comply with legal requirements.
    - Confirm the legal language is clear and actionable for end users.
- **Security measures:**
  - **Inform legal:**
    - Detail the security protocols in place, such as encryption, firewalls, or access controls.
    - Highlight any planned changes to security architecture.

- o **Alignment needed**:
  - Ensure that the security measures align with regulatory obligations (e.g., GDPR mandates for data protection).
  - Confirm compliance with cybersecurity frameworks, where applicable.

- **Risk assessment**:
- o **Inform legal**:
  - Provide an overview of identified risks, including:
    - ◆ Potential breaches or vulnerabilities.
    - ◆ Compliance risks with new features or initiatives.
    - ◆ Share mitigation strategies planned or in progress.
- o **Alignment needed**:
  - Confirm that identified risks are legally acceptable or require additional mitigation measures.

- **Business goals and constraints**:
- o **Inform legal**:
  - Share key business goals and how the product supports them (e.g., monetization through data analytics).
  - Identify constraints or trade-offs impacting compliance (e.g., budget limits, time constraints).
- o **Alignment needed**:
  - Ensure business objectives are free from legal conflicts.
  - Validate plans for third-party integrations, data monetization, or feature launches align with compliance requirements.

Best practices for collaborating with legal

Mentioned as follows are some of the best practices to keep in mind when having a conversation with the legal team:

- **Transparency:** Keep the legal team informed early and often, especially during the discovery and planning phases.
- **Documentation:** Maintain clear records of all decisions and inputs shared with the legal team.
- **Proactivity:** Identify potential legal issues before they escalate and work with legal to address them promptly.

Negotiation

Negotiation is one of the most critical and nuanced skills in a PM's toolkit. Whether aligning priorities with stakeholders, securing additional resources, or advocating for a product's placement within a competitive roadmap, negotiation plays a pivotal role in shaping outcomes. Importantly, negotiation in product management is not about dominance or winning; it is about finding common ground and generating mutual value.

PMs are frequently at the center of high-stakes conversations where decisions can significantly influence a product's direction and success. In these situations, effective negotiation helps ensure that all parties feel heard, aligned, and committed to the shared vision. Understanding how negotiation works, why it matters, and how to approach it strategically is essential for any PM aiming to lead with influence and drive meaningful results.

Negotiation in product context

At its core, negotiation is the art of reaching an agreement through dialogue and compromise. In the context of product management, this often involves navigating conflicting priorities, limited resources, and diverse stakeholder perspectives. For example, engineering may advocate dedicating time to address technical debt, while marketing pushes for new features to align with an upcoming campaign. In such scenarios, negotiation becomes the essential tool for aligning these competing interests and ensuring the product and the business continue to move forward effectively.

Internal negotiations, particularly with cross-functional teams such as engineering, marketing, or operations, are centered on balancing priorities and achieving alignment. Unlike external negotiations, which are often governed by contracts or formal agreements, internal discussions rely heavily on trust, shared objectives, and open communication. The aim is not to win but to create collaborative outcomes that support both product goals and organizational success.

Best practices in internal negotiation include transparency, active listening, and framing discussions around shared goals. PMs should avoid relying on authority or exerting undue pressure. Instead, they should present their case through a lens of mutual benefit, demonstrating how the proposed direction supports collective outcomes. Flexibility and a willingness to make trade-offs are key sometimes; success involves deferring one priority to gain alignment and support for another.

Negotiation is also deeply rooted in relationship-building. It is not a one-time conversation but an ongoing process of cultivating trust and demonstrating a genuine investment in the success of all stakeholders involved. When practiced effectively, negotiation not only resolves conflicts but also strengthens partnerships and fosters a culture of collaboration—one that ultimately drives better product outcomes.

Types of negotiation

Not all negotiations follow the same structure or intent. In some situations, the goal is to reach a mutually beneficial agreement through collaboration and compromise. In addition, the PM may need to take a firmer stance to protect the product's interests or strategic direction. The nature of the negotiation often depends on the context, stakeholders involved, and what is at stake. Here is a breakdown of the key approaches.

Collaborative negotiation

Collaborative negotiation centers on achieving win-win outcomes for all parties involved. In this approach, stakeholders work together to identify solutions that address their respective needs, with an emphasis on building trust and fostering long-term partnerships rather than focusing solely on short-term gains. For instance, a PM might negotiate with the sales team to adjust delivery timelines in support of a major client opportunity. At the same time, they ensure that engineering resources are not overstretched, preserving the team's ability to maintain quality and meet existing commitments.

This negotiation style is most effective when all participants are aligned around a common objective, such as the successful launch of a product or the achievement of a critical business goal. By prioritizing shared outcomes and encouraging open communication, collaborative negotiation creates an environment where alignment and mutual support thrive.

Distributive negotiation

Distributive negotiation is inherently competitive and often characterized as a zero-sum game, where one party's gain directly results in another's loss. This approach typically arises when key resources such as time, budget, or personnel are limited. For example, in a situation where two product initiatives are competing for the same engineering resources, allocating those resources to one project inevitably means deprioritizing the other.

In these scenarios, successful negotiation hinges on strong prioritization and clear justification. PMs must effectively communicate the strategic value of their initiative, highlighting how it aligns with broader organizational objectives, its potential impact on end users, and the expected **return on investment** (**ROI**). A compelling case is often supported by data, including customer insights, competitive analysis, market trends, or projected revenue gains.

This is precisely why proactive preparation is so important. Having a well-documented **product requirements document** (**PRD**), stakeholder alignment, and supporting data in place, ideally a quarter in advance, positions the PM to advocate confidently and persuasively when resource conflicts arise.

Integrative negotiation

Integrative negotiation focuses on creating value for all parties by expanding the scope of possibilities rather than competing over existing constraints. This approach encourages creative problem-solving and reframing discussions to uncover shared benefits and hidden opportunities. For instance, engineering may advocate for dedicating time to address technical debt, while the PM faces pressure to deliver a new feature for an upcoming release. Instead of treating these goals as mutually exclusive, an integrative strategy would explore how resolving certain aspects of technical debt could, in fact, accelerate future feature delivery. In some cases, the technical improvements may directly support the infrastructure required for the new functionality.

By shifting the conversation toward shared outcomes and long-term benefits, integrative negotiation transforms potential conflict into collaboration, allowing multiple objectives to be achieved simultaneously and strengthening cross-functional alignment in the process.

Best practices for negotiation

Preparation is one of the most critical components of successful negotiation. Entering a discussion without a clear understanding of one's own goals, the motivations of the other party, and potential areas for compromise often leads to misalignment and frustration.

The following best practices can help PMs negotiate more effectively and constructively:

- **Do the homework:** Before any negotiation, it is essential to gather relevant data. For example, if a PM is requesting additional engineering resources, they should be prepared to demonstrate how this investment will affect delivery timelines, customer satisfaction, or revenue potential. A well-supported case built on data is far more likely to be taken seriously and less easily dismissed.

- **Listen actively:** Negotiation is as much about listening as it is about presenting a position. Understanding the other party's motivations can reveal opportunities for alignment. For instance, if the marketing team is advocating for a tight timeline, the reason may be a high-impact industry event. Recognizing this context allows the PM to explore compromises that meet marketing's goals without compromising product quality.

- **Prioritize objectives:** Not every request carries equal weight. Effective negotiators know which items are essential and where they can be flexible. When discussing a roadmap, for example, it may be critical to push for one high-impact feature while being open to deferring less time-sensitive items. Negotiation should not be viewed as a contest where every demand must be met. Success often involves strategic trade-offs.

- **Focus on the bigger picture:** The ultimate goal of any negotiation should be to support the success of the product and the broader business. By framing proposals in terms of company objectives and shared outcomes, PMs can help shift conversations away from individual wins and toward collective progress.

- **Stay calm and professional:** Tensions can arise during negotiation, particularly when priorities clash. Maintaining a calm, respectful demeanor is essential. The PM's role is not to argue, but to facilitate problem-solving. A composed and professional approach strengthens relationships and sets the tone for productive dialogue, even in the face of disagreement.

Common pitfalls and how to avoid them

Negotiation is not only about applying the right strategies, it also involves steering clear of common missteps. One frequent mistake is approaching negotiation with too much rigidity. Flexibility is essential; treating negotiations as all-or-nothing scenarios often leads to stalemates and missed opportunities. Effective PMs remain adaptable, seeking workable compromises that still support their core objectives.

Another critical error is failing to align negotiation efforts with the broader company strategy. For instance, advocating for a feature that lacks alignment with organizational goals can quickly undermine a PM's credibility. It is essential to ensure that any request or proposal is clearly connected to measurable outcomes that advance the company's vision, whether through revenue growth, user engagement, or operational efficiency.

Equally important is follow-through. Agreeing to a compromise is only the first step; delivering on those commitments is what truly builds trust. Consistent follow-through not only strengthens professional relationships but also lays the groundwork for smoother and more productive negotiations in the future.

Stakeholder management

Throughout this book, stakeholder management has been referenced repeatedly, and for good reason. Stakeholders are essential to a product's success. They serve as guiding forces, much like stars that help navigate a product's journey. Stakeholders come in many forms: Executives, engineering leads, designers, marketing teams, end users, and others, depending on the nature of the product.

Effective stakeholder management goes beyond simply addressing concerns. It involves aligning diverse goals, actively listening to input, and uniting all parties around a shared product vision. A PM who excels at managing stakeholders transforms potential friction points into opportunities for collaboration, innovation, and long-term alignment. This skill not only enhances execution but also helps build a culture of trust and mutual ownership across the organization.

The art of understanding stakeholders

Effective stakeholder management begins with a clear understanding of who the stakeholders are and what they care about. Each stakeholder brings a unique perspective, shaped by their specific role within the organization. Executives may focus on revenue growth and market positioning, while engineers are typically concerned with feasibility and timelines. Designers often prioritize UX, and marketing teams seek compelling narratives to drive engagement and adoption.

A crucial early step in this process is stakeholder mapping. This involves identifying key individuals or groups, assessing their levels of influence and interest, and categorizing them accordingly. For example:

- High-influence, high-interest stakeholders, such as executive sponsors, require regular updates and close collaboration to stay engaged and aligned.

- High-influence, low-interest stakeholders may need targeted communication to ensure they remain informed without being overwhelmed by unnecessary detail.

Understanding these dynamics allows PMs to tailor communication strategies and engagement approaches that are both efficient and impactful. At the heart of stakeholder management is trust. Stakeholders who trust the PM are far more likely to offer support, approve decisions, and allocate critical resources. Building trust involves consistent, transparent communication; reliably delivering on commitments; and demonstrating a deep understanding of the product and its broader business context.

For example, when presenting a potentially controversial product pivot to an executive stakeholder, it is essential to support the recommendation with relevant data and to clearly explain how the change aligns with company objectives. Transparency is key, honestly addressing potential risks, trade-offs, and challenges helps build credibility. When stakeholders see that decisions are grounded in thoughtful analysis and strategic alignment, they are more likely to respond with confidence and support.

Effective communication with tailored message

Communication is the glue that holds stakeholder relationships together, yet not all stakeholders speak the same language. Tailoring messages to suit different audiences is essential for ensuring clarity, alignment, and influence. For technical stakeholders, such as engineers, communication should focus on feasibility, dependencies, timelines, and potential technical risks. In contrast, when engaging with executives, the emphasis should shift to high-level insights, business impact, ROI, and alignment with strategic objectives.

The choice of communication medium also matters. While some stakeholders prefer detailed written updates, others may respond more effectively to concise slide presentations or in-person discussions. Establishing regular touchpoints, such as bi-weekly stakeholder meetings or **quarterly business reviews (QBRs)**, helps maintain alignment, track progress, and foster two-way dialogue. These sessions should not only serve as progress reports but also as opportunities to gather feedback, surface concerns, and reinforce shared goals.

Conflicts among stakeholders are inevitable, especially when cross-functional teams have competing priorities. For example, engineering may resist compressed timelines due to resource constraints, while sales may push for rapid feature delivery to meet client demands. Managing these tensions requires a diplomatic, solution-oriented approach, and often, skilled negotiation. By understanding each stakeholder's perspective and seeking common ground, PMs can mediate effectively, maintain momentum, and keep the product vision intact.

Rallying support for vision

Securing stakeholder buy-in goes beyond presenting a polished plan, it requires engaging stakeholders early and consistently throughout the product lifecycle. Involving them from the outset fosters a sense of ownership and investment in the outcome. During the discovery phase, for example, PMs can invite stakeholders to participate in workshops or brainstorming sessions. When shaping the roadmap, seeking stakeholder input and addressing concerns transparently helps build alignment and trust.

Stakeholder management often involves navigating complex power dynamics. Some stakeholders may hold significant influence over decisions, while others may feel their input carries less weight. It is the PM's responsibility to manage these dynamics thoughtfully, balancing the priorities of high-impact decision-makers with the perspectives of less influential voices to ensure the product addresses the needs of all users, not just the loudest or most powerful. For instance, if executives advocate for a high-visibility feature that may alienate core users, the PM should bring relevant data to the discussion. Highlighting potential risks to retention or user satisfaction metrics and proposing alternatives that achieve strategic goals without compromising UX demonstrates thoughtful leadership and a balanced approach.

Importantly, stakeholder management is not a one-time task; it is an ongoing process. Maintaining open lines of communication, celebrating shared wins, and demonstrating the impact of stakeholder contributions all help to reinforce long-term engagement. As market dynamics, internal priorities, or product direction evolve, so too will stakeholder expectations. Regular check-ins help ensure continued alignment. Ultimately, effective stakeholder management requires as much listening as it does communication. By treating stakeholders as partners rather than obstacles, PMs foster a collaborative environment, one in which the product is more likely to thrive and deliver lasting value.

Art of storytelling

As this journey through this book draws to a close, it is worth reflecting on the path traveled from the start. The readers have explored the intricacies of product development, mastered the nuances of stakeholder management, and gained insight into negotiation and team utilization. Along the way, the importance of communication has emerged as a central theme. Yet, communication alone is not enough. The true impact lies in how a message is delivered, how a PM connects with their audience, conveys a vision, and inspires meaningful action. This is where storytelling becomes an essential, final skill in the PM's toolkit.

Storytelling in product management is not about embellishment or theatrics. It is about shaping a narrative that resonates, whether the audience is composed of executives, engineers, designers, or end users. Storytelling allows complex ideas, such as product roadmaps, business cases, or technical challenges, to be communicated in ways that are both compelling and accessible. A well-crafted story aligns diverse stakeholders, bridges gaps in understanding, and gives depth and meaning to a product vision. Ultimately, storytelling is the thread that ties strategy, execution, and emotion together. When done well, it transforms abstract plans into shared purpose, inspires collaboration, and drives products forward with clarity and conviction.

The power of a well-told story

Stepping back to reflect on the chapters explored throughout this book, from understanding business models and managing contracts to collaborating without authority, a common thread emerges: The ability to influence people. The tools and techniques covered, leveraging data to support decisions, managing conflict with diplomacy, and prioritizing with focus, are all critical components of effective product management. Yet even the most compelling data, the strongest rationale, or the most well-structured roadmap can fall short if it fails to resonate on a human level. This is where storytelling becomes indispensable. Storytelling transforms information into meaning. It creates emotional connection, inspires action, and elevates communication from transactional to transformational. In product management, where alignment and buy-in are essential, the ability to tell a compelling story is often what turns a good idea into a shared mission.

Bringing it all together

Throughout this book, the importance of alignment has been a recurring theme: aligning stakeholders, aligning priorities, and aligning the product with market needs. Storytelling is the thread that weaves all of these elements together. It serves as the bridge that connects vision to execution, strategy to action, and people to purpose. For instance, when collaborating with engineering to address technical debt, storytelling can be used to convey the broader impact of inaction: A gradually slowing system, rising user frustration, and competitors gaining an edge. In stakeholder negotiations, framing requests within a narrative of shared success helps illustrate how their support contributes to wins not just for the product team but for the organization and its users.

Storytelling has also proven invaluable in navigating difficult conversations. As highlighted in earlier chapters on managing without authority and negotiating trade-offs, a well-crafted narrative can de-escalate tension, foster empathy, and build a sense of shared ownership. Rather than stating, *we cannot implement this feature due to limited resources*, a PM might instead guide stakeholders through the decision-making journey: *Here is what users are telling us, here is the impact we are targeting, and here is how this decision supports our shared goals.*

In this way, storytelling becomes more than a communication tool, it becomes a strategic asset, helping PMs inspire, influence, and lead with clarity and purpose.

Template for storytelling

Effective storytelling often follows a structured approach that ensures clarity, emotional engagement, and relevance. For PMs, using a repeatable framework helps transform complex information into compelling narratives that resonate across audiences. The following adaptable template offers a straightforward way to craft impactful stories in any product context:

1. **Start with the problem:** Begin by identifying the challenge or pain point faced by users or stakeholders. Make the problem relatable and human-centered to build empathy and set the context for your solution.

    Example: Imagine a small business owner, *Sarah*, struggling to manage her inventory with outdated tools. Every month, she spends hours reconciling mismatched data, losing valuable time that could be spent growing her business.

2. **Introduce the solution:** Position your product, feature, or idea as the solution to the problem. Clearly explain how it addresses the identified challenge.

    Example: Now, picture Sarah using our streamlined inventory management app. With just a few clicks, her inventory syncs in real time, saving her hours each week and giving her back control of her business.

3. **Explain the impact:** Demonstrate the tangible benefits and outcomes of your solution. Use real data, metrics, or user stories to validate the impact.

    Example: Within the first month of using the app, Sarah increased her sales by 15% due to improved stock visibility. And she is not alone—our data shows that small businesses using the tool save an average of 10 hours per week.

4. **Call to action:** Conclude with a clear takeaway or next step, whether it is gaining stakeholder support, prioritizing a feature, or aligning on a decision.

    Example: This is why we believe this feature should be our top priority for the next sprint, it directly drives user success and retention. Together, we can make stories like Sarah's a reality for thousands of small businesses.

By following the above simple storytelling structure, PMs can communicate more persuasively, inspire action, and build stronger alignment across teams.

Best practices for storytelling

While storytelling is a powerful tool for PMs, delivering an effective narrative requires more than just following a structure; it demands intentionality. To truly resonate with an audience, stories must be tailored, clear, and purposeful. Below are key best practices to elevate storytelling in product management:

*   **Know your audience:** Tailor your message to the needs and priorities of your listeners. Engineers may appreciate technical depth and clarity around feasibility, while executives are more likely to focus on business impact, strategic alignment, and ROI.

- **Be authentic:** Genuine communication creates connection. Avoid overly polished language or exaggerated claims. Audiences respond to sincerity, and authenticity fosters trust and credibility.

- **Use data wisely:** Data should support your story, not replace it. Well-placed statistics add weight and credibility, but too many can overwhelm. A statement like, *80% of users reported increased satisfaction,* is powerful when embedded within a human-centered narrative.

- **Create a narrative arc:** Effective stories follow a natural flow: a clear beginning that introduces the problem, a middle that builds tension or highlights challenges, and a conclusion that presents the solution and its impact. This structure helps audiences stay engaged and understand the bigger picture.

- **Use visuals and Analogies:** Visual aids and relatable comparisons can make complex topics more accessible. For instance, describing technical debt as *a leaky boat we need to patch before adding more passengers* can make the concept more tangible and easier to grasp.

- **Keep it concise:** Respect your audience's time by focusing on what matters most. A concise, well-structured story is more impactful than one filled with unnecessary detail. Clarity and brevity help ensure your message lands effectively.

Methods to refine storytelling

Storytelling is not just an art, it is a repeatable discipline that can be practiced, refined, and mastered. To help PMs integrate storytelling into their everyday communication, a few proven frameworks offer structure, clarity, and emotional resonance. The following are two popular storytelling models, followed by practical methods for putting them into action:

- **The Pixar method:** This classic storytelling framework, popularized by Pixar, offers a simple yet effective narrative arc. It creates emotional connection and forward momentum by presenting a relatable problem and a satisfying resolution.

  o **Structure:**
    - Once upon a time...
    - Every day...
    - One day...
    - Because of that...
    - Until finally...

  o **Example:** Once upon a time, customers struggled to track their fitness goals. Every day, they logged data in separate apps, losing motivation. One day, we launched our integrated fitness tracker. Because of that, they could see all their progress in one place. Until finally, user engagement and goal achievement rates soared.

- **The HERO Method:** This framework positions the user as the hero of the story, with the product acting as the guide that helps them overcome challenges. It emphasizes empathy and outcome-driven narratives.
  - **Structure:**
    - **Hero:** Identify the user or stakeholder.
    - **Empathy:** Understand their challenges and aspirations.
    - **Resolution:** Present your solution and how it helps.
    - **Outcome:** Highlight tangible, meaningful results

Methods to practice effective storytelling

Storytelling is a skill that develops through intentional practice. While understanding frameworks and structures is important, true mastery comes from applying these techniques in real-world scenarios, refining them through feedback, and adapting to different audiences. The following methods provide practical ways for PMs to strengthen their storytelling abilities and integrate them seamlessly into their daily communication and leadership practices.

- **Storyboarding:** Visualize your story by sketching out the key elements, problem, turning point, rezsolution. This helps clarify the flow and identify gaps before presenting.
- **Peer feedback:** Test your narrative by sharing it with someone unfamiliar with your project. If they understand and stay engaged, your message is likely to land well with broader audiences.
- **Iterate and refine:** Storytelling, like product development, improves with feedback. Adapt your narrative based on what resonates most with your audience and remain flexible in your delivery.
- **A final reflection of turning vision into story:** As this book ends, it is worth pausing to reflect. Across each chapter, whether it was understanding business models, navigating stakeholder dynamics, managing without authority, or aligning teams, there was a common thread: influence through connection.

  Storytelling is not simply the last chapter; it is the skill that binds all the others together. It is what turns insights into inspiration and strategy into shared purpose. With the storytelling frameworks and best practices now in hand, PMs can do more than deliver features; they can build alignment, spark action, and lead with purpose.

Conclusion

The tools, perspectives, and lessons shared in this book were designed to equip PMs for the complexities of their role. From balancing priorities to leading cross-functional teams, from negotiating trade-offs to fostering trust, you've explored the wide spectrum of what it means to lead products to success. And now, with storytelling, you hold the final piece of the puzzle: the ability to connect emotionally and bring your product vision to life.

As you continue your journey, remember every product, every pitch, and every decision carries a story waiting to be told. Craft those stories with empathy, authenticity, and intention. Use them not just to inform, but to inspire. Let storytelling be your compass guiding your team, your users, and your stakeholders toward a future you helped shape.

This may be the end of a book, but it is the beginning of your next great story.

Points to remember

- Project management basics equip PMs with the tools to plan, coordinate, and deliver projects effectively, even without a dedicated PM on the team.

- Leading without authority emphasizes influence over command, building trust, and aligning teams through shared goals and clear communication.

- Effective team utilization ensures optimal allocation of resources, balancing workload, and leveraging individual strengths while accounting for PTO, vacations, and unforeseen capacity changes.

- Managing contracts and legal considerations involves aligning agreements with product realities, clarifying data usage, and ensuring compliance with regulations like GDPR or CCPA.

- Negotiation skills are essential for securing resources, resolving conflicts, and aligning priorities both within internal teams and with external stakeholders.

- Stakeholder management requires empathy, clear communication, and the ability to align diverse priorities while keeping everyone informed and engaged throughout the product lifecycle.

- Storytelling is a powerful tool for PMs, enabling them to connect with audiences, convey product visions effectively, and inspire action among stakeholders.

- Collaboration between product and engineering drives successful project execution, particularly when managing technical debt and capacity planning in Agile environments.

- Data-driven decision-making supports credibility and builds trust, ensuring PMs can justify their choices with evidence.

- Adaptability and flexibility are critical skills, allowing PMs to pivot strategies, address challenges, and keep teams aligned in dynamic environments.

Multiple choice questions

1. **Why is understanding project management important for PMs?**
    a. To manage team budgets
    b. To coordinate timelines and align teams
    c. To take over engineering tasks
    d. To draft legal documents

2. **What is the primary method of leading without authority?**
    a. Using hierarchical directives
    b. Building trust and aligning shared goals
    c. Delegating all decision-making
    d. Creating detailed task lists for teams

3. **How can PMs effectively utilize their teams?**
    a. By focusing solely on high performers
    b. By balancing workloads and leveraging individual strengths
    c. By assigning tasks randomly to save time
    d. By avoiding discussions about capacity constraints

4. **What is one of the key roles of a PM in legal contract management?**
    a. Drafting contracts from scratch
    b. Ensuring contracts align with product realities
    c. Handling all regulatory approvals independently
    d. Negotiating employee benefits

5. **In negotiation, what is a distributive approach?**
    a. Finding win-win outcomes for all parties
    b. Expanding the pie through creative solutions
    c. Dividing limited resources where gains for one party mean losses for another
    d. Focusing on building long-term relationships

6. **What is the biggest challenge in stakeholder management?**
    a. Scheduling meetings
    b. Aligning diverse priorities and expectations
    c. Handling technical issues
    d. Creating financial projections

7. **Why is storytelling important for PMs?**

    a. It replaces data in presentations

    b. It bridges technical details and stakeholder understanding

    c. It removes the need for team meetings

    d. It ensures faster project completion

8. **What is a critical aspect of collaboration between product and engineering teams?**

    a. Delegating all decisions to engineering

    b. Avoiding discussions about technical debt

    c. Prioritizing tasks and managing capacity together

    d. Managing budgets for the team

9. **How can data enhance stakeholder trust?**

    a. By replacing narratives with charts

    b. By supporting decisions with evidence and credibility

    c. By overwhelming them with complex metrics

    d. By focusing solely on financial performance

10. **What defines a great PM's adaptability?**

    a. Sticking to rigid plans despite challenges

    b. Flexibility to adjust strategies in dynamic environments

    c. Delegating all responsibilities to others

    d. Avoiding stakeholder interactions

Answers

1	b
2	b
3	b
4	b
5	c
6	b
7	b
8	c
9	b
10	b

Join our Discord space

Join our Discord workspace for latest updates, offers, tech happenings around the world, new releases, and sessions with the authors:

https://discord.bpbonline.com

Index

www.ingramcontent.com/pod-product-compliance
Lightning Source LLC
Chambersburg PA
CBHW061808210326
41599CB00034B/6921

* 9 7 8 9 3 6 5 8 9 9 8 1 8 *